ALSO BY ORVILLE SCHELL

The China Reader

Mandate of Heaven

Discos and Democracy

To Get Rich Is Glorious

Modern Meat

Watch Out for the Foreign Guests

Brown

Modern China

In the People's Republic

VIRTUAL TIBET

VIRTUAL TIBET

Searching for Shangri-La from the Himalayas to Hollywood

Orville Schell

METROPOLITAN BOOKS

HENRY HOLT AND COMPANY

NEW YORK

Metropolitan Books
Henry Holt and Company, LLC
Publishers since 1866
115 West 18th Street
New York, New York 10011

Metropolitan Books™ is an imprint of
Henry Holt and Company, LLC.

Published in Canada by Fitzhenry & Whiteside Ltd.,
195 Allstate Parkway, Markham, Ontario L3R 4T8

Portions of this work have appeared, in slightly different form,
in *Tricycle*, *The Nation*, and *Harper's*.

Library of Congress Cataloging-in-Publication Data
Schell, Orville.
Virtual Tibet : searching for Shangri-la from the
Himalayas to Hollywood
p.   cm.
"Metropolitan books."
Includes index.
ISBN 0-8050-4381-0
1. Tibet (China)—History. 2. Tibet (China)—In motion pictures.
3. Tibet (China)—Foreign public opinion.   I. Title.
DS786.S295   2000   99-088146
951'.5—dc21

Henry Holt books are available for special promotions and
premiums. For details contact: Director, Special Markets.

First Edition 2000

Designed by Lucy Albanese

Printed in the United States of America

1   3   5   7   9   10   8   6   4   2

FOR TOM ENGELHARDT:

my dear friend and editor.
A person of unparalleled insight,
integrity, ability, and dedication.

Wreathed in the romance of centuries, Lhasa, the secret citadel of the "undying" Grand Lama, has stood shrouded in impenetrable mystery on the Roof-of-the-World, alluring yet defying our most adventurous travellers to enter her closed gates. With all the fascination of an unsolved enigma, this mysterious city has held the imagination captive, as one of the last secret places on earth, as the Mecca of East Asia, the sacerdotal city where the "Living Buddha" enthroned as god, reigns eternally over his empire of tonsured monks, weaving their ropes of sand like the schoolmen of old, or placidly twirling their prayer wheels, droning their mystic spells and exorcising devils in the intervals of their dreamy meditations.

L. Austine Waddell,
Lhasa and Its Mysteries (1905)

CONTENTS

PART II

PART III

VIRTUAL TIBET

MY TIBET AND OURS

Never have I encountered weather that changes so precipitously, so unpredictably. As we leave camp with a yak caravan on our trek around the base of Mount Amnemachen, which local Golok tribespeople have worshiped for centuries as a "spirit mountain," the snowy peak is sawtoothed against a cobalt blue sky. The sun bakes relentlessly down on us as we slowly make our way up a pass. Then, unexpectedly, a wind arises. The sky changes color. A storm suddenly boils up the valley. Snow begins to fall. The shimmering white peak disappears and the vastness of the landscape shrinks to a flat, disorienting whiteness. Soon, the only visible landmarks are the blurred outlines of occasional *lahtse*s, cairns of stones piled on top of boulders, offerings to local spirits by centuries of Tibetan Buddhist pilgrims who have made ritual circumambulations around this awe-inspiring mountain. Otherwise, even the ink-black yaks carrying our things have vanished before our eyes into snowy whiteness.

Not until we reach the top of the next pass, where just as suddenly the weather clears, do I spot our yaks and Daejung again. He is responsible for the six mounted Golok herders and twenty beasts of burden accompanying us on this trekking and climbing expedition.

From a distance Daejung has an almost yetilike appearance, suggested by the long sleeves of his *chuba*, a Tibetan garment resembling a cloak and fastened at the waist with a brightly colored sash into which he has thrust the silver scabbard of a dagger. Tibetan nomads keep many of their effects tucked inside their *chuba*s against their bodies and are capable of astounding the uninitiated with the strange inventory of things they can produce from within, somewhat in the fashion of a magician pulling outlandish objects out of a hat: a plastic bottle of yak yogurt, a pack of cigarettes, a box of rifle cartridges, a can of pineapple, even a half-eaten leg of mutton.

Daejung stands on a rocky, windswept ridge, overlooking a rolling valley called the Place of a Thousand White Tents. It was here that pilgrims once pitched their cloth tents as they made their traditional pilgrimages around Amnemachen before ascending this pass the next day. As I approach, Daejung remounts his horse, wheels, and giving a whoop, half sung and half shouted, charges up a snowy incline. I breathlessly clamber up behind him, and there on the rocky crest at the very summit of the pass are banks of prayer flags hung on rough juniper wood posts with yak-hair lanyards. Tibetans believe that each time one of these prayer-imprinted flags flaps in the wind, its prayer is transmitted heavenward, propitiating spirits that are said to abound in almost every mountain peak, pass, or lake, thus earning its owner merit for the next life.

Like the spars of a phantom ship trailing tattered sails after a storm, the prayer flags whip and snap in the brisk, cold breeze. Beneath them lie banks of *mani* walls, piles of prayer stones, each inscribed over and over with the sacred mantra *Om mani padme hum*—literally, "The jewel and the lotus," an invocation of the mythic bodhisattva Avalokiteshvara who, depicted holding a jewel and a lotus, suggests how the Buddha grew out of the depravity of life into a pure state just as the blossom of a lotus, or wisdom, springs forth unsullied from the impurity of mud. As Catholics recite Hail Marys, so this mantra is chanted tirelessly by devout Tibetans in hopes of gaining a measure of enlightenment and good karma for their next incarnation. Indeed, among these lofty mountains that vault into the sky like open-air cathedrals, there is a ghostly majesty whose religious power derives not from the few paltry monuments to the spirits that men have succeeded in erecting, but from the grandeur of the landscape itself.

"Each year in the old days thousands upon thousands of pilgrims used to make circumambulations around Amnemachen," Daejung announces in his guttural, almost unintelligible Mandarin Chinese. "But then the Chinese came and soon no one dared worship or even hang prayer flags around their tents. Everything old was considered bad and we Tibetans could get into trouble if we followed our traditions." He gives a nervous laugh and glances toward the representative from the provincial office of the Chinese Mountaineering Association who is also accompanying us.

"But in 1979," he says, suddenly smiling, "after the fall of the Gang of Four, in the earth-sheep year, thousands of pilgrims appeared around Amnemachen again. Even to old people it was a surprise."

Were it not for distant wisps of smoke, visible for only a moment before they are caught by the wind and erased, the tent by the river might easily be mistaken for just another of the large boulders that dot this valley. But as we move closer, I begin to make out a string of tethered yaks and a lone figure, evidently watching the slow approach of our phalanx of Caucasian trekkers wearing brilliant red, blue, green, and orange parkas, wind pants, and hats.

"Pilgrims," says Daejung bluntly and rides forward to greet them. These will be the first pilgrims we have seen.

How Daejung is explaining our bizarre presence, I do not know—after all, virtually no Westerners have been here in the Golok Autonomous Region for decades. As he talks, the tent flap opens but then almost immediately closes again like the shutter of a camera. I hear the murmur of agitated voices within. The next time the flap parts, I catch a fleeting glimpse of several female faces.

Finally, curiosity triumphs over alarm. The flap opens wide and two women, wearing yak-hide boots with felt soles and dressed in flowing robes encrusted with silver jewelry and coral ornaments, step shyly out. Their long black hair is meticulously plaited into scores of slender braids that cascade thin as veins down their shoulders and are joined like a bridal train behind them. The oldest woman clutches a Buddhist rosary in her chapped, arthritic hands, the beads passing ceaselessly through her gnarled fingers as she mutters nonstop prayers. The women stare in mute stupefaction at the unlikely procession that has not only inexplicably materialized in their camp but done so in utter contravention of Tibetan Buddhist tradition, circling the mountain from the wrong direction. (Tibetans always circumambulate, or pass around, holy places from left to right. In order to avoid climbing a very high pass on our first day out, however, we have chosen to navigate this sacred mountain from right to left.) The notion that we might be trekking around this sacred mountain as a form of recreation would undoubtedly be incomprehensible to these women. In short, we are performing an act of Buddhist absurdity.

I wrote the above words in 1981, when, after several decades of strict closure, the Beijing government finally gave foreign tourists, trekkers, and climbers limited access to the Tibetan Plateau. Even though this was the first time that I had been in an ethnically Tibetan region, it could have been said of me, as of so many other Westerners, that I had long been journeying toward Tibet. In a manner of speaking, I had many times before reached "Tibet," that fabulous land of our Western imagination which I had inhabited vicariously in various books of exploration and adventure, novels, and articles in *National Geographic*s of my youth, even though I had never actually set foot on Tibetan soil.

If there was a beginning milestone in my progress toward Tibet, it would be the moment in 1953 when at age thirteen I happened to pick up Heinrich Harrer's classic tale, *Seven Years in Tibet*. The book recounts that Austrian mountain climber's riveting flight in 1944–45 from a British prisoner of war camp in India, over the Himalayan massif, and across the "roof of the world" to the closed Tibetan capital of Lhasa. There Harrer managed to become a tutor of the fourteenth Dalai Lama, who, although still a boy, was the spiritual leader of all Tibetans and the head of an ancient Buddhist theocracy.

For an American boy growing up in New York City during the gathering Cold War and in the midst of a cornucopia economy headed into the high tide of 1950s consumerism, Harrer's book offered a fabulous escapist tale of an isolated, ancient, forbidden, and mysterious land whose untouched open spaces, towering mountains, and mystical religion and exotic monasteries filled with colorful pageantry were the very opposite of anything I had experienced.

Although I had no way of knowing it then, I was taking my place among the many Westerners who had become entranced by Tibet, or rather by the fantastic reports of those few European travelers who had managed to penetrate its peripheries. Harrer's *Seven Years in Tibet* was but the most recent in a long lineage of accounts of Tibet by Western missionaries, diplomats, explorers, adventurers, freebooters, soldiers, dreamers, spiritual seekers, geographers, ethnographers, mountain climbers, and scam artists that extended back to the middle of the seventeenth century.

First came the impressions of Catholic missionaries in the seventeenth and eighteenth centuries, then the dispatches of British East India Company officials in the eighteenth century and of the Indian cartographers sent secretly by the British Raj to map Tibet's "blankness" in the nineteenth century; next followed the reports of colonials such as Francis Younghusband, who led a British military expedition into Tibet just after the turn of the century, and finally the writings of a diverse wave of seekers who came on the scene in the early twentieth century. The one recurring word that appears in almost all their texts is *mysterious*. "No country in the world had exercised a more potent influence on the imagination of men," writes Sir Thomas Holdich in his 1906 book, *Tibet, the Mysterious.* "Through all the ages Tibet has held a paramount position among those regions of the world which have been popularly invested with a veil of mystery because they are inaccessible and unknown."

By the latter part of the nineteenth century, the "race" among Europeans to be the first to reach Lhasa rivaled in its obsessiveness the races to find the headwaters of the Nile or reach the North and South Poles. But because Lhasa was imagined as a spiritual El Dorado, journeys to Tibet were often conceived of and viewed as pilgrimages rather than as simple geographic expeditions or explorations. Even for people with little interest in Buddhism, penetrating Lhasa, the sacred heart of Tibet, was viewed as something akin to an infidel's reaching the holy city of Mecca by stealth, as Sir Richard Francis Burton had in 1853. Turn-of-the-century European explorers were drawn to Tibet in part by the urge "to fill in the white spaces on the map where no humans but Tibetans had ever been before," as the great Swedish explorer Sven Hedin writes in his classic, *A Conquest of Tibet.*

In the minds of Westerners, especially those curious about Tibet's unique and colorful form of Buddhism, a whole series of Tibets, each more fabulous than the last, arose. These conjuries were built up from the often overheated accounts of those who had actually been there—as well as those who claimed to have been there. In the course of time, they accumulated until they began to form a multilayered structure of fact and fiction, something like slowly deposited strata of silt that ultimately form the striated geology of sedimentary rock.

Tibetan fantasies rooted themselves in almost every form of popular entertainment: in magazines, newspapers, books, comics, children's stories, stage productions, and finally on the screen. When James Hilton's 1933 novel, *Lost Horizon,* was released as a film in 1937, it was the apotheosis of Tibet as fantasy realm. With it, the notion of that land as the paradisiacal Shangri-La entered both the imagination and the vocabulary of Western popular culture, becoming one of the most powerful utopian metaphors of our time.

Tibet had now become the last place on earth still abounding in true "mysteries," including lamas who could fly, magicians who could stop rain, oracles who could foretell the future, and yetis, a probably imaginary race of apelike half-human creatures said to inhabit the snowy wastes of the Himalayas and the Tibetan Plateau. If Buddhists saw the world as illusory and deemphasized the difference between dreams and waking consciousness, Westerners blurred the distinction between what Tibet actually was and how they imagined it, or wanted it to be, so that it, too, became the dreamiest of realities. And so, like a split image in the viewfinder of a reflex camera, Tibet developed a divided persona in the public mind of the West. On the one hand, it retained all its associations of being a paradisiacal Shangri-La. On the other, after China's occupation in the 1950s, it also came to be viewed as a victimized land and culture laid waste by an invading colonializing power.

It is a tricky thing to reprise one's murky memories of youth in search of those influences that determined one's later life. However, when I took a leave from Harvard College in 1960 after studying Far Eastern history, vaguely planning to make my way to Asia via the South Seas to study Chinese, something of Harrer's hunger for adventure had already taken root in me. My ultimate destination, then as impossible for an American to visit as Tibet had been for so many centuries, was the People's Republic of China, the land of Chairman Mao, his much-vaunted revolution, and untold millions of "blue ants" (as the American media dubbed the Chinese in those days). At that point in history, there was something deeply alluring to a young Western student of the area in the very fact that as outsiders we were not welcomed; indeed, we were not even permitted to travel there by our own government.

It took me more than twenty years to make it to the Forbidden City in Beijing on assignment for the *New Yorker* magazine. Since few Chinese in those early years of China's Open Door policy had laid eyes on *laowai,* or "old foreigners," as we were known in Mandarin, our very presence produced the same effect of remote worlds colliding that had so thrilled me in *Seven Years in Tibet.* And when at last I returned home to write, I felt somewhat like Harrer bringing news of an unknown land to the outside world.

As anyone discovers upon approaching a long-dreamed-of place, reveries are most vivid and poignant when they remain undisturbed by the waking world. Those who have read my various reports over the years know that the China of Mao's epic revolution turned out, not surprisingly, to have its own reality—and a rather unmysterious one at that. By 1981, when I made my first trip to Tibet, reality had begun to encroach on my fantasy of that fabled land as well. As the first groups of Westerners were allowed into Tibet, and as even the Dalai Lama's government in exile was permitted to send several "fact-finding delegations" to Tibetan ethnic areas, a clearer picture of what had happened during the Cultural Revolution began to take form. Tibet, it turned out, had undergone an interregnum of savage attacks—in many ways even more extreme than those that had been visited on Central China itself—against almost all aspects of its traditional society and culture. And by the time I arrived in Lhasa as a correspondent for a 1995 PBS *Frontline* documentary on Tibet's agonized relationship with China, I, too, had come more or less fully down to earth. In reality, Tibet was more a tragedy of outside incursion and brutalization than a Shangri-La–like refuge protected from the encroaching outside world.

But as my knowledge increased about what had happened in Tibet under Chinese occupation, I simultaneously found myself becoming somewhat out of sync with the way many Westerners living abroad were coming to apprehend Tibet. After decades of relative quiescence, Western fascination with and fantasies about old Tibet were being reawakened—in part by the prospect of actually being able to go there. In fact, fascination with Tibet, Tibetan Buddhism, and the fourteenth Dalai Lama—the same Dalai Lama whom Harrer had tutored as a boy, who had fled into exile in 1959, and who had won the Nobel Prize for Peace in 1989—had been growing throughout the 1990s as he began traveling more extensively in the West. Pieces on Tibet were beginning to pop up everywhere in the media; Tibetan Buddhist monasteries and study centers were springing up all across the country; support groups for the Dalai Lama's exile movement were proliferating; and the entertainment industry was being drawn into the vogue, sponsoring political events, fund-raising banquets, concerts for "Tibetan freedom," and even "major motion pictures" on the subject. Having become acquainted with the Dalai Lama and some of the officials in his government in exile through my work on several documentary films about China and Tibet, I now found myself in the odd position of serving as a conduit of sorts for some of America's most recent infatuation with things Tibetan.

When I read that Sony-TriStar (which later became Columbia Tri-Star) was pursuing the idea of making a film of *Seven Years in Tibet,* a certain residual spark of curiosity about our—and my own youthful—fantasy about Tibet was rekindled within me. And the fact that Heinrich Harrer, a man who claimed not to have had a sexual relationship while in Tibet, would be played by Brad Pitt, a hot young star who had burst on the movie scene, his washboard abs exposed, making torrid love to Geena Davis in the 1991 film *Thelma and Louise,* only added a certain touch of delicious irony to this newly promised incarnation of latter-day Tibetan mythology.

Since Harrer's time in Lhasa, an unparalleled confluence of media, entertainment, and technology had merged with global commerce in our society to create the most powerful mythmaking machine of all time. How, I wondered, was Hollywood's "dream factory" now going to mine remnants of the "real" but vanished Tibet to create another version of this suggestive land that had haunted the Western imagination for centuries? Given our boundless ability to catalyze our dreams into virtual lands, it was irresistible to ponder what this newest episode of our evolving love affair with Tibet would look like.

Having once left college and America to plumb the depths of my fantasy about the South Seas and then China, so now I decided to follow a similar urge to explore the depths of our collectively imagined Western version of Tibet just as it seemed on the brink of reemerging in popular culture in a new and vivid form. Like any other fantasies cobbled together from fragments of suggestive reality, our fantasies of places on or off this earth generally reflect far more about ourselves and our own yearnings than we perhaps care to know. This verity certainly seemed to me to be as true of Tibet as of any other place I knew. So I set out to write a book that was not about Tibet itself but about the kaleidoscope of "virtual Tibets" created over the past two and a half centuries, one that would conclude with an exploration into those updated versions still being created today. Even more, I imagined the effort as an attempt to explore why we Westerners—indeed, I myself—have cared so much about Tibet, why we have spun such a fabulous skein of fantasy around this distant, unknown land.

PART I

1

TIBET AS PLACE AND MYTH

One may debate, of course, whether any place on our increasingly small planet remains untouched by the homogenizing effects of jet travel and the global marketplace. What is not in question, however, is the yearning of disenchanted Westerners to believe in such places. Indeed, to acknowledge that such lands may no longer exist has seemed too bleak a thought for most of us in modern life to bear.

When in 1869 the British colonial government in India posted Elizabeth Sarah Mazuchelli's husband to Darjeeling in the Himalayan foothills, she immediately fell in love with the area's "fierce majesty and barren grandeur." What appealed to her about those "perpetually snow-clad" and remote mountains was the thought that "no solemn garden parties or funeral dinners, no weary conventionalities of society, follow us here." Similarly, Leslie Weir, the first Englishwoman to reach Lhasa, told the Royal Asiatic and Royal Central Asian societies in 1931, "We cannot realize how much we have sacrificed during these late years of scientific advance and of accelerated speed ... [while] the Tibetans have retained poise, dignity, and spiritual repose," all things, she insisted, that modern Westerners had "lost in [their] hectic striving."

Few places on the globe have been afforded better geographical conditions for remaining isolated than Tibet, protected as it is from Central Asia by the Kunlun Mountains and the deserts of Qinghai and Xinjiang to the north, from China by the rugged foothills of the Tibetan Plateau, and from India by the Himalayas. Never mind that it was not the quaint pocket-sized kingdom tucked behind the mountains that many in the West came to believe it to be but instead a vast, arid, and sparsely populated land as large as Western Europe. What mattered was how people wanted to imagine it.

Fantasies of escape are naturally more powerful when rooted in real geography; the concreteness of an actual place helps us believe our romantic myths are something more than baseless, chimerical dreams. As the explorer Sven Hedin wrote in his book *To the Forbidden Land: Discoveries and Adventures in Tibet,* "Romantic pleasure must arise from what is firmly believed, at least for the nonce, to be an aspect of reality. . . . The antique and the exotic, war and warlike adventure, chivalrous love and duty, the supernatural in many shapes, which were once *de rigueur* as some of the ingredients of Romance, could only move on the strict assumption that they were real and even actual—that they had happened somewhere and to somebody, either in this world or in another."

More than any other land, Tibet has provided just such an enticing target for a corpus of romantic transferences and has continuously fired the imagination of Western escape artists. Its very name—generally believed to have come from the combination of two Tibetan words, *To,* meaning "upper," and *Po,* the name that Tibetans themselves call their land—has long summoned forth images of a quintessentially exotic fairy-tale kingdom distinguished by spiritual attributes whose loss we lament in our own contemporary lives: "uncompromised faith, simplicity, isolation, calm, and spiritual mystery" is how Mazuchelli described them after visiting Pemionchi monastery while on a trek in 1869 to view Mount Everest. "Strange as were the surroundings of these pagans, and grim as were their symbols, how can I find language to express the majesty and grandeur of their worship, which impressed me more deeply than anything I have ever seen or heard?"

The Himalayas, which separate Tibet from the Indian subcontinent (and whose name is derived from the ancient Sanskrit words *hima* and *alaya*, meaning "abode of snow"), were created by a geological upthrust of rock as India, then a vast island, collided with the Eurasian landmass some forty-five million years ago. That tectonic collision of geological plates created a fifteen-hundred-mile-long range of mountains that rises from the tropical rainforests above Burma to form a great snowy arc running westward through Bhutan, Sikkim, Tibet, and Nepal to Pakistan and boasting the highest and youngest peaks in the world. Sven Hedin called the Himalayas "the most stupendous upheaval to be found on the face of our planet." The British explorer Edward Amundsen described them as "like a sea, the gigantic waves of which, driven by northern and southern winds, have changed to stone at the moment of their worst fury," and as Edwin Bernbaum writes of the Himalayas in his gorgeously photographed book, *Sacred Mountains of the World,* "The sight of their sublime peaks, soaring high and clean above the dusty, congested plains of India, has for centuries inspired visions of transcendent splendor and spiritual liberation."

In the late nineteenth century, when "wonders" had become by definition scientific, when the church had increasingly lost power, and when the divine rights of kings and royalty were fast falling to democracies and dictatorships, the idea that somewhere there existed a feudal theocracy ruled by a compassionate God-king and a colorful aristocracy that labored not for industrial production or colonial expansion but for the spiritual enlightenment of humanity—and did so under golden monastery roofs—proved irresistibly attractive to a disenchanted West.

It hardly needs to be said that Tibet's snow-capped mountains and alpine deserts do not, in fact, offer the easy gratification of our earthly needs promised, for instance, by our fantasies of tropical island paradises with their palm-fringed beaches and azure lagoons. Indeed, until recently, Tibet was entirely devoid of most amenities. Tibetans did not even adopt the wheel—except for purposes of prayer—until the second half of the twentieth century, when Chinese occupiers finally arrived. Most of Tibet is thousands of feet above sea level and possesses one of the more inhospitable climates on earth. It has an indigenous cuisine made up of things that most Westerners have found virtually inedible, and through most of this century was populated by a largely nomadic people who engaged in only the most rudimentary personal hygiene. What is more, Tibetans have shown themselves to be capable of considerable savagery against one another, not to mention outsiders. Yet this catalog of dubiously utopian attributes has seldom hindered rapturous Western dreams.

To this day, Tibet is still imagined as "the cure for an ever-ailing Western civilization, a tonic to restore its spirit," as Tibet scholar Donald Lopez writes in his recent book, *Prisoners of Shangri-La*. "To the growing number of Western adherents of Tibetan Buddhism 'traditional Tibet' has come to mean something from which strength and identity are to be derived . . . a land free from strife, ruled by a benevolent Dalai Lama, his people devoted to the *dharma*." Though many Europeans and Americans have been captivated by other forms of "Oriental" religion, Tibet's brand of Buddhism—steeped as it is in tales of magic and mystery, including accounts of unbelievable spiritual feats—continues to hold a special fascination.

Buddhism, which ultimately mixed with nativist shamanism in Tibet, was originally founded by Prince Siddhartha Gautama. Born in the middle of the sixth century B.C. into a wealthy family on the border between present-day Nepal and India, he set out to wander as an ascetic to acquaint himself with the suffering of ordinary people. The experience is said to have caused him to renounce his life of privilege in order to search instead for the true nature of reality and existence. Through his efforts he came to be known as the Shakyamuni, meaning "the hermit of the Shakya clan" in Sanskrit. His teachings, or the dharma, grew out of his realization while meditating under a *bodhi* tree that human existence is bounded by the "four noble truths," namely that life is filled with suffering, attachment and desire are the root of most suffering, liberation from desire and the self is possible, and such liberation, or enlightenment, can be attained by leading a compassionate life of virtue, meditation, and wisdom.

According to the Shakyamuni Buddha, or "enlightened one"—whose recitations were transcribed by one of his disciples, Ananda, in sutras, literally meaning "threads" or "strings"—the way to enlightenment requires adherence to a "noble eightfold path" that commits followers to strive to maintain right views, right resolve, right speech, right action, right livelihood, right effort, right mindfulness, and right concentration. In the Buddhist view, life's endless sufferings can be escaped only by accepting the impermanence and illusionary nature of reality. As the Buddha says in the *Prajna Paramita,* a group of his most famous sutras, "Regard this fleeting world like this: like stars fading and vanishing at dawn, like bubbles on a fast moving stream, like morning dewdrops evaporating on blades of grass, like a candle flickering in a strong wind, echoes, mirages, phantoms, hallucinations, and like a dream."

Buddhism does not promise salvation by a supernatural God residing in some cosmic heaven. Instead, it promises release from *samsara,* the painful cycle of birth, death, and rebirth, to *nirvana,* a state of everlasting enlightenment and liberation. This freeing of one's essential consciousness from endless reincarnations caused by karma, the residue of one's earthly actions, can be attained only by showing compassion in one's corporeal life toward all sentient beings. In the words of the Buddha, "Do not do anything harmful; do only what is good; purify and train your own mind."

Within a century and a half of his death, Buddhism had divided into two main schools: Hinayana (the so-called lesser vehicle, still practiced in parts of South and Southeast Asia today, also known as Theravada Buddhism) emphasized the salvation of the individual, while Mahayana (the greater vehicle, variants of which are practiced in Tibet, Mongolia, China, Korea, Japan, and certain parts of Southeast Asia) emphasized the need to strive for the collective salvation of all human beings. Neither tradition believed in a supernatural God the creator. In this sense,

Buddhism was as much a set of ethical teachings, a philosophy of life that could lead to a form of earthly enlightenment, as the theology of a transcendental faith.

It was Mahayana Buddhism that was first transmitted to Tibet sometime around the seventh century A.D. There, over the next few centuries, it slowly fused with Bon, an indigenous animistic faith centered on a priesthood whose role was to ensure the happiness of the deceased in the afterlife by propitiating myriad spirits, deities, demons, and demigods whom Tibetans imagined to inhabit every part of the natural landscape. The clerics of this new fusion became known in Tibetan as *lamas*, the Tibetan translation of the Sanskrit *guru*, a word meaning "heavy" or "weighty," suggesting that a guru is weighty with good spiritual qualities. L. Austine Waddell somewhat disparagingly writes in his pathbreaking 1895 book on Tibetan Buddhism, "Lamaism [as it was then known] is only thinly and imperfectly varnished over with Buddhist symbolism, beneath which a sinister growth of poly-demonist superstition darkly appeals."

If Buddhism changed Bon in Tibet, Bon also changed Buddhism. Into the Buddhist pantheon were incorporated Bon's spirits as new protective demons—the ghoulish, macabre figures that one still encounters in Tibetan art. Also incorporated into its practice were aspects of its elaborate rituals, sacrifices, exorcisms, and prognostications by oracles and wizards allegedly able to communicate with the deceased. Indeed, even today in India, where he lives in exile, the Dalai Lama regularly consults the Nechung oracle, who has long been considered his personal protector and who offers him advice on grave matters while in a trancelike state of possession and speaking in tongues.

In A.D. 779, the Buddhist master Padmasambhava, or guru Rinpoche, journeyed from India to Tibet to help found the first Buddhist monastery, Samye, just south of Lhasa. By the thirteenth century, Buddhism had spawned a complex series of monastic orders whose rival monasteries mirrored the land's fragmented political structure. The distinctive brand of Buddhist teaching that we know today as Tibetan Buddhism, or Vajrayana (the diamond vehicle), had been codified and accepted as Tibet's prevailing faith. Vajrayana Buddhism added to the by then standard Buddhist spiritual practices of meditation and chanting an assortment of other techniques, including yoga, tantric sexual rituals, visualizations, and repetitive prayers to the Buddha himself that are carried out through recitation and the use of prayer wheels and prayer flags.

One of the most important features of Mahayana and Vajrayana Buddhism is the notion of the *bodhisattva,* or "enlightened being," who out of universal compassion for the suffering of others seeks Buddha-hood in order to better help save those still trapped in the inescapable cycles of samsara, the conditionality of a worldly existence. Tibetan Buddhism's most fundamental precept is that motivation determines actions and that if one wishes to act compassionately and gain enlightenment, one must vigilantly strive to cultivate a high state of consciousness about what one does and how it may affect others. Why? Because upon death, what the Dalai Lama has described as the "imprint" of a former being's consciousness, or karma, will remain as a residue that is "reincarnated" in a new animal, human, or divine form.

According to Tibetan Buddhist belief, when the reincarnation of a particularly enlightened being occurs in human form, that person is known as a *tulku,* which literally means "emanation body." (*Tulku*s are often referred to in English as "living Buddhas," a literal translation of the Chinese characters *huofo* but a somewhat misleading expression of this uniquely Tibetan institution.) The most eminent Tibetan *tulku* is the Dalai Lama. Traditionally, the Dalai Lama has been viewed as both the spiritual and the temporal leader of all Tibetans. The traditional belief that he is also the reincarnation of the mythic bodhisattva Avalokiteshvara (Chenrezig in Tibetan), the transcendent Buddha of compassion, did not become part of the institution's mystique until around 1650, when the fifth Dalai Lama, still known as the Great Fifth to Tibetans, sought to add a measure of religious depth to his official persona. At the same time, the Great Fifth also declared that his old master at Tashilhunpo monastery in Shigatse was the reincarnation of Amitabha, the Buddha of light, reputed to be the father of

Avalokiteshvara, thus creating the institution of the Panchen Lama, whose name derives from his Tibetan appellation, Panchen Rinpoche, "The Great Gem of Learning."

Another distinctive characteristic of Tibetan Buddhism is the monastic life it spawned. Each monastery was traditionally organized around one or more *tulku*s, just as the Tashilhunpo monastery in Shigatse was organized around the Panchen Lama. But monasteries were more than just ascetic religious retreats for the land's hierarchical priesthood. Since Tibet had virtually no cities, monasteries also became the focal point of social life for the land's largely nomadic populace. Monasteries were where Tibetans were educated, where commerce was conducted, and where society interacted during religious festivals. (There was also a parallel structure: large estates farmed by feudal serfs whose lands were held by members of the aristocratic class, who helped run the temporal side of Tibetan governance.) By the time of the Chinese Communist occupation of Tibet in 1950, there were said to be over twenty-five hundred monasteries spread throughout Tibetan ethnic areas, almost all of which would be destroyed or severely damaged in the decades of Maoist political upheaval that followed.

While the Himalayas served as a natural barrier against intruders from the south, the approaches to Tibet from the east and north were less formidable. In truth, however, it was Tibetans who first broke out of their natural geographical isolation, not outsiders who broke in. By the end of the seventh century A.D., King Songtsen Gampo had begun to unify Tibet's disparate clans and created the semblance of a capital in Lhasa, which controlled a powerful Tibetan empire in Central Asia in which an increasingly sophisticated culture arose. Its influence came to extend from Nepal in the south and Kashgar in the west to Khotan in the north and the Chinese border regions to the east. In fact, in A.D. 763, Tibetans attacked and pillaged the Tang dynasty capital of Chang'an (today's Xian), then perhaps the most cosmopolitan and cultured city in the world. While Tibet's current relationship to China is one of subordination, during imperial times there were long periods when the connection was far more ambiguous.

In the ninth century, however, the power of the Tibetan empire waned and it was not until the rise of the Mongols four centuries later that Tibet once again broke out of its isolation, this time by allying itself with the Great Khan. While Tibet submitted to Mongol temporal power, Mongol leaders gave Tibetan Buddhism a central place in their religious life; the result was a curious synergy between the two Central Asian peoples that came to be known as the *yon-chö,* or "patron-priest" relationship. The Mongols (*yon,* or "patrons") "protected" the Tibetans (*chö,* or "priests"), including the Dalai Lama, who in turn provided spiritual guidance to Mongolia. In fact, the name *Dalai Lama* (*dalai* means "ocean" in Mongolian) was conferred in 1578 by Altan Khan, a Mongolian prince, on Sonam Gyatso, the third Dalai Lama, because *gyatso* means "ocean" in Tibetan.

When Kublai Khan conquered China and set up the Mongol Yuan dynasty in Beijing in 1279, Tibet became a peripheral part of this new empire, wedded to China, in a manner of speaking, by a "barbarian" matchmaker. Under the Ming dynasty (1368–1642), Tibet's relations with China continued, although in a considerably diminished manner. While Chinese emperors conferred honorific titles on certain Tibetan notables, they exerted none of the political authority that the Mongols had enjoyed. In 1662, however, when another "barbarian" tribe, the Manchus, overthrew the Ming to set up the Qing dynasty, they began to jockey for power over Tibet. A complicated series of shifting alliances between the Tibetans, the Mongols, and the Manchus finally brought Qing troops, allied with the seventh Dalai Lama, to Lhasa itself in 1720; and in 1721, in a decree issued in the name of the Qing court, Tibet was declared a vassal state. To consolidate their protectorate, the Manchus henceforth posted a military garrison and a handful of imperial representatives, or *amban*s, in Lhasa.

Until the twentieth century, the West was little more than a footnote in Tibetan history. An irony of Tibet's current relations with the West is that for two centuries its celebrated resistance to Western intrusion, its very "forbiddenness," was as much imposed by a wary and conservative Tibetan clergy as by suspicious Chinese *ambans* who did not want to see that land become a back door into China for European imperialists.

In 1904, the worst fears of both came to pass when Colonel Francis Younghusband's expeditionary force set off from India for Lhasa. Worried that czarist Russia had designs on this remote region, the British viceroy in India dispatched Younghusband with just over a thousand British and Indian troops to force the Tibetans to renounce any intention of allying with Saint Petersburg. The expedition would ultimately march all the way to the "forbidden city" and leave a toll of several thousand dead and wounded Tibetans behind.

In the wake of this incursion, the ailing Qing dynasty sent an army of its own to Lhasa to reassert its administrative and military authority. But time had run out on China's last imperial dynasty. In 1911, the Qing was overthrown, its troops were expelled from Lhasa, and Tibet entered a period of almost forty years during which it exercised virtual independence over its affairs.

During these decades, Tibet achieved many of the hallmarks of self-rule: a functioning government, a tax system, its own currency, a postal system, and a small military. The Tibetans even negotiated certain agreements directly with the British as if they were a sovereign power. "Whatever political theorists might say," Hugh E. Richardson, former head of the British mission in Lhasa, would write in his 1962 book, *Tibet and Its History,* "the Tibetan government could and did follow a course of action completely independent of the government of China." Indeed, even the representative of Chiang Kai-shek's Nationalist government, Shen Tsung-lien, who arrived in Lhasa in 1946, acknowledged in his own book, *Tibet and the Tibetans,* that the country had enjoyed de facto independence since 1911.

Yet Tibet was not quite a nation in the European sense. Indeed, at no time did any Western power come out in favor of its independence or grant it diplomatic recognition, and in the minds of the Chinese Nationalists and Communists alike, Tibet, like Taiwan, continued to be viewed as a de jure and integral part of China.

After the Communist Party's victory over Chiang's Nationalists in

1949, Mao Zedong set about reunifying all the errant pieces of China's old multiethnic empire, traditionally viewed as including *han* (Central Chinese), *man* (Manchus), *meng* (Mongolians), *hui* (Moslems), and *zang* (Tibetans). Indeed, as it had been for the founders of so many previous Chinese dynasties, the task of reunification was viewed by Mao's revolutionary government as an almost sacred obligation. Since it was the official Party view that China had been "dismembered"—literally *fen'gua,* or "cut up like a melon"—by predatory imperialist powers, reunification was a tangible way for Mao to show the world that China had, in fact, finally "stood up" and would henceforth strive aggressively to restore and defend its sovereignty and territorial integrity.

Officials in Lhasa responded with alarm to China's declarations that it wished to "liberate" Tibet from feudal bondage. They tried to beef up their backward military and break out of their self-imposed isolation. In October 1950, however, after negotiations failed, the People's Liberation Army (PLA) began a military occupation of Eastern Tibet, and soon thereafter the Dalai Lama fled Lhasa with his cabinet for the Indian border. In the spring of 1951, after the United Nations refused to consider Tibet's appeals for help, a Tibetan delegation finally went to Beijing and signed an accord, the Seventeen-Point Agreement for the Peaceful Liberation of Tibet, but without the Dalai Lama's approval. The agreement acknowledged Chinese sovereignty—"The Tibetan people shall return to the big family of the motherland"—in return for a promise of "national regional autonomy" that would allow Tibetans to maintain their traditional religious, political, and economic systems until "the people raise demands for reform." But it also granted China the right to set up a military headquarters in Lhasa.

After the Dalai Lama's return to Lhasa, for a while a fragile peace looked like it might hold. Indeed, it is often forgotten now that in the early 1950s the Dalai Lama himself was quite sympathetic to some of the liberationist sentiments then sweeping Mao's China. In a conversation several years ago, he told me that, threatening as he found the Chinese, the Communist Party's emphasis on serving the oppressed and championing the commonweal over the interests of private individuals appealed to him. In fact, in 1954 he traveled to Beijing to meet Mao and even dared hope that the Party might prove to be the savior of the poor and downtrodden in Tibet as well as in China. "I began to get very enthusiastic about the possibilities of association with the People's Republic of China," he later wrote. "The more I looked at Marxism, the more I liked it. Here was a system based on equality and justice for everyone."

Although he also received "a strong impression of rigidity" and of "paranoia" while in Beijing, he expressed a willingness to become a Party member and to try to "work out a synthesis of Buddhist and Marxist doctrines that really would prove an effective way of conducting politics." One day shortly before the Dalai Lama left for Lhasa, however, Mao reportedly turned to him and whispered, "Your attitude is good, you know." Then, in a way that chilled him, Mao added that "religion is poison" because "it neglects material progress."

The Chinese Communists, of course, viewed old Tibet through their own ideological lenses as a decadent and oppressive society in which ordinary people had been exploited by serfdom, theocratic rule, and a land-tenure system stacked in favor of the aristocracy and the clergy. Indeed, there were many aspects of Tibet's feudal social and political system that were deeply unjust and autocratic. What held the fabric of Tibetan life together, however, was the common bond of Buddhism, which gave at least the illusion of a shared purpose and meaning to every level of society. But where this belief system might have seemed to a nomad or serf a sacred and unalterable fact of life, to Communists steeped in the notion of religion as the opium of the masses, it was anathema. They viewed Tibet's traditional society, where the vast majority of the population were illiterate and many were virtually "owned" by noble landholding families or monasteries, as feudal in the extreme. As Marshal Chen Yi described it on a visit to Lhasa, China's ultimate commitment was to "rid Tibet of its backward situation."

When China began dismantling monasteries, forcing the organization of agricultural cooperatives, and initiating "democratic reforms" in Kham, or Eastern Tibet, conflict quickly arose. By 1956, opposition had catalyzed into armed resistance. It was at this time that the American

Central Intelligence Agency began aiding Tibetan guerrillas, even transporting several hundred of them to Camp Hale in Colorado for military training.

The fighting culminated in 1959 with an uprising in Lhasa against the Chinese occupation. In March of that year, the Dalai Lama fled once again, this time all the way to Dharamsala, India, where he set up a government in exile. He would sadly remember departing Lhasa "in a daze of sickness and weariness and unhappiness deeper than I can express."

When the Cultural Revolution swept through Tibet in the mid-1960s, Red Guards, not a few of whom were themselves young Tibetans, launched a form of class warfare, savagely attacking what the Party described as all "remnants of old customs, values, and beliefs." Before the political paroxysm was spent, almost all Tibet's monasteries were in ruins, thousands of monks had been imprisoned or murdered, almost every aristocrat had had his property expropriated, and ordinary people had had their religious lives radically circumscribed. Animosity between Tibetans and Han Chinese rose to dangerous levels.

After Mao's death in 1976, the relatively liberal Hu Yaobang became Party general secretary and Beijing's policy toward Tibet softened considerably. Returning from a 1980 trip to Tibet that evidently shocked him, Hu called on all Party cadres to implement new "flexible policies suited to conditions in Tibet," including more autonomy and support for indigenous Tibetan culture, albeit still "under the unified leadership of the party Central Committee." Negotiations with representatives of the Dalai Lama were then initiated and several fact-finding missions composed of supporters of the government in exile were allowed to visit Tibet.

What finally ended these few years of hopeful moderation when reconciliation might have been possible was a spate of anti-Chinese riots in support of Tibetan independence that broke out in Lhasa in September 1987. By the end of October, a number of Tibetan monks had been shot by the police and Lhasa was again seething with tension. When in March 1988 and again in 1989 anti-Chinese proindependence demonstrators once again took to the streets of the city, Beijing declared martial law. The crackdown represented a stark end to Beijing's willingness to resolve the Tibet question through compromise. These disturbances and Beijing's ongoing militant insistence that Tibet was a sovereign part of China set off a global debate over the rights of an ethnically distinct, linguistically different, culturally unique, geographically separate people who had attained a high level of de facto self-rule to gain self-determination from the sovereign claims of a multiethnic state like the People's Republic of China.

Needless to say, each side of this unequal standoff had an elaborate and carefully, if selectively, researched version of history that supported its own claims. That both versions have a certain polemical coherence and a certain quotient of truth only makes sorting out the intricacies of this fractious relationship all the more daunting.

During these years of upheaval, the Tibetan government in exile adopted an aggressive new strategy for gaining support for their cause: a global publicity campaign to portray Tibetans as the victims of Chinese oppression. Instead of simply seeking to win concessions through negotiations, they also began vigorously to court world opinion through organizations like the International Campaign for Tibet, an advocacy group based in Washington, D.C., and through more frequent high-visibility trips abroad by the Dalai Lama. Unfortunately, the effort succeeded in antagonizing China even as it ignited new support for a Tibet already on the figurative hard drives of many Westerners. And so, a whole new chapter in the history of the West's vicarious involvement with that land began. Western respect for and fascination with the Dalai Lama took a quantum leap in 1989 when he was awarded the Nobel Peace Prize. But it was a grand humiliation for China to have its first Nobel Peace Prize winner be a minority dissident in exile, and Sino-Tibetan relations entered an even more intractable phase.

Often forgotten in this controversy was the fact that by 1994 China had invested over $4 billion in Tibet and had initiated over sixty major new infrastructure projects there. In 1996 alone, Beijing pumped another $600 million into this essentially nonproductive protectorate. The rights and wrongs of the situation aside, many were left wondering whether Tibet could realistically hope to make it alone, should independence ever be offered.

As of today, Beijing's position remains more rigid than ever, even as the posture of the Dalai Lama has become considerably more flexible, especially on the question of independence. In 1988, he suggested that Tibet be granted not outright independence but some kind of political autonomy "founded on a constitution of basic law" and a form of government that would give Tibet "the right to decide on all affairs relating to Tibet and Tibetans," while leaving matters of defense and foreign affairs in the hands of Beijing.

China, however, has shown few signs of reappraising its hard-line approach. Indeed, even President Clinton's unusual exchange with President Jiang Zemin of China during a June 1998 summit in Beijing did little to thaw the situation. "I have spent time with the Dalai Lama," Clinton cheerfully quipped to Jiang. "I believe him to be an honest man, and I believe if he had a conversation with President Jiang, they would like each other very much." Two years later, China's posture toward Tibet was as uncompromising as ever. Raidi (some Tibetans use a single name), the chairman of the People's Congress of Tibet, and Legqog, the head of the Beijing-appointed Tibetan Autonomous Region government, were blaming the United States, Britain, and the Dharamsala government for its support of Tibetan separatists and vilifying the Dalai Lama as "the chief representative of the feudal serf system" that had reduced the Tibetan people to "animal status." Of course, Jiang, like other Chinese, tends not to romanticize Tibet as many Westerners do. Indeed, he expressed incredulity that those who live in countries where "education in science and technology has developed to a very high level" and where "people are now enjoying modern civilization" should still "have a belief in Lamaism."

Many observers believe that Beijing has simply decided to wait until the sixty-five-year-old (as of July 6, 2000) Dalai Lama passes from the scene and is counting on Tibet to become ever more Sinicized and so more amenable to Chinese rule. (The area currently included in the so-called Tibetan Autonomous Region contains fewer than half the ethnic

Tibetans in China. And due to the massive PLA presence and the recent wave of government-sanctioned immigration from the border regions of Qinghai, Gansu, Sichuan, and Yunnan provinces, the Tibetan Autonomous Region now has almost as many Han Chinese as Tibetans.)

Unexpectedly, though, the Beijing government has found itself confronting a new problem nearly as intractable as the Tibetan activists and independence seekers. To their dismay, Party leaders began to realize that China somehow had to find a way to rule over another Tibet, a symbolic one championed by a far more fantastic kingdom than any that had ever existed behind the Himalayas—the kingdom of Hollywood. Its coin of the realm was far more persuasive and influential than sutras, monks, and monasteries, and as the 1990s proceeded, the citizens of this kingdom threatened to take possession of this other Tibet as a form of intellectual property—to internationalize it and challenge China's version of its "liberation" in ways that seemed beyond the ability of Party leaders to grasp, much less control.

Aided by Hollywood's global public relations machine, the West did, in fact, come to project a new set of assumptions, this time political, on its Shangri-La. The realities of the emotion-laden China-Tibet question were anything but simple, but to foreigners looking on from afar, the Chinese occupation and the destruction of Tibetan culture seemed similar to some brutal forms of nineteenth-century Western colonization, which were also based on no more than the flimsiest claims to sovereignty. For such Westerners, to whom the International Campaign for Tibet was now appealing from its Washington, D.C., office, the Chinese were crushing not only a traditional society but the dream of Shangri-La itself. For many Westerners who had allowed themselves to dream the dream of Tibet, Chinese rule represented a paradise lost.

The kingdom of Hollywood's fin de siècle seizure of Tibet as a subject for its films raised a curious new question: Who in this global era would be the final arbiter of which version of Tibet would triumph—the real Tibet, China's Tibet, or the "virtual Tibet" that was being elaborated anew in the West and in a host of new Hollywood films?

2

THE KINGDOM OF THE SCREEN

If Tibet was once a highly stratified feudal society jointly controlled by an aristocracy and a theocracy replete with forms of exotic pageantry and flamboyant dress meant to fill Tibetans with awe, then Hollywood *kultur* is in certain ways not so dissimilar to that of old Lhasa. Indeed, with its own nobility of stars and celebrities, distinctive rites, costumes, festival-like awards ceremonies, celebrated monuments, potent mythologies, studio complexes as vast as monasteries, and a reigning pantheon of semidivine deities worshiped around the world, Hollywood might well appear as alien and mysterious to outsiders as the forbidden city of Lhasa once did to those Westerners who first breached its carefully guarded perimeters.

Compared with those of Hollywood, ancient Tibet's powers to create fantasies were actually quite limited. After all, the American film industry has long had the capacity to take almost any dream, yearning, or projection and write it large as the heavens for the whole world to see. Indeed, whatever has ended up catching the attention of Hollywood's celebrity-struck culture has often become part of the globe's collective fantasy life, for Hollywood films are the most powerful vectors of fantasy ever known to humankind. And by the mid-1990s, this unparalleled engine of invention had alighted on Tibet as one of its chosen subjects. Almost everywhere one looked in the film world, Tibet, Tibetan Buddhism, and the Dalai Lama were being acclaimed and generating waves of collateral interest in other media and entertainment forms.

After ignoring Tibet almost completely for decades, Hollywood made an oblique sortie into the field in 1986 with *The Golden Child,* an unlikely film that featured African-American actor Eddie Murphy coming to the rescue of a young lama who has fallen prey to a band of kidnappers in an ersatz Tibet. Then in 1994 the Italian film director Bernardo Bertolucci released *Little Buddha,* a film about a middle-class American couple in Seattle, played by rock idol Chris Isaak and actress Bridget Fonda, whose son turns out to be the reincarnation of a high Tibetan lama. At the kitsch heart of this film was Keanu Reeves playing the Lord Buddha.

By 1996, when I began to follow the film world's interest in Tibet, more than a score of documentaries and a scattershot of new feature films were in development. *Dixie Cups,* an action pic centering on the CIA's efforts to aid Tibetan guerrillas in the 1950s and 1960s was reputedly being produced by actor Steven Seagal. *The Buddha from Brooklyn,* the story of a Jewish-Italian cosmetologist who is designated the reincarnation of the high lama Jetsunma Ahkon Lhamo, had reportedly been bought by Turner Films. *Windhorse,* a low-budget feature about a contemporary Lhasan family rent asunder by tensions between Chinese occupiers and Tibetan nationalists was about to be secretly shot in Tibet and Nepal by the Academy Award–winning documentarian Paul Wagner. *Mystics and Magicians in Tibet,* a historical drama about Buddhist scholar and mystic Alexandra David-Neel's explorations in Tibet, was also in development, to be produced by Ismail Merchant. And a script based on Blake Kerr's book *Sky Burial,* about a 1987 Chinese police crackdown in Lhasa, had been bought by Merchant-Ivory Productions. But there were also two large-budget Hollywood films by well-known directors under way. The first, a version of Heinrich Harrer's classic *Seven Years in Tibet,* was to be directed by Jean-Jacques Annaud, whose *Black and White in Color* had won an Oscar for the best foreign language film in 1977. Its script was being written by Becky Johnston, who coscripted *The Prince of Tides,* and it was being produced by Reperage and Vanguard Films–Applecross Production in conjunction with Peter Guber's Mandalay Entertainment. Annaud had also hired composer John Williams, whose credits included *Jaws, Superman, JFK, Schindler's List,* and *Star Wars* to do a score that would feature cellist Yo-Yo Ma. Budgeted at $65 million, it was to be released in the United States by Sony-TriStar Pictures.

Annaud had a polyglot string of film credits to his name, including *Quest for Fire* (1981), *The Name of the Rose* (1986), *The Bear* (1988), and *The Lover* (1992). His urge to put Harrer's tale on screen, he explained, grew out of his fascination with the paradox that, while Westerners have many things and are often unhappy, Tibetans have few things and often seem unusually happy. "We have been told since we were born that the ultimate goal in life is to get as much money as you can, and have fame, success, and be on TV," he told me. "Why is it then, that most people that you find in Los Angeles will go on TV, have fame and a lot of money, but are so unhappy? On the contrary, why is it that people who have absolutely nothing and who are going along the tracks of Tibet prostrating themselves and have no possessions glow with happiness?"

What gave Annaud's production real Hollywood buzz was Tibet's marriage to the film's star, Brad Pitt. Unable to shoot in Tibet itself because of China's sensitivity toward the subject and having been refused permission by an Indian government nervous about antagonizing China to go on location in the Indian territory of Ladakh (a region inhabited by Tibetan Buddhists and possessing a landscape similar to parts of Tibet), Annaud decided to build his version of Lhasa in the Argentine Andes, a terrain remarkably like Central Tibet.

Hollywood's second major Tibet film was to be entitled *Kundun* (meaning "the presence"), the Dalai Lama's diminutive name used by his family members. Slated as a $28-million production, it had as its sole star director Martin Scorsese, who had created such movies as *Taxi Driver* (1976), *Raging Bull* (1980), *The Last Temptation of Christ* (1988), and, more recently, *Casino* (1995). *Kundun* was to tell the story of the Dalai Lama's life from his birth in Amdo in 1935 to his flight to India in 1959. It was being coproduced by the Walt Disney Company's Touchstone Pictures and Scorsese's Refuge Productions and its score was to be written by the contemporary avant-garde composer and Buddhist practitioner Philip Glass.

Scorsese had been urged to undertake the project by scriptwriter Melissa Mathison, wife of actor Harrison Ford, who had become an ardent supporter of the Dalai Lama. She had previously written scripts for such films as *The Indian in the Cupboard* (1995) and *E.T.* (1982), which led the British *Sunday Telegraph* to describe her as "something of an expert on loveable bald exiles." What evidently convinced Scorsese to do *Kundun* was meeting the Dalai Lama himself. "Something happened," he told an interviewer. "I became totally aware of existing in the moment. It was like you could feel your heart beat; and as I left, he looked at me. I don't know, but there was something about the look, something sweet. . . . I just knew I had to make the movie."

While *Seven Years in Tibet* cast Western actors in its principal roles, all the parts in *Kundun* were to be played by non-Caucasians, many by Tibetans who had never acted before. Since Scorsese, too, was unable to get permission to shoot in either Tibet or Ladakh, he chose an equally improbable venue, the Atlas Mountains in Morocco. An edgy competition soon developed between the two famed directors shooting on different continents.

Undeniably, there was something of a craze brewing around Tibet. Like a radioactive core emitting uncontainable energy, Hollywood's sudden interest was helping to fuel what some observers started to call a "Tibet phenomenon." Indeed, as the buzz about the film productions increased, media outlets of all kinds soon gravitated to the story, so that everywhere one looked the subject of Tibet had a way of popping up.

Books about Tibet and Tibetan Buddhism had long been pouring into bookstores, sometimes even garnering special sections. But now the stream turned into a torrent. Amazon.com's Web site offered some twelve hundred Tibet-related titles, ranging from *A Cultural History of Tibet* and *The Tibetan Book of the Dead* to *If the Buddha Dated: A Handbook for Finding Love on the Spiritual Path* and *Awakening the Buddha Within,* by Long Island–born Lama Surya Das (né Jeffrey Miller), who, being Jewish, had been dubbed the "Deli Lama."

From *Newsweek* ("Tibet Goes Chic") to the *New York Times* ("The Hollywood Love Affair with Tibet") and the *Boston Globe* ("Spiritual Happening: Buddhism Is a Newly Popular Way to Nurture the Soul"), magazines and newspapers were highlighting and headlining things Tibetan. Even *USA Today,* that voice of the American heartland, joined the stampede of Tibetiana with a front-page story, "The Littlest Lama," about a four-year-old Seattle boy who had been designated the reincarnation of a high lama and was being sent off to a monastery in Nepal in a manner eerily similar to the plot of Bernardo Bertolucci's *Little Buddha.*

Prime-time television, too, managed to capitalize on the fad when ABC premiered *Dharma and Greg,* a sitcom about the unlikely relationship between Dharma Finkelstein, the sexually liberated daughter of a "flower generation" Jewish father who always "wished he was Buddhist," and her WASP yuppie stockbroker husband.

Manifestations of Tibet's beachhead in popular culture appeared in many unlikely places. Technogeeks searching for nirvana could access a Tiger Team Buddhist Information Network Web site that promised a twenty-four-hour-a-day "single source for all that is Buddhist in today's Internet community." Benefit speeches, celebrity cocktail parties, photo show openings, congressional gatherings, meditation retreats, concerts, experimental theater productions organized by Tibet support groups, and other improbable events became commonplace in large cities. In May 1998, for example, disco punk diva Nina Hagen (known as the "Banshee from Berlin") performed a benefit evening in San Francisco with her group, Trance Mission, for Tibetan refugee children as part of an exploration of what she called her "sacred cabaret."

In June 1996, I attended a huge Tibetan Freedom Concert in San

Francisco's Golden Gate Park featuring the Smashing Pumpkins, the Red Hot Chili Peppers, Rage Against the Machine, and the Beastie Boys, among other bands—one of several such concerts that would take place around the country in the years to come. Over 100,000 young people emblazoned with tattoos and bristling like pincushions with body-piercing accoutrements mixed with gaggles of elderly berobed monks, some of whom would testify about Chinese torture as a kind of political entr'acte for the big-name bands. As the musicians wailed away, young dancers careened and ricocheted around a huge mosh pit, kicking up clouds of dust until some, almost stripped of their clothes, their eyes rolled back in near delirium, fell in trancelike exhaustion, to be carried off by blue-shirted monitors who dutifully presided over this Western ritual of ecstasy. (What all this had to do with Tibet sometimes seemed remote, though, oddly, it brought to mind old footage shot in Lhasa during the 1940s of swarms of Tibetans streaming after the possessed Nechung oracle as, in a trance and staggering under the weight of an enormous ceremonial headdress, he prognosticated the future.)

If these young people, drawn by their favorite bands rather than by global politics, had a minimalist conception of Tibet ("You know, maybe some mountains, monks, and stuff like that," was all that one young concertgoer could manage for me) or its political plight ("It has lots of romantic appeal because it has real natural people with a lot of heart," was another typical response), they were certainly willing to scream "Free Tibet" when led in ritual chants from the stage. On the other hand, Beastie Boy Adam Yauch, the celebrity moving force behind the concert, was a man transformed by his encounter with Tibet and its representatives in exile.

A singer who first burst on the punk scene in the 1980s in a haze of drugs and bravado and once sang such anthems as "(You Gotta) Fight for Your Right (to Party)," Yauch is now a man passionately involved in Tibet and its religion. In recent years he has taken to singing songs like "Boddhisatva Vow" and "Shambhala." When I met with him on the last day of the two-day concert, I was surprised by his mild and unassuming manner. Indeed, in his brown windbreaker and tan slacks and with his buzz cut, pale complexion, slightly undershot jaw, and reddish nose, he might be mistaken for a UPS deliveryman rather than a rock superstar. He explained his attraction to Tibet as part sympathy ("On a micro level China has been destroying Tibet") but mostly admiration: "Tibetans have been refining what it means to be human and then, by a miracle, dispensing this around the world. Tibet is a model of what a society can be when people start to realize that we are dependent on one another. The animal, plant, and insect kingdoms all keep us alive, not just water and oxygen. Tibetan culture represents a people living truly in balance with themselves and the world. The purpose of the concert is to make kids more aware of what Tibet stands for and that every time we go shopping, we are supporting those corporations which are fueling China's human rights abuses.

"The point is, we are directly involved every day. It's our responsibility to change the situation in Tibet, because all of the nuns and monks you saw here today have friends and relatives who have been tortured and killed as a result of the Chinese occupation. Paldin Gyatso, who spent thirty-three years in Chinese prisons, had cattle prods rammed into his mouth. For them to stand out there on that stage and know that others care, and to feel that emotion, is important."

The concert was organized by the nonprofit Milarepa Fund, named after an eleventh-century Tibetan ascetic and poet and set up by Yauch and a group of other Gen Xers who have continued to organize annual Tibetan Freedom Concerts. Their goal is to create greater public awareness among young people about Tibet's plight and the Dalai Lama's mission. Whatever these concerts say about the West's fascination with Tibet, they are impressive evidence of the degree to which that fascination is being translated into highly visible action. Indeed, the Milarepa Fund is only one among a growing federation of new groups organized by Western Buddhists, lawyers, students, editors, publishers, artists, musicians, mountain climbers, movie stars, environmentalists, politicians, and human rights activists to help Tibetans. By 1999, another Tibet support group, Students for a Free Tibet, had established chapters in nearly four hundred high schools and colleges across North

America. Operating in conjunction with the nonprofit advocacy group the International Campaign for Tibet, these nongovernmental organizations were helping to turn the grim pas de deux between China and Tibet into an oddly triangular affair. If Tibetans abroad lacked diplomatic recognition, embassies, or representation in important international organizations, they were gaining crucial access to power, money, and the media through their newly forged partnership with these unofficial and ardent American groups and supportive celebrities. Thanks to the appeal of these organizations' cause, the compelling personality of the Dalai Lama, and the shrewdness of their tactical planning, they had managed to circumvent many of the conventional structures of intercourse between nation-states.

As interest in Tibet seemed to gain a certain critical mass, Madison Avenue, too, began to take notice. An Anheuser-Busch TV commercial showed a clutch of robed lamas gazing longingly up at a Budweiser beer blimp; a Gatorade commercial showed Michael Jordan trekking toward a mountain peak for a bearded guru's oracular advice: "Life's a sport. Drink it up!"; and MasterCard began using a Buddha image in a commercial as if enlightenment were only a piece of plastic away. Slick catalogs now addressed the "needs" of a growing number of Buddhist faithful. The J. Peterman catalog offered that hard-to-find Tibetan shaman's jacket. "It's official," proclaimed another catalog blurb. "Crystals are out. Tibetan Buddhism is in." Steve Smith promised that the Livingarts catalog, of which he was founder and president, "will help you start the new year with exploration of your inner self and the world around you." He also guaranteed free delivery on all orders (over a hundred dollars) of yoga videos, meditation ensembles, weight-loss programs, natural headache-relief remedies, tape cassettes for "15-Minute Acupressure Facelifts," *Secrets of Sacred Sex* videos, and sets of Chocolate Body Paints. ("Turn your loved one into a delicious dessert. Simply heat to a pleasant 98.6 degrees, apply liberally, and let your imagination go wild!")

Western Buddhist journals like *Tricycle, Shambhala Sun,* and *Mandala* enjoyed a surge of subscribers as their pages bulged with ads featuring grinning gurus offering dharma-center study sessions;

Buddhist retreats; tours and treks to Tibet, Nepal, and Ladakh; and endless assortments of Buddhist tchotchkes, including a shovel-billed *Om mani padme hum* baseball cap. ("A mantra on a baseball cap, what's the connection?" went the pitch. "Well, there are 106 stitches on a baseball, 108 prayer beads on a *mala* [a Buddhist rosary]. . . . So, step up to the plate with your compassion on your forehead.") And for those Buddhist aficionados who had not become spiritually evolved enough to extend the notion of "nonattachment" to their financial lives, George D. Kinder, a balding middle-aged man, smiled out of ads that offered "Fee Only Financial Planning & Money Management." Lest someone think that Kinder's eightfold financial path was base profiteering in disguise, his ads explain that each year "at least 20% of the firm's net earnings are given to Buddhist and other charitable causes."

At the same time, dharma centers were springing up like Starbucks coffee bars. As of 1997, a database at the Pluralism Project, a Harvard University group researching religious diversity in America, listed over a thousand Buddhist centers nationwide. Exiled lamas found ever more enthusiastic groups of American followers as they traveled from center to center giving "teachings" like so many circuit preachers. While many followers were serious about their "spiritual practice" of Tibetan Buddhism, pop cultural manifestations of this new movement were sometimes distinctly low in spiritual calories. As Jo Jo Kwong, designer of a line of crystal meditation beads, admitted to the *New York Times,* "I'm a modern person; I can't spend years of my life meditating." So Kwong created a line of beads just right for busy entrepreneurs like herself because, as she declared, they "do the meditating for you."

Even the FBI was drawn into the expanding aura of the Tibet vogue. When in 1995 David Koresh's Branch Davidians defied the combined forces of the U.S. constabulary in Waco, Texas, the FBI attempted to "cool them out" by blasting their compound with the high-decibel chants of Tibetan Buddhist monks from the Gyuto monastery.

The infatuation with Tibet was, in fact, part of a larger fascination with Asia. DeeDee Gordon of the *L-Report,* a "trend encyclopedia aimed at manufacturers," observed in a *Vogue* article that the world was being swept by "inflasian," an upwelling of Asian influence on pop culture. It's "not just a Japanese thing," she explained, "but also about Thailand, Tibet and about how everybody wants to be Buddhist."

One impressive manifestation was Odyan, the huge mandala-shaped Tibetan temple and study complex that opened in northern California's Mendocino County in 1996. Modeled after the great Samye monastery in Tibet itself, Odyan was built over two decades by the American followers of Lama Tarthang Tulku of the Nyingma Buddhist sect. With its perimeter surrounded by a chain-link security fence topped with razor-sharp accordion wire, Odyan included six temples; a huge underground meeting hall; a large library; a 108-foot-tall Vajra temple with 108,000 statues of the founder of Tibetan Buddhism, Padmasambhava; 750 stupas, including a gold-plated Enlightenment Stupa over 100 feet tall; the largest prayer wheel in the world (motorized and weighing over 15,000 pounds); and 1,272 smaller prayer wheels (capable of spinning 100 billion prayers a minute!). The vast moat around its circumference was stocked with a flock of white swans.

Whatever in the zeitgeist was conspiring to make this particular moment in pop culture a Tibetan one, as soon as Hollywood bonded with its version of Tibet and turned its attention toward the Himalayas, the lives of Tibetans, at least those in exile, were bound to be affected. Historically speaking, much of Tibet's mythic power in the West derived from its defiant isolation. Since Tibet would not come to us, if we wished to touch up against its presumed magic and mystery we had to find a way to get to it. And now, it, or a replica of it, would be coming to us through every cineplex in America. In the meantime, a dense concentration of star power, media attention, money, and public relations would be focused directly on the figure of the Dalai Lama.

While it seemed a genuine opportunity for his government in exile, it was also a moment of potential peril. Like chunks of some remote Antarctic ice shelf, one piece of Tibet after another now seemed on the verge of breaking off and floating into the meltingly warmer oceans of the world, far beyond the control of Tibetans and Chinese alike. Such a process had, in a sense, begun at that moment in 1959 when the twenty-three-year-young Dalai Lama appeared at the Indian border as a refugee and was exposed to the mass public scrutiny of a curious world for the first time. In India over the years, he had been slowly forced to exchange inaccessibility for accessibility and aloofness for involvement, thus risking the very cachet that distance and detachment had once so effectively spun around him. It was a great paradox that by being exiled to Dharamsala, India, the Dalai Lama and his closest advisers had, after a fashion, undergone an earthly reincarnation. Deprived of their homeland and access to their people, with little money and fewer resources, bereft of diplomatic recognition, and ever aware of how badly fellow Tibetans were being treated back home, they could not but welcome Hollywood's sudden fascination with their plight. Without a full understanding of how Hollywood worked or of its legendary appetite for consuming subjects and stories only to move on, many exiled Tibetans dared to hope that with images of His Holiness the fourteenth Dalai Lama (admittedly played by actors) on movie screens worldwide, global attention might lead to some sort of cathartic salvation, however ill-defined, for their country.

In the early months of 1996, the productions of both movies—*Seven Years in Tibet* and *Kundun*—were gearing up to re-create Tibet in an elsewhere vaguely here on earth, with all the power, financial backing, and punch of a colonial expedition. Intrigued by the thought that Tibets of all sorts—*ours* and *theirs*—were to be caught in this powerful Hollywood updraft, I caught my own updraft, a United Airlines shuttle flight from my home near San Francisco to Los Angeles International Airport. There I picked up a rental car and set off in a one-man caravan to explore the kingdom of Hollywood and take measure of its latter-day pilgrims as they put their prodigious energies toward the fabrication of a new virtual Tibet.

3

THE DALAI LAMA COMES TO HOLLYWOOD

A gridlock of limousines with opaque smoked windows chokes the narrow cobblestoned entranceway that divides the two wings of the Beverly-Wilshire Hotel, one of the palaces at which Hollywood royalty gather to attend the endless fund-raising events they are called on to support. The sense of congestion is heightened by the throng of onlookers. In front of the main entrance to the hotel's grand ballroom, an unruly mass of TV cameramen, news crews, print journalists, and still photographers with huge bazookalike lenses face a scrum of autograph seekers, fans, and gawkers—the kind of inchoate crowd that assembles at a moment's notice in Hollywood whenever word spreads that a celebrity may be about to appear. Both groups are penned behind crimson lanyards on either side of the entranceway to the ballroom, jockeying for position under the scrutiny of liveried doormen in gray jackets and black bow ties whose job it is to keep these unruly aggregations inside their confinement areas.

Every time a limousine pulls up and its doors open, sun guns—bright battery-powered lights mounted on TV cameras—flash on in anticipation, for tonight His Holiness the fourteenth Dalai Lama will be the guest of honor at a dinner for the American Himalayan Foundation, a philanthropy run by financier Richard Blum, the husband of Senator Dianne Feinstein of California. Although the foundation's mandate is to fund community projects in the Himalayan region, few of those gathered outside are thinking about clinics, small-scale hydroelectric dams, restored monasteries, or even the Dalai Lama himself. Instead, in a state of high excitement they await the galaxy of celebrities about to arrive.

Suddenly, a murmur ripples through the press area and the sun guns brighten, bathing an incoming limousine in a blaze of light. Its doors open to the chatter of camera shutters as Meg Ryan and Dennis Quaid, fortified behind dark glasses, sweep up the steps past reporters and autograph hounds alike. They quickly disappear as if sucked into the refuge of the lobby by a powerful current of air.

"Hey! Who's that?" someone cries out as a man, hair sleek with pomade, in a black shirt buttoned at the neck with no tie, exits from the next limousine with a woman half his age.

"It's nobody!" a loud voice answers. The sun guns switch off and the humiliated couple is left to walk the gauntlet to a ripple of laughter.

As a doorman meets the next limousine, a rumpled-looking middle-aged man emerges, blinking like some unexpectedly awakened nocturnal animal.

"Garry! It's Garry!" Another blaze of light and signature books are thrust ardently over the red lanyard toward the advancing star of cable television's *The Larry Sanders Show.*

"Hey, Garry! Why are you here?" a reporter calls out. Shandling pauses. Then a wry smile spreads across his face. "Because I heard the Dalai Lama was great live," he replies before vanishing.

As the line of limousines lengthens, the gaggle of tourists also grows. An American family comes on the scene. The mother wears a yellow pantsuit emblazoned with yachtsmen's signal flags; the balding, overweight father sports a San Diego Chargers athletic warm-up; the teenaged son in rapper shorts that hang almost below his slender hips has a moussed coiffure that looks something like an oily tossed salad. Standing transfixed under the portico of this five-star luxury hotel surrounded by more elegantly dressed international guests, these heartland Americans remind me of the nomad pilgrims one sees in Lhasa wearing ragged *chuba*s and staring in wonder at the sites of the sacred city. Indeed, these three tourists look hardly more sophisticated, although at least marginally more hygienic, than their Tibetan counterparts. And presumably they do not keep legs of half-cooked mutton tucked inside their athletic warm-ups.

"Hey! Why's the lama still not here?" one of the autograph seekers behind me yells.

"Do you think he'll sign?" counters a young man in a "Live Hard" T-shirt who clutches a dog-eared autograph album for dear life.

"You dream, man. Anyway, the guy probably doesn't even do English."

Their conversation is truncated as actor Richard Gere, the Hollywood star most identified with the Dalai Lama and the Tibetan freedom movement, steps from a limousine. Mayhem breaks loose as supplicants cry out for autographs or interviews. Gere pauses respectfully just in front of the steps, shielding his eyes against the blinding glare of the lights. He thrusts his hands deep into his pockets, seems to hesitate, starts for the ballroom door as if to breeze past everyone, and then at the last second veers abruptly toward the press area, where he comes to rest in front of a crew from *Entertainment Tonight,* the popular NBC show about Hollywood. As Gere patiently answers questions, every TV cameraman in the press corral strains to get a shot.

No sooner does Gere disappear than Harrison Ford appears with his two young children and his wife, *Kundun* scriptwriter Melissa Mathison. Showing little of the boyish charm that first brought him to the world's attention as Han Solo in *Star Wars,* he looks as somber as someone crossing a treacherous no-man's-land where even eye contact might unleash a withering blaze of unfriendly fire. He makes a beeline for the hotel entrance, his children tucked protectively between him and his wife.

"Fuck, man! He dissed us!" exclaims the young man in the "Live Hard" T-shirt. But there's no time to dwell on hurt feelings. Like a Swiss clock striking the hour and emitting a circular procession of figurines, one after another the stars are now popping from their limousines.

Here come R.E.M. singer Michael Stipe and Red Hot Chili Peppers bassist Flea. While the still photographers are hunched over their cameras firing away with automatic drives like tail gunners in a dogfight, a white stretch limousine of such epic length that it seems to sag in the middle noses up to the curb. Out steps action-adventure-film star Steven Seagal, who has reportedly contributed substantially to this benefit event. A meaty six-foot-tall man, he wears a yellow brocade Chinese-style silk jacket with a high mandarin collar embroidered with golden dragons. His hair is gathered in a close-cropped pigtail and he clutches an elaborate Tibetan talisman of silver that looks like a small lantern. He is accompanied by a complement of hefty, gum-chewing retainer/bodyguards in dark suits, a retinue that makes him look somewhere between a 1950s banana republic potentate and a mutant Gilbert and Sullivan mikado.

Unlike the paparazzi, I have been invited to the three-hundred-dollar-a-person banquet and the seven-hundred-dollar VIP reception that is to precede it. From the hallway outside the reception, where coordinators equipped with earphones and head mikes are on patrol, comes the distinctive high-pitched din of cocktail voices competing to be heard. Inside, several hundred guests network their way around the large room, sip drinks, and nibble on baby asparagus spears wrapped in prosciutto. The Dalai Lama stands at the far end of this plushly designed room, a diminutive red-robed figure, in a receiving line that includes Richard Gere, Melissa Mathison, and Harrison Ford. One after another, he greets the hundreds of guests who wait patiently in line to shake his hand. He smiles, welcoming each with a deferential little bow, and then warmly clasps their hand in his own as a photographer clicks the crucial snapshot to verify a moment that might otherwise pass and be as unsubstantial as an illusion.

Reaching for a tray of hors d'oeuvres, I find myself elbow to elbow with actress Sharon Stone, resplendent in an off-white silk pantsuit and pale white makeup that lend her the air of a Greek statue come to life. A young robed and obviously enamored monk approaches her. In stuttering English, he nervously asks if she will pose with him for a snapshot, a request to which she agrees with good cheer.

Later, when Stone finally reaches the head of the receiving line, the Dalai Lama grasps her hand with no sign of recognition. Only after frenzied whispering and prompting from Gere and Mathison does his body suddenly jolt upright. For a moment he fixes his grinning gaze on her beautiful Hollywood face, makes a little cooing noise of delight, and then clutches her hand with extra vigor and holds it for a long moment.

It takes well over an hour before all the faithful have trooped reverently by in a process headlined by the *Los Angeles Times* the next day as "Hollywood Elite Says Hello, Dalai." Of the receiving line itself, the paper's reporter offered this comment: "It's at potentially tedious times like this that His Holiness's role as an incarnation of the bodhisattva of compassion would appear to be an advantage."

If the throng outside the entranceway is enamored of movie stars in general, in this food chain of celebrity worship the stars inside are enamored of the Dalai Lama himself. They exhibit a respect bordering on veneration that few besides Nelson Mandela or Mother Teresa could have elicited here in Hollywood. Yet what the Dalai Lama has to offer the denizens of this rarefied world is actually quite fragile—his unbesmirched spiritual integrity. Paradoxically, in his new relationship with the West his allure still depends on the very aloofness long associated with Tibet in the popular mind and the assumed mystery of its spiritual essence. In Hollywood, where everyone is out hustling something, there is nothing more beguiling, even unnerving, than someone in the limelight who restrains him- or herself. Thus, the Dalai Lama finds himself enmeshed in a contradiction. He must give face time to stars such as these if he is to serve his cause, raise money, and acquaint more people around the world with Buddhism and the plight of his people. He must also, however, carefully guard against any act that might seem to debase his moral and spiritual currency, thereby making him appear mundane.

Indeed, nowhere does familiarity breed so much contempt as here;

to be too readily possessable in L.A. is to become uniquely undesirable. As in Buddhism, an excess of visible desire is a distinctly negative currency. Indeed, perhaps something is already draining from his presence. As venerated as he still is, many of his Hollywood admirers and supporters have come to view him not so much as awe-inspiring in his ineffability but as lovable—a warmhearted, even cuddly religious icon whose appeal derives in part from his unpretentiousness and the fact that his fame in no way threatens theirs. "His own manner is so down-home and folksy that, with all due respect to his wisdom and position," proclaimed the film magazine *Premiere,* "it would be fair to say that the Dalai Lama is, well, cute."

But, of course, what is wanted of the Dalai Lama here is not really cuteness, money, power, or beauty but pure intentions, goodness, and spiritual wholeness. What helps make him and his Buddhist philosophy of nonviolence and compassion so winsome and alluring here is the sense that he wants nothing for himself. Though he is a canny politician searching for ways to rescue his people from Chinese domination, it is his apparent selflessness—the visible holiness of His Holiness—and the thought that it might somehow rub off relatively effortlessly that give him his special magnetism and so confer on Tibet as a whole a similar aura. When counterpoised against China—the brutal, censorious, godless Communist occupier of Tibet known also for throwing endless roadblocks in the way of movie companies frantically interested in reaching that mass market of 1.3 billion souls with their products—all the elements of a major morality play are in place.

"Let's face it, the Dalai Lama is a great guy to hang out with," writes Bill Higgins, a columnist for the *Los Angeles Times* who spends time each year on spiritual retreats in India. "He's warm, he's friendly. Since the age of two he's studied being a great guy, and he's had the best teachers. He's trained to see everyone as the Buddha."

Apparently a lot of other people in the world of entertainment agree, because tonight's event has been so oversubscribed that auxiliary tables have had to be squeezed into the grand ballroom. Because this is a Melissa Mathison–Harrison Ford–*Kundun*–sponsored night, no one is in attendance from the *Seven Years in Tibet* camp. With legal sabers rattling over who controls the story of the Dalai Lama's life, this evening is something of a symbolic *Kundun* coup in the sweepstakes to receive the Dalai Lama's foremost cinematic blessing.

Just as the huge throng of well-wishers—including director Oliver Stone, transcendentalist and actress Shirley MacLaine, the rock group Lama Boys, film star Rebecca de Mornay, producer Sidney Pollack, Star Trekker Leonard Nimoy, composer Philip Glass, lounge singer Jim Nabors, and Beastie Boy Adam Yauch—finally settle down to a radicchio and roasted garlic salad, a troop of yellow-bonneted monks of the Gelugpa lineage, the sect to which the Dalai Lama belongs, ascend to the stage and begin a guttural chanting of prayers. I'm reminded of the chanting halls of monasteries I have visited in Tibet, although here, of course, no rancid yak butter burns in the votive lamps, no pilgrims clamor, there is nothing, in short, of the grimy, greasy, smoky, dark atmosphere of real monasteries filled with real monks.

The Dalai Lama, who sits to one side of a stage on a raised dais between Mathison and Gere, gazes around at this ocean of glitterati and the sumptuously arrayed tables decorated with more than ten thousand roses, a gift from one of his California admirers, and a sly smile crosses his face. Taking Gere's hand in his own, he chuckles in wonderment and shakes his head in evident disbelief, as if, even after these many years of exile and globe girdling, he still retains the power to be amazed by the incongruities that can arise around his public presence.

Others begin eating their sumptuous dinner, but he sips only tea. When it comes time for him to address the crowd, he is greeted with a thunderous ovation. Then a silence descends so profound that most guests do not even dare sip their water for fear of clinking ice cubes in their glasses. He begins by talking about the need to promote tolerance, nonviolence, and compassion, then segues into an expression of ardent hope that China's leaders will soon sit down and talk with him about his country's future. Sharon Stone is so moved that she must dab tears away with a napkin.

Unexpectedly, he talks for almost an hour, so that it is nearly nine by the time the main course can be served. When his speech finally ends, hundreds of guests—who may have been hoping for a more pithy display of Oriental wisdom—quickly steal away, leaving hundreds of expensive dinners behind. But then, this is the city where people regularly eat (or, at least, order) meals in serial fashion as they wedge multiple business appointments into a single breakfast or lunch hour. Who can say what events still beckon the powerful and famous gathered here tonight?

In any case, the dinner is counted a great success. The illustrious crowd of stars seems ample testimony to the continuing allure of Tibet and the ability of its singular emissary to translate his spiritual message and the tragedy of his people into an international cause célèbre. And it is these aristocrats of the kingdom of entertainment who will, mostly unwittingly, help write a new chapter in the history of Western mythology about Tibet.

4

TINSELTOWN *TULKUS*

Like the myth of Tibet, the idea of Hollywood's having an actual geographical center has died hard. At the intersection of Hollywood and Vine, impresario Sid Grauman's Chinese Theater, opened in 1927, still aspires to be viewed as the Hollywood equivalent of Lhasa's monumental Potala Palace, an exotic emblem of a fabled city. Earlier, Grauman had opened the Egyptian Theater, which featured hieroglyphic murals and a huge golden scarab above its proscenium. The El Capitan, which boasted the unlikely combination of a Spanish Colonial–style exterior and interiors decorated with East Indian–Hindu–style motifs, burst on the scene in 1926. But his Chinese Theater was the theater of theaters, for which the only possible premiere could have been Cecil B. DeMille's opulent and fantastic biblical extravaganza, *King of Kings*.

Orientalism was alive and well in the Hollywood of that era and Grauman's Chinese Theater was a reasonable gauge of the "good" Asia that then inhabited the American imagination, a counterpart to Ming the Merciless, the Mongol monster who fought Buck Rogers in outer space, and Fu Manchu, who plotted his dastardly earthly conquests. His British creator, Sax Rohmer, described Fu as "the greatest and most evil genius whom centuries have provided," a being "inspired by the cool, calculated cruelty of his race." These were, of course, the years when Chinese were still unable to purchase land anywhere in California except in the small urban Chinatowns to which they had been largely confined.

Grauman's Chinese Theater was designed to look the way Westerners imagined a Buddhist temple in some etherealized China ought to look. That is to say, it was—and remains—a garish extravaganza of traditional Chinese architectural elements and Orientalist kitsch. The theater's towering pagodalike roof, adorned with bronzed dragon gargoyles, is supported by two huge vermillion columns topped by wrought-iron ceremonial masks done in a vaguely South Seas style reminiscent of the decor of Trader Vic's "Polynesian" restaurants. Its grand entrance is surrounded by a walled courtyard garnished with two thickets of bamboo, a pair of imperial stone lions, and clusters of Oriental bells that hang like bunches of grapes.

But where the magnificent Potala in Lhasa is a real palace and entombs the remains of actual Dalai Lamas, the high priests of Hollywood have left nothing more substantial here than fossil-like prints in the most base of building materials, concrete. It is in the theater's forecourt that Hollywood's most famous celebrities have left imprints of their hands and feet in wet concrete, a practice oddly suggestive of the Confucian tradition of setting up tablets to departed family members in ancestral temples. But it was these curious ersatz relics that made Grauman's Chinese Theater Tinseltown's most iconic spot.

The real business of Hollywood, however, has moved away from this increasingly honky-tonk precinct to the balmy, palm-fringed coastline at Santa Monica. And Orientalism, too, has undergone a process of modernization, shifting from exotic architectural fantasies to hopes for mystical personal transformation from Asian religions.

In the film enclaves of Los Angeles, spiritual searching is now second only to making money. While Tibetan Buddhists were a real rarity in Grauman's time, today Buddhism and other imported faiths have proliferated with unforeseen rapidity. In the kingdom of Hollywood, where the shaping of the self for public consumption has become something of an art form, where the boundaries between real and unreal, the self and the self projected on-screen often blur, morphing everything into a whirlpool of celebrity, beauty, publicity, power, money, fame, and spiritual hunger, a religion had better be an adaptable commodity to survive. If in New England Puritanism "reached its limits unconstrained by a parent church or by any external social or institutional authority," as the historian of early America Bernard Bailyn writes, and if in early Pennsylvania various German Protestant sects bore "the strangest and most plentiful fruit"—so many bizarre cultic manifestations in a wilderness without bounds—it is not unreasonable to find this American tradition of religious adaptability alive and well in Hollywood.

In an unprepossessing tidal flatland between the canals of the beachfront city of Venice and Los Angeles International Airport stands a replica of the alleys of old Beijing. This is the set for a thriller called *Red Corner,* whose script calls for death, abuse in prison, an interracial love affair, and a chase over Beijing rooftops as an American businessman, played by Richard Gere, finds himself framed for murder. My quest to make sense out of Tibetan Hollywood would lead me to an array of celebrity incarnations, but my first stop had to be with Gere, who is viewed by many as one of the main progenitors, the Grand American Lama, of Buddhism's Hollywood beachhead.

If Hollywood's fascination with Tibet and the Dalai Lama were to be personified, Gere would certainly be the prime candidate for the role. Born in 1949, he grew up in a very American small town in upstate New York, studied philosophy at the University of Massachusetts, joined the anti–Vietnam War movement and the radical group Students for a Democratic Society, then began acting in regional theater. Gere did not attract international attention until his starring role in the 1972 London production of *Grease.* Thanks to his performances in the 1982 film *An Officer and a Gentleman* and in *Pretty Woman* eight years later, he has become one of Hollywood's best-known and most-bankable stars. He has also long been interested in international political causes, particularly the plight of refugees from Central America and Tibet. It was Gere who fired Hollywood's first Tibet-related shot heard round the world, at the 1993 Academy Awards ceremony, where he startled global viewers by using his time at the microphone to protest China's occupation of Tibet. Since then, he has been tireless in his support of the Tibetan exile cause and an uncompromising critic of China's human rights abuses, which partially explains his interest in the script for *Red Corner.*

As a movie star and the former husband of supermodel Cindy Crawford, Gere the Buddhist celebrity has been an easy target to lampoon. "Gere is supposed to have progressed quite far in the mystical hierarchy for a Westerner, and to have gained admission to some of its [Buddhism's] 'secret practices,' " *Premiere* magazine has written. "No one is very forthcoming as to what those secret practices entail, but scholars and observers agree that the higher achievements include telepathy, levitation, control of body temperature and even the ability to pass through solid objects."

In fact, Gere's search for an Asian spirituality that might give his life direction and meaning is more than a quarter of a century old. He first became interested in Transcendental Meditation, a form of contemplative practice made popular by the Indian religious figure Maharishi Yogi, who during the sixties experienced his own version of celebrity as a guru to the stars, including the Beatles. While stage acting in New York City in the seventies, Gere also began studying Zen Buddhism and practicing *zazen*—Zen meditation—at the First Zen Institute. He read W. Y. Evans-Wentz's translations, including *The Tibetan Book of the Dead,* and studied briefly with Joshu Sasaki Roshi in Los Angeles. In an interview in the Buddhist journal *Tricycle,* Gere recalls his painful early attempts at mastering the rudiments of Zen Buddhist practice.

"Every day . . . there would be four or five people who would be rushing to do *dokusan* [face-to-face study with the *roshi,* or master]. They all had something to tell the *roshi,* and I would think, 'Oh, fuck, I've got nothing, absolutely nothing.' The first time I started mumbling, and he just stopped me and said, 'More *zazen*!' and threw me out. And then the next day it was the same.

"Another twelve hours go by, and I'm starting to break down. My back's killing me, my legs are killing, my everything's killing—I mean screaming! Dealing with my brain at that point was also very painful. . . . So I don't want to go in there because I've got nothing. I'm stupid and I'm lost and I've got no right to be here and I'm scum! So I start crying. I want him to really like me and think I'm sensitive. So I cry. And he laughs and tells me to go out and do more *zazen*! Anyway, you try every possible thing that you can to avoid the fact that your brain cannot wrap itself around this." Eventually, Gere gave up trying. "[But] they made me go in to see Roshi . . . and I was so lost I just sat there silently. He sat there with me and said, 'Okay, now we can begin.' "

Gere says that he has only missed three or four days of meditation—because he was "too drunk, too fucked-up"—in the more than two decades since. Confessing that he found Zen practice "dry," he says that when he began meeting Tibetans and learning about their religion, he suddenly felt a new "energy was brought up into the heart. Love is really the emphasis for Tibetans: compassion, kindness, *bodhicitta,* or selflessness." His first meeting with the Dalai Lama provoked in Gere a simple but heightened sense of feeling "safe." The Dalai Lama, explains Gere, "very subtly destroys all your expectations of him as a god figure who's going to make all your problems go away."

Since then, Gere has gone to Dharamsala, the seat of the Dalai Lama's government in exile, every year. He cofounded Tibet House in New York with Robert Thurman, the Columbia University Tibetan scholar and father of actress Uma Thurman, is currently chairman of the International Campaign for Tibet in Washington, D.C., and has become one of only a handful of Westerners who have developed a truly close relationship with the Dalai Lama.

"When I first got involved with the Tibetans, they could have really just glommed on to me as a movie star," Gere tells me as we talk in his trailer on the *Red Corner* set. "I mean, I've been glommed on to by other people in political or social ways, trying to get money and what-not. Instead, they gave me a book, a flyer, and some cookies and tea. They never asked for anything! In the end, of course, it was an extraordinary strategy because it made me give more in return by making me feel, 'Hey! These people don't want anything but my own happiness!' "

Gere began making trips to Tibetan refugee settlements in India and Nepal and then was finally allowed by the Chinese authorities to visit Tibet itself. "It wasn't so much the geography of 'place' but the geography of mind and heart that interested me," he says. "Tibet is bigger than Western Europe but has only a few million people, so there is still a sense of solitude about it. The height of the mountains is a symbol of Tibetans being somehow close to heaven. After all, the human body is constructed with the highest chakra, or energy center, being located at the top of the head. So, like mountains, there is something symbolic about the Tibetans themselves."

Just then Gere is summoned to the makeup trailer, and so we continue our conversation from adjacent barber chairs, staring at each other's reflection in a wall mirror. A cosmetologist armed with a toolbox of brushes, sponges, compacts, eyebrow pencils, bottles of blush, canisters of spray, and an arsenal of combs, curlers, and hair dryers dabs pancake on him like an art restorer touching up the work of a great master.

Gere thinks there has been a change in how people see Tibet. "While there still is a tendency to romanticize Tibet, much of the earlier romanticism has been replaced by a more realistic view," he says. "Because of the Chinese occupation, Tibet no longer just conjures up images of mountains, isolation, and yogis. The whole new political thing, however, has sometimes been extremely difficult for people to bring together with the older spiritual element. I mean, with Tibet, you have two things that do not instantly fit together. You've got ideas of nirvana, peace, love, and meditation. Then you have human rights abuses and genocide.

"With the Chinese it's David and Goliath, and I think that's clearly

how the Tibetans have managed to consolidate whatever outside support they have. Many of us constantly remind our Tibetan friends, 'You
must maintain that sense of uniqueness and that genuine cultural commitment to nonviolence. If you pick up arms and become like the
Palestinians, you'll lose your special status.' In other words, whatever
they do politically has to be in keeping with who they are as a culture.
To do that has been extremely difficult. Nonviolence takes a long time."

Gere notes that people demand of the Dalai Lama that he behave as
the personification of both Buddha and Jesus Christ. "On the other
hand," he tells me, "there is the reality of him as an ordinary person. But
somehow he delivers on both levels. I mean, there is no question that
we are all suffering to various degrees. Americans, Chinese, Tibetans,
Russians—we're all trying to get away from that suffering. And here's
someone who speaks about that constantly and says, 'Yes, we're all
suffering and here's a system. If you follow it, you will achieve happiness.' Intuitively I feel his happiness. He is available. What he has
achieved is available to us. He is worthy of our projections.

"To me he's incredibly polite, gracious, giving, and generous. In his
presence, one feels that this man wants nothing except for you to be
happy, even though there is nothing for him in the bargain. So when
you're with him, all the facade, all the armor falls away. He reduces us to
the simplicity of a child, to the motivation of a child who just wants
things to be right in the universe."

As I watch Gere in the mirror carefully considering each of my questions before answering, I find myself marveling anew at the way that
Tibet invites even those long acquainted with it to fashion their own distinctive versions of the place and its spiritual leader. I ask what Gere
views as the West's main projection. "It's that just by proximity to *him,*
you will get spiritually healed," he suggests. "Although that's a pretty
silly thing, every time I'm around His Holiness I must confess that I do
sort of hope to get 'zapped.' " And because the Dalai Lama is synony-
mous with Tibet, Tibetans, too, are granted spiritual authority by Westerners, says Gere. Because of him, they are thought of as good people.

"Traditionally," he goes on, "Tibetans didn't let anyone in and no
one wanted to get out because they thought they were already in heaven.

Outsiders hurt each other and killed each other. They were seen as having duplicitous emotions and drives. Tibet tried to keep everything out, and so they didn't create any bonds with other countries. They weren't part of any web of alliances and so ultimately they had no protection." But Tibet has remained, he believes, "the last real, living 'wisdom' civilization. The culture, the society, everything is wrapped around this all-encompassing idea of the bodhisattva, an enlightened being who returns in mortal form to help free others from suffering. Tibetan institutions have been created to produce more bodhisattvas, not more cars.

"Jesus is very much accepted by the Tibetans, even though they don't believe in an ultimate creator God," Gere notes. "I was at a very moving event that His Holiness did in England where he lectured on Jesus at a Jesuit seminary. When he spoke the words of Jesus, all of us there who had grown up as Christians and had often heard them before could not believe their power. It was . . ." Gere suddenly chokes with emotion. For a few moments he just stares into the makeup mirror, waiting to regain his composure. "When someone can fill such words with the depth of meaning that they are intended to have, it's like hearing them for the first time."

Of Hollywood's recent urge to put Tibet on the big screen, Gere says: "In the end, they're all just movies. They will be transformative only to the degree that one wants to be transformed and is capable of being transformed. The dangers are that one will get a kind of wet catharsis from them. Namely, people will think that because they've lived through a movie, they have somehow lived through the Tibetan experience and had an effect on it. In that way, people may just allow Tibet's problems to be put back into their compartment, while they move on to the next film."

What is striking about Gere is not just his sincerity but that for fully half his life—he is now fifty years old—he has been studying and practicing Buddhism, while at the same time serving as one of the most visible supporters of the Dalai Lama's efforts to solve the problem of Tibet and return home to Lhasa. In Hollywood, land of the ephemeral, one meets few people whose interest in and commitment to anything are as durable.

❧   ❧   ❧

Oliver Stone, a twice-wounded Vietnam veteran and the controversial Academy Award–winning director of films ranging from *Platoon* (1986), his epic tale of Vietnam, and *JFK* (1991), a conspiracy-minded account of the assassination of the former president, to *Natural Born Killers* (1994), a violent tale of spree killing, is a large bear of a man with a brooding countenance. He is also a devotee of Tibetan Buddhism. His film production company, Illusion Entertainment, is situated on Santa Monica Boulevard in a glass-walled high-rise several blocks from the ocean. It buzzes with the hectic energy unique to Hollywood.

Stone came back from Vietnam in 1968 not only with a Purple Heart and a Bronze Star but with a manic energy all his own, feeling, as he says, "real visceral," even "rabid." The intensity would soon translate itself into a frenetic and assaultive on-screen style and would help create a reputation for wildness offscreen. In the many contradictions of his real life as well as his screen life, he is something of a Hollywood Buddhist pioneer.

Buddhism first came to Stone's attention through his work on *Heaven and Earth,* his 1993 film based on the harrowing Vietnam memoir of Le Ly Hayslip. Undergoing a painful divorce at the time, he was impressed by the way Hayslip's Buddhism had helped her through her own wartime hardships. Although the film was a great disappointment at the box office, making it served as a spiritual journey for Stone that he claims helped change his life.

Soon after the film was finished, he made a pilgrimage to Tibet accompanied by Richard Rutowski, a friend and Buddhist practitioner. In hopes of finding some measure of spiritual enlightenment, Stone acted out an age-old Western dream: he went in search of a certain high lama in Kham, the Tibetan-populated southeastern region adjacent to the Tibetan Autonomous Region. On returning to the United States, he helped set up a dharma center in Los Angeles for Kusum Lingpa, a Tibetan monk who, after two decades in prison, escaped from China and became Stone's spiritual teacher.

Raised as a liberal Episcopalian on New York's wealthy Upper East Side, Stone considers his interest in Buddhism largely a private affair. But in a barely audible voice that suggests control rather than inner calm, he acknowledges that he has always been spiritually inclined and has always had to "wrestle with" faith and God. But, he complains, "Christ was all about pain and suffering—about a guy dying on a cross—whereas Buddhism is about detachment from suffering. I've identified with pain and Puritan Anglican guilt all my early life. Now I don't choose to live like that." So, he welcomes Buddhism for having helped him "get out from under the monstrously oppressive God the Father.

"I'm happier just living my life and meditating every day on the concept of emptiness," he tells me. "Buddhism is sometimes hard to grasp, but it's the road to happiness and to reconciliation with the idea of death." He clasps his hands in front of him in a prayerlike gesture and sits silently for a moment. "There's a lot of preparation to be done for dying, something that was forever in my face in Vietnam, where the chaplains were always saying, 'You gotta go out and kill for Christ!' There is a shallow form of every religion, even of Christianity. But unlike fundamentalist Christianity or Islam, I've never seen any kind of harmful Buddhism develop. Tibetans seem to regard the practice of Buddhism as a kind of play."

Even when he is talking about Buddhist compassion, there is a brooding, tense quality to Stone that suggests inner struggle. A part of Stone always seems on the brink of losing control, a part he refers to as his "reptile brain," as if an unreformable segment of his psyche lived in a state of constant friction with the rest of his being. As he once told *Esquire* columnist Ron Rosenbaum, for him life is "continual conflict," "a raging sea," "a war."

It may seem odd that a film director possessed of such a dark, violent, even apocalyptic view of life should be drawn to Buddhism and its tenets of contemplation, nonviolence, and compassion toward all living creatures. But Stone insists that violence is an inherent part of every human being that cannot be completely escaped. What offends him on-screen is not the cinematic depiction of violence but films where its consequences aren't shown—where, as he says, "people just fall dead and that's it."

Not insignificantly, he finds Tibetan Buddhism a little more forgiving of his "wild Western practices" than Vietnamese or Japanese Buddhism. "I don't subscribe to the asceticism of Buddhism," he says, a sly, gap-toothed smile creeping across his face.

Perhaps part of what draws Stone and others in the film community to Buddhism and Tibet is that they are able to construe it as being absolving of their particular sins of choice. Not only is "the church" far away and alien, but its priests, in southern California at least, seem to allow for flexible interpretations of their doctrine.

"One of the reasons Buddhism has been so successful in Hollywood is because it's nonjudgmental," a colleague of Stone's tells me. "Oliver says that he has been running away from judgment his whole life. The fact that his Buddhist gurus seem to have told him that it's okay to be *himself,* even to lead a life with certain excesses, comes as an incredible relief, especially to someone so used to judging himself."

There are, of course, vows in Tibetan Buddhism and rules, but as Becky Johnston, scriptwriter for *Seven Years in Tibet,* reminds me one day as we talk about this paradox and Stone, "Buddhism is guilt-free. Karma frees us from a sense of having sinned and having to feel guilty in the eyes of God."

What Tibet, Buddhism, and the Dalai Lama seem to personify in Hollywood is, then, a kind of uncritical acceptance. While Christianity offers mercy, it can also be suffocatingly censorious of sinners. In its place, Buddhism offers the dharma—Buddha's teachings—and Hollywood's version of the dharma does not usually involve browbeating or stern admonishments to followers to take hold of themselves and live in a "godly" way. Christ, of course, promised forgiveness, but in the Christian scheme of things, without repentance and the abandonment of one's iniquitous ways, there is no escape from guilt.

A tolerant interpretation of any faith has an undeniable appeal to those who have gained wealth, are living the good southern California life, and have acquired certain confirmed habits of self-indulgence. For such people, Tibetan Buddhism, at least the Los Angeles version of it, seems to offer an especially convenient way to graft a spiritual dimension onto their lives without being forced to sign up for self-denial or ultimate judgment. It also avoids the need for a time-consuming, potentially agonizing commitment to totally transform one's life by willpower, faith, or hard work. In this scheme of things, to be a believer almost all you have to do is believe.

A short time after speaking with Stone, I received a flyer in the mail for an event in Los Angeles featuring Stone's guru, Kusum Lingpa. A spokesperson writing on behalf of the Orgyen Khachod Ling Dharma Center announced that one of Lingpa's upcoming teachings would be "a Phowa transference of consciousness empowerment ceremony," described as being "extremely expedient" and of a "particular benefit to those individuals who do not have a great deal of time to practice."

Of course, many Tibetan Buddhists would claim that any theological view of their religion as being obligation-free or as a convenient shortcut to enlightenment is misguided and self-serving. Robert Thurman cautions those Westerners who, because of their "anti-Christian or anti-Jewish" disposition, think of Tibetan Buddhism as a purely meditative tradition that does not make judgments or lay down rigid moral prescriptions for behavior. This view, he emphasizes, is "simply wrong." On the contrary, in Buddhism, "the foundation of meditation is a strong ethical system."

Perhaps. But America, and Hollywood in particular, has long held out the promise of reinventing the self, and both are uniquely adept at creatively reconceiving established creeds to fit the needs of the moment.

Among the most extravagant self-styled Tibetan Buddhists in the Hollywood pantheon is action-pic superstar Steven Seagal. Martial arts expert, actor, director, and producer, Seagal has done a whole series of action-adventure films, from *Hard to Kill* in 1990 to *The Glimmer Man* in 1996, singlehandedly dispatching more bad guys amid explosions and volleys of high-powered-weapon fire than anyone except, perhaps,

Jackie Chan. Offscreen, Seagal's life story has merged so inextricably with elements from his films that he has acquired almost as many renditions of himself as the reincarnations of a high lama. He has variously alluded to having been a member of the *yakuza,* the Japanese mafia; a Zen adept; a CIA operative; a *tulku,* or reincarnation of a high lama; a Green Beret; and a Navy Seal. He is rumored to be in the habit of carrying a gun and to have threatened to "take out" people who crossed him. Simply put, he seems to thrive by using his acting to turn himself into whoever he wishes to be. After all, as he acknowledged once on *Larry King Live,* Hollywood is "full of illusions and delusions . . . and a lot of people who come to Hollywood—and I would not exclude myself—are, you know, slightly delusional." Indeed, by surrounding himself with a phalanx of bodyguards, publicists, coproducers, assistants, and other factotums, Seagal has managed to generate a phantasmagoric aura of power and enigma, not to mention menace, as if he ruled over some unseen fiefdom, even if partially of his imagination.

Still, there are a few things about Seagal that can be known with relative certainty. Born in 1952 in Detroit, Michigan, the child of an Irish Catholic mother and a Jewish father, he grew up in Los Angeles until, at age seventeen, fascinated by the martial arts, he left for Japan. There, in 1974, he married Miyako Fujitani, a black belt in aikido whose family owned a dojo, or martial arts training center, where Seagal himself soon began studying aikido, ultimately earning a black belt of his own.

While in Japan, Seagal became interested in spirituality, Zen Buddhism, and the traditional Chinese medical practice of acupuncture. In those years abroad, Seagal claims that because of his knowledge of acupuncture he was asked to work with groups of Tibetan monks who had been badly tortured by the Chinese and that he thereby gained some familiarity with Tibet's political situation as well as a respect for the compassion with which these monks regarded even their tormentors. In 1980, Seagal left not only Japan but his wife and their son to set up a dojo of his own in Los Angeles and to seek his fortune in Hollywood. Over the next decade, he married again and divorced before meeting actress-model Kelly LeBrock, with whom he had two more children. He came to the attention of Creative Artists Agency mega-agent Michael Ovitz, who was impressed with his martial arts prowess and befriended him; the result was a production deal with Warner Bros. The third of Seagal's Warner Bros. films, *Marked for Death,* turned into one of the top moneymakers of 1990.

No one searching for the various manifestations of Tibetan Buddhism in Hollywood could long escape Steven Seagal. But it was a particular bit of rumor that drove me his way. David Breashears, a friend of mine then in the process of making a 3-D IMAX movie about climbing Mount Everest, told me he had heard that Seagal had a Tibet film project "in development," provisionally entitled *Dixie Cups,* a name Central Intelligence Agency operatives once used for expendable allies in covert operations.

The script, it turned out, was based on stories an American named Jeff Long had heard while locked up in a Nepali jail in the mid-1970s. Having been arrested in Kathmandu as part of a wristwatch-smuggling ring run by foreign mountain climbers, he found himself imprisoned with a group of Tibetan freedom fighters who had been launching hit-and-run raids from the Mustang area of northern Nepal against People's Liberation Army convoys in Tibet. Rounded up and jailed by a Nepali government fearful of antagonizing China, they told Long of their heroic but essentially futile guerrilla efforts, supported and organized by the CIA, which even airdropped weapons and supplies to them behind Chinese lines. Indeed, in 1999 a book entitled *Orphans of the Cold War: America and the Tibetan Struggle for Survival* was published by John Kenneth Knaus, one of the American CIA operatives responsible for this covert operation.

At the time of Long's incarceration, these Tibetan freedom fighters had just lost their American patronage in the wake of President Richard Nixon's initiatives to regularize relations with Beijing and his historic 1972 trip to Beijing to meet with Mao Zedong. Seagal commissioned Long to work on a script based on some of the stories he had heard in prison that centered on one CIA operative—to be played by Seagal, of course—heroically helping the guerrillas.

Because Hollywood is a veritable dynamo of gossip and rumor, it is often hard to know what to believe; and since the system so often works on patronage from above, people are generally reticent about saying anything against anyone who is in a position to help or hurt them. Nonetheless, the reluctance of people to talk critically about Seagal seemed extreme. To ask about him in the movie community is, atmospherically speaking, to enter one of his films. Although many people have worked with him, virtually no one wanted to be quoted by name, which gave an otherwise ordinary journalistic exercise an eerie cloak-and-dagger feeling. Much of what former cohorts had to say about Seagal was unflattering and they feared the consequences—though what these might possibly be were unclear—of divulging their views.

Dora M., who was familiar with the early stages of the development of the *Dixie Cups* script, refused to speak with me unless I guaranteed her anonymity. "I'm a little afraid of him," she said over the phone. "I've already been warned against talking to the media and I've heard Seagal's notorious for wanting to wipe people out just like in his films."

According to Dora, in 1994 Seagal split with Kusum Lingpa, the exiled Tibetan lama also then favored by Oliver Stone and a number of other Hollywood stars, when Lingpa refused to declare him a *tulku.* Then in 1995, Seagal went to India and chartered a plane to tour Tibetan monasteries looking for another spiritual master.

"He really wanted to meet the Dalai Lama while he was in India and was just salivating when the occasion for an audience arose," Dora told me. "All these kinds of Hollywood people want to be legitimated and confirmed by someone like the Dalai Lama, because they feel that they can get some authority from it. I guess Seagal felt that an audience would allow him to legitimize his whole bonzo Tibet fascination."

In his audience, according to Dora, Seagal felt that something "unique" had transpired between him and the Dalai Lama. "He claimed that His Holiness bent down and kissed his feet," she said. "And Seagal took that to mean that the Dalai Lama was proclaiming him a deity. Hollywood people live in such a weird rarefied atmosphere of their own creation where you are what you say you are. If you tell people you are a scriptwriter or a producer, then that's what you are, even though you may have never written a script or had a film made. And after getting an audience with the Dalai Lama, you could say purple yaks grow on trees and no one would challenge you. Seagal just likes to put on these roles like clothes. What started as a Walter Mitty–like fascination with being a guerrilla adviser in Tibet began to get really overblown in his mind. Lately, Seagal's even started intimating that he worked for the CIA."

Dora M. sees the whole Tibet craze as high comedy. "You've got all these egomaniac movie stars, self-absorbed, money-grubbing gurus, and flocks of Buddha groupies looking for 'the path.' And then all the rich people are buying Tibetan art that has probably been stolen from Tibet by the Chinese and sold in Hong Kong."

Nonetheless, she believes that, if it ever gets made, *Dixie Cups* could be a good thing for the Tibetan independence movement. "Seagal could turn Tibet into a real human rights abuse story. Seagal could ironically be a great teacher about what has happened to Tibet politically, because he knows how to appeal to the crowd with violence. And he always goes for the underdog."

In February 1996, I learn from Seagal's Steamroller Entertainment production office in Hollywood that the *Dixie Cups* script has been retitled *The Soldier and the Snow Lion* and is still a long way from being shot. Furthermore, I learn that Seagal is now in the midst of shooting another film, *The Glimmer Man,* in which he plays a CIA agent turned cop with a Buddhist bent. According to a production assistant, the film is a "buddy action thriller"; the title, she explains, "refers to the hero's stealthiness in doing in his enemies before they even have a glimmer of anyone's being there."

It's an intriguing prospect, I think to myself—watching a Buddhist homicide cop play his part. But when I ask about visiting the set, which is in downtown Los Angeles, the production assistant assures me that it is closed.

Soon after, I happen to have a conversation with a representative of the Dalai Lama who is an old friend. He tells me that the following week he is planning to have dinner with Seagal, who often gives financial support to the government in exile's efforts. When he asks whether I might like to join him, I feel as if locked gates might suddenly swing open. Armed with this invitation, I call back Steamroller Entertainment. So respectful is Seagal of the Dalai Lama and his aides that several hours later permission has been granted for me to go on *The Glimmer Man* set.

I head toward downtown Los Angeles, marked by a lonely thicket of skyscrapers rising into an ozone glare like some desert mirage off the flatness of East L.A. A block or two past this copse of high-rises, the downtown tapers off into lower-lying brick buildings filled with parking garages, job-lot stores, porno arcades, and sweatshops. Turning in at a sign that says, "Hotel Cecil: Precios Muy Economicos—Low Daily, Weekly Rates," I find Seagal's film crew mustered in a parking lot so packed with mobile equipment that it looks like a supply depot for an army on the move. The lot is beside an abandoned building whose interior has been converted into a police station for *The Glimmer Man*.

Inside a production-office trailer, I meet Carl Goldstein, first assistant director. "We need three or four stuntmen for tomorrow's chase," he is saying into a phone. "We gotta get some broads into the cars and then shoot them with the techno-crane."

When Goldstein hangs up, I ask what *The Glimmer Man* is about. "Oh, it's East meets West in a very philosophical manner," he replies distractedly, reaching for another ringing phone. "Yeah, I need to ask you about the autopsy room," he barks into the receiver.

During the course of the day, I learn that in *The Glimmer Man* the homicide detective played by Seagal "went native" somewhere in the jungles of Southeast Asia and became a self-styled Buddhist. Upon returning to the United States he is detailed to hunt down a serial killer who murders whole families and hangs them crucifixion-style from the walls of their homes. Armed with such ingenious weapons as a credit card fortified with a snap-out razor, Seagal is to make his way through a mind-bending world of copy-cat murderers, Russian mafia members, and Serbian terrorists while fingering his Buddhist rosary.

When the Buddhist journal *Shambhala Sun* later asked Seagal how he reconciled all the carnage in his films with the lifestyle of a man presumably dedicated to practicing compassion and nonviolence, he replied, "Well, I don't think one has anything to do with the other. . . . I was under a contract with Warner Bros. I could not get out of, and what they wanted me for was male action films. I was offered extraordinary sums of money by other studios to do different types of movies and Warner Bros. would not let me go. Now that I'm out of that situation, this will enable me to do the kinds of films I would really like to do, which certainly are spiritual in nature and which will lead people into contemplation and offer them joy."

I ride an old freight elevator up to the sets for the interior of a police station, where a throng of extras and crew members mill around, drinking coffee, munching donuts, and awaiting the arrival of Seagal. And indeed, like the glimmer man himself, he makes no grand entrance, but instead just seems to materialize. Coiffed in his trademark pigtail, he has a Tibetan rosary looped around his left wrist and a gold chain around his right one. He is wearing his signature high-collared, Chinese-style silk jacket, only this time it's pitch black and embroidered with yellow dragons. The rest of his ensemble consists of tight black trousers and lizard-skin cowboy boots. His somewhat puffy face boasts an unnatural tan tinged with a suggestion of boiled-shrimp pink that gives him a babylike blush. His expression is a smoldering glower.

Seagal repairs to a canvas director's chair inscribed with his name; almost immediately, a young female retainer appears with a stool marked "S.S. Boot Rest," onto which Seagal regally hoists his feet. A cell phone is proffered like a scepter by another retainer. As he speaks into it, a third assistant in a Mao cap uses a makeup sponge to daub at his beefy brow, already glistening with perspiration from the hot stage lights.

Today, the production is shooting a scene in the police station men's room in which a lawyer informs Seagal that his client needs psychological treatment rather than jail. Seagal ad libs new lines on each successive take, each line more abusive than the last, as if any shred of Buddhist compassion in him were slowly being vanquished by an irrepressible and deeply rooted hostility welling up from within. Before long, Seagal has ratcheted himself into such a state of aggression that he is clutching his prayer beads in a clenched fist and snarling at his counterpart, "Tell your asshole boss that nobody, *nobody* threatens me! Now get your ugly white ass out of here!"

As lunchtime approaches, another young assistant glides over to me and whispers that "Steven" has agreed to see me during the break. When the shoot wraps, she ushers me down the elevator and across the lot to where Seagal's personal trailer is parked. There, I find Seagal sitting out front in another long-legged director's chair with his feet up on the same boot rest. As several female attendants serve him a lunch of miso soup, raisin bread toast, mushrooms, oatmeal, and minced egg whites, he looks like an Oriental potentate.

Since I am seated in a folding chair of ordinary height, I feel something like a commoner about to petition a monarch. But Seagal greets me graciously and asks what I'm up to. As I describe my project, he munches thoughtfully on a piece of toast, then explains his interest in Tibet. "My involvement has been quite secret up until now," he says in a hushed tone. "There are still many things I cannot talk about, actions to be taken in real life on behalf of the Tibetans that will not just be in movies." His eyes narrow against the sun's glare as he fixes me with a well-rehearsed look that mixes self-importance with a hint of menace.

"People say I only have a recent interest, but it's been twenty-five years. Really, it's just karma. I missed the seventies and all the drugs and craziness here because I was sitting Zen in Asia and actually practicing mysticism with Shinto and Buddhist priests. That was when we started getting all these Tibetan monks with broken bones and wounds—lamas who couldn't speak—coming out. I nursed a lot of them back to life. Once, when I myself almost died, I promised God that I would spend every hour helping people who are suffering. I ended up having a deep spiritual connection to these lamas. I attribute that to my past lives. I'm clairvoyant and have compassion.

"I've kept my spiritualism secret because people don't understand it. Friends have never gotten this part of my life, but there are many great lamas who recognize me as someone strange and from another time, who refer to me as one of them. I feel a kinship beyond words with them, something really deep. People all over the world come up to me and recognize me as a great spiritual leader." He gives me another penetrating stare. "I'd like to spread any kind of light I can and lead people into the dharma."

An assistant urgently hands him a cell phone. Seagal murmurs a few terse orders about a pending deal into it, clicks it closed like a switch-blade, and takes a few sips of miso soup.

"I do films because I can put little seeds in them that can become spirituality," he continues. "But Hollywood is a dream by people whose demonic impulses have kept me under their thumb. I have one more Warner Bros. film to do and then I'm on my own and can make the kind of spiritual Tibet films I want."

"Like *Dixie Cups*?"

He looks at me as if I had just breached security, then nods gravely but says nothing.

"And how do you view the Dalai Lama?"

"I've seen so much bullshitting from people who just want to be associated with the Dalai Lama," he replies, his voice tinged with barely suppressed scorn. "But the Dalai Lama gave me a spiritual blessing that would not have been given to anyone who was not special. I don't think he has given such a blessing to another white person. The Dalai Lama's been a great friend to me and I don't want to use that for anything but my personal spiritual sustenance. He is the great mother of everything nurturing and loving. He accepts all who come without judgment. He has a very serious impact on the degenerate times in which we live and on bringing us back to a more pure realm."

Again our conversation is interrupted by a call. After he finally surrenders the cell phone to his assistant, he goes on. "China understands Tibet only enough to generate fear." His eyes narrow. "At my audience, the Dalai Lama gave me a hug, put his head next to mine, and said, 'I'll see you again—in the Potala.' And I had a vision that I would be with the Dalai Lama in the Potala Palace someday despite the Chinese." He pauses, then in a deeply conspiratorial tone adds, "I want to have certain things happen so badly that I don't want to talk about them too much."

By now one of his assistants is pointing at her watch, so I thank Seagal and mention that I look forward to dinner at his Bel Air house that evening. He presses his hands together in the mudra gesture of prayer and gives me a silent nod as if to bestow a blessing on me before my dismissal.

Bel Air is Hollywood's residential ground zero. The map of movie stars' homes that is hawked by young Mexicans along Sunset Boulevard is most densely crowded here with little red stars connoting the haciendas of legendary entertainment greats. The houses of deceased stars such as Greer Garson, Henry Fonda, and Dean Martin share the area with the residences of relative newcomers like Barry Manilow and Steve Martin. Tonight, several of these opulent and lushly landscaped estates are illuminated in the darkness by banks of lights as if they were objets d'art in a sculpture garden. One with elaborate terraced grounds has a phalanx of white-jacketed parking attendants out front unburdening guests of their expensive, perfectly laundered cars. Passing another, I catch glimpses of tuxedoed waiters offering flutes of champagne to a milling poolside crowd.

Steven Seagal's house is surrounded by a high iron fence. The only way in is via an electronically controlled steel-plated gate. Inside, however, I find a relatively modest house by Hollywood standards. The door is answered by a tall, beautiful young woman, one of a myriad of comely women constantly in Seagal's presence who help create a sense of enigma, at least for an outsider. Are they assistants, lovers, starlets, producers, wives, friends, or some combination of the above? This one abandons me in the living room, so that I suddenly feel rather like a patient in a doctor's waiting room. It is panelled in dark wood to look like an English manor house and features a gas log in its ample fireplace. On one side is a grand piano under which rests a curious array of moose antlers, as if in Seagal's world, the yin of the piano needed to be balanced by the yang of something more masculine and outdoorsy. A welter of mementos from Seagal's life and films also converge in the room: a Western saddle heaped with lariats, some Japanese armor, a Persian rug, a few Tibetan beads, a selection of Native American art, and a collection of citation plaques from groups like the Coalition of Italo-American Associations.

I spend twenty minutes alone contemplating the motifs of the room until a white limousine glides through the gate and berths beside the door like an ocean liner. The Dalai Lama's representative, himself a

Tibetan *tulku,* disembarks, looking somewhat out of place beside this
massive conveyance that Seagal has respectfully dispatched to fetch him.

When Seagal appears to welcome his guest, a robed Tibetan lama is
beside him. He later introduces himself as Lama Chonam and tells me
he has only recently escaped from the Golok Autonomous Region in
China's Qinghai province. Seagal, he adds, has generously invited him
to live in this house while he studies English. As he speaks, I cannot help
recalling a friend's somewhat cynical remark that Hollywood stars have
gone from keeping staffs of private gardeners, cooks, butlers, and personal trainers to having their own live-in lamas.

When we sit down to dinner, Seagal takes his place like a paterfamil-
ias at the head of the table. Only instead of Dad, Mom, Grandma, Sis,
and Junior, our happy family consists of a Tibetan lama in robes, a
Hollywood action-pic megastar clad in a silk Chinese-style jacket, a
tulku cum high *rinpoche* in a business suit and tie, a young woman with
the aura of a would-be starlet, and an interloping writer. We dine on
distinctly un-Buddhist fare—grilled squab. As we eat, we chat about
China's unyielding posture toward the Dalai Lama and the way in which
"the Tibet question" is emerging in American popular culture.

Sensing that Seagal wishes to speak privately with his other guest,
after dinner I take my leave. As I drive away, I find myself still wondering about Seagal's love affair with Tibet, the Dalai Lama, and Tibetan
Buddhism, indeed about Hollywood's fascination with this unlikely trio.
Then Dora's words come to mind: "He always goes for the underdog."
It is a strangely incongruous thought here in the middle of all the glitz,
wealth, power, and urge to dominance that the opulence of Bel Air represents. I wonder if Seagal and many other Tibet supporters here as
well, having had to triumph over adversity themselves, aren't inclined to
identify with the Dalai Lama and Tibetans as underdogs—the little guy
against the big bully.

During a trip to Washington later that spring, I encounter Seagal
again at a second dinner, hosted by the American Himalayan Foundation
for the Dalai Lama. Having heard that he was slated to do yet another
action film, called *Blood on the Moon,* described by the *Hollywood*

Reporter as about a man who "seeks revenge on modern-day pirates when his family is killed during a pleasure cruise off the Hong Kong coast," I ask Seagal how *The Soldier and the Snow Lion* is coming.

"Cool," he says nonchalantly, his hand working his prayer beads like Captain Queeg.

"So when are you going to start shooting?"

"If I get the call, tonight, tomorrow."

"What studio is going to do it?"

"I'm doing it myself."

"Where are you going to shoot it."

"Probably on my ranch, which is twice as large as Hong Kong. Then we'll also shoot in Ladakh."

"But the Indian government is refusing to allow either Jean-Jacques Annaud or Martin Scorsese to shoot in Ladakh. Do you really think they'll allow you to do a film featuring CIA-backed Tibetan guerrillas killing People's Liberation Army soldiers?"

"No problem," he replies, cocking his head jauntily and raising an eyebrow. "I'm not like Scorsese and Annaud. I know all the guys in the Indian government—the prime minister, the foreign minister, you name it. I've been into their houses and eaten with them. What you don't understand is that a lot of India's rulers are actually very spiritual people and I think they recognize my own spirituality. There's no problem getting permission. Why? Because I'm one of them."

"Well, good luck," is all I can muster by way of reply.

That was the last time I spoke to Seagal. In June 1997, a little more than a year later, however, the media blossomed with a rash of articles about him, as well as cartoons and photographs. Headlines proclaimed him "The Tao of Pow" and a "Tinseltown *Tulku*." Seagal, it was reported, had been declared a "living Buddha." According to the flurry of news articles, while on a trip to India, Seagal had met Penor Rinpoche, the eleventh throne holder of the Palyul tradition from Eastern Tibet and the supreme head of the Nyingma lineage of Tibetan Buddhism, the oldest and most mystically inclined of the four main lineages presided over by the Dalai Lama. Penor Rinpoche had already attracted much skeptical attention in the American Buddhist community when, while on a trip to the United States in 1988, he canonized the middle-aged hairdresser and purveyor of cosmetics from Brooklyn Catherine Burroughs as Jetsunma Ahkon Lhamo, the reincarnation of a seventeenth-century saint who was the sister of Kunzang Sherab, the founder of the Palyul tradition in Tibet. It was she who became known as the "Buddha from Brooklyn." Penor was in the process of setting up dharma centers around the world when Seagal invited him to L.A. and reportedly made a substantial contribution to Kunzang Palyul Choling, his "seat in the West," located in Poolesville, Maryland, already under the direction of Burroughs.

What Seagal, who had long hoped to be "found" to be the reincarnation of a high Tibetan lama himself, wanted of Penor Rinpoche was a "clarification" of his status in hopes that some evidence of Buddhahood might be officially discovered. Indeed, after consultations with other lamas, Penor did conveniently confirm Seagal's intimations of spiritual greatness. It was reported in the press that, according to Khenpo Tsewang Gyatso, an assistant to Penor Rinpoche, an actual investiture ceremony had been held that February at Namdroling monastery in Bylakuppe, India. At the ceremony, Seagal was formally recognized before a crowd of some fifteen hundred people not only as a *tulku* but as the reincarnation of Chungdrag Dorje, a revered seventeenth-century *terton,* or "revealer of the treasures of Padmasambhava," the grand progenitor of Tibetan Buddhism. Chungdrag Dorje was reputed to have discovered sacred texts and objects hidden away by Padmasambhava and not only was founder of the Nyingma lineage but came from the Palyul monastery, Penor's own, which today is, ironically, without any monks in residence.

Why did it take so long for Chungdrag Dorje to be reincarnated as Steven Seagal when the process usually takes place several years after the death of the preceding lama? And why did not Seagal get recognized while still a child, as is usually the case?

"With regard to the particular circumstances of Steven Seagal's recognition, while it is generally the case that *tulku*s are recognized young in life, this is not always so," explained Penor Rinpoche. "In the Tibetan tradition, there is nothing unusual about recognizing a *tulku* late in their life. . . . It is not uncommon for there to be a lengthy span between the death of a master and the reappearance of his or her subsequent reincarnation."

Penor Rinpoche went on to elaborate. "As for Steven Seagal's movie career, my concern is with the qualities I experienced with him which relate to his potential for benefitting others and not with the conventional details of his life, which are wholly secondary. . . . Some people think that because Steven Seagal is always acting in violent movies, how can he be a true Buddhist? Such movies are for temporary entertainment and do not relate to what is real and important. . . . It is possible to be both a popular movie star and a *tulku*."

When asked specifically about Seagal's violent roles, Penor responded, "He's just acting. He probably hasn't killed anyone in his whole life." But then Penor Rinpoche seemed to step back just a bit from his creation. "Such recognitions do not mean that one is already a realized teacher. The next step of 'enthronement' may or may not occur for a *tulku*. . . . In the case of Steven Seagal, he has been formally recognized as a *tulku*, but has not been officially enthroned . . . [or] undergone the lengthy process of study and practice necessary to fully realize what I view as his potential for helping others." Such statements did little to allay suspicions that Seagal had bought his *tulku*-hood with a substantial donation.

The editor of the Buddhist journal *Tricycle*, Helen Twerkov, was blunt about her suspicions: "It's a difficult situation, because no one who knows Steven Seagal—who's been around him—seems to think he demonstrates any elevated spiritual wisdom." Activist scholar Robert Thurman, who begged Seagal not to go public with his *tulku*-hood, wryly observed that "God works in mysterious ways." But he also noted that the idea of an apostle of movie violence ending up as a bodhisattva was actually very Buddhist. "I like the idea that the 'good guys' could be anywhere and that a miracle can occur anytime," he said glibly.

5

THE EVANGELIST

The fourteenth Dalai Lama is not just the leader of one of the world's great religious traditions but, of present necessity, a prodigious juggler of several other disparate causes as well. He is the symbolic protector of an oppressed and dispossessed people who might otherwise be forgotten by a world increasingly focused on the sort of commerce in which Tibet can have virtually no role; he is the head of a small and tenuous government in exile that must raise the wherewithal to support itself; he is an international politician who must find some resolution with powerful opponents in Beijing and who is called upon to comment on issues ranging from South Africa to Kosovo; he is a religious teacher who travels the world giving complex discourses on Buddhist philosophy; he is also a very popular globe-trotting celebrity who, like it or not, has become part of a Tibetan fantasy much treasured in the

West. Overemphasizing any one of these roles can harm his advocacy of the others, making him vulnerable, for instance, to criticism by Communist Party leaders in Beijing that his religious leadership is only a mask hiding a covert political agenda aimed at spliting China apart or to accusations that he gratuitously involves himself in the affairs of other states, as some suggested when he expressed reservations about NATO's 1999 air strikes against Serbia.

As might be imagined, when the Dalai Lama finds himself in Hollywood, these roles fit together uncomfortably at best and not at all at worst. This particular morning in July 1996, as a steady stream of people floods toward Pasadena Civic Auditorium (which is inescapably within Hollywood's gravitational pull), he will have to juggle several of these contradictory roles for different constituencies. He must address the well-scrubbed young Americans who wear shirts embossed with the logo of the Compassion and Wisdom Buddhist Association, which is helping sponsor this three-day event; sustain the dreams of young countercultural Caucasians in jeans and tie-dyed shirts who will be in attendance; engage the middle-aged Chinese Buddhists in suits and ties who are sponsoring the event; and speak to the Tibetan women in traditional garb and monks in saffron and purple robes who are his people.

Suddenly, heads in this odd confluence of disparate types entering the auditorium turn together as if at a tennis match. A white stretch limousine is pulling up to the curb. As its doors swing open, a young Tibetan woman in traditional garb standing near me gasps, "It's him!" Expecting to see the Dalai Lama, I am surprised—though by this time I shouldn't be—when Steven Seagal steps out and, surrounded by his usual retinue, is ushered into the auditorium. A rumor has it that despite Seagal's offer to make a substantial financial contribution, the Dalai Lama's aides have decided to maintain a certain distance between the star and their charge. They evidently fear the Dalai Lama's becoming too closely identified with such a loose cannon of a celebrity.

Certain sources of financial support can create difficult situations for the Dalai Lama here in America, where "buying access" is everyday business for the rich, the famous, and the powerful. They are often

eager to unburden themselves of substantial sums for the interest that
accrues in status from being listed as a host or sponsor of an event for a
venerated personage whose particular brand of celebrity drawing power
is otherwise beyond their grasp. After all, whereas the rich are many,
there is only one Dalai Lama. And when it comes to placing a price on
drawing power and uniqueness—as with, say, van Gogh's irises or the
singular funeral objects from the tomb of a well-publicized Egyptian
pharaoh or Inca noble—sometimes the sky is the limit. So the Dalai
Lama's advisers, despite their always urgent need for financial support,
have had to learn vigilance when swimming in entertainment or political
waters, where everyone wants what they don't have and believes that
money and power ought to be able to get it for them.

Inside the Civic Auditorium, where a sold-out crowd awaits him, the
Dalai Lama is today on religious, and thus relatively safe, ground. For
the next few days he will teach what he knows better than any other
human being on earth, Tibetan Buddhism. He will also perform an
Avalokiteshvara Bodhisattva initiation ceremony, a ritual named after
the thousand-armed Indian Buddha of compassion whose earthly manifestation Tibetan Buddhists believe each reigning Dalai Lama to be. In
fact, the fourteenth Dalai Lama is said to be the seventy-fourth reincarnation of Avalokiteshvara in a lineage that can supposedly be traced
back to Shakyamuni, the Lord Buddha himself.

The architectural motif of this vast 1920s hall is Art Deco, but the
stage has been decorated to look like the chanting hall of a Tibetan
monastery. Large *thangka*s, Tibetan wall hangings, are part of a colorful, eye-pleasing backdrop. Beneath a banner reading "The Great Lord
of the Snow and Land and Emanation of Great Compassion,
Avalokiteshvara, Tenszin Gyatso the 14th Dalai Lama, May You Be
Victorious in All Directions, and May You Stay a Long Time for the
Happiness of All Beings" is a raised thronelike chair and a golden altar
festooned with flowers, fruit, butter lamps, and images of a host of protective Tibetan deities bathed in stage lights. Arrayed around this centerpiece are robed monks, devotees, and supporters from the world of
entertainment. They represent a by now familiar cast of characters—
Richard Gere, Robert Thurman, Adam Yauch, Dennis Quaid, and

Melissa Mathison. Only Steven Seagal has been relegated to an offstage seat, albeit in the front row of the orchestra.

Although the Dalai Lama will focus on the purely religious task of teaching (while making sure that the informal entourage of entertainment stars who support him financially receive their due), he will also engage in a subtle political initiative directed at events taking place thousands of miles away. For he has decided to aim his teaching at members of the local overseas Chinese Buddhist community—a strategy that also has a secular edge to it. Overseas Chinese, many of whom are quite dedicated to the Dalai Lama, are actually superfluous to what everyone knows is Tibet's real "China problem," namely, Beijing officials who steadfastly refuse to have anything to do with him or his government in exile. But symbolically, much is at stake in any demonstration that the Dalai Lama and the Tibet he represents can coexist peaceably in some kind of ecumenical relationship with Chinese in general. Thus, the Chinese in attendance here are actually surrogates of sorts for the Dalai Lama's adversaries in Beijing. By showing that he can work with this lost tribe from the "Chinese motherland," he is visibly demonstrating that he is not anti-Chinese. In deference to the targeted audience, the entire teaching will be simultaneously translated from Tibetan into Mandarin by an onstage translator. (Those who speak neither Tibetan nor Mandarin Chinese will listen to an English translation over earphones.)

When at last the Dalai Lama emerges onstage, a murmur hums through the crowd. In a slightly crouched pose, a position of humility, he presses his hands together in the mudra posture of prayer, bowing first to the altar and then to the audience. Ascending his temporary throne, he flips the end of his *chogo,* or monk's habit, over his shoulder, clips a microphone onto its cowl, and begins chanting, "Om mani padme hum." Meanwhile, a young monk adjusts an electric fan that is to cool His Holiness under the hot stage lights. We are in almost every sense a long way from the Potala.

In the middle of his chanting the Dalai Lama stops, cocks his head, looks quizzically at the monks and film stars seated below him, smiles, and then emits a mirthful giggle. It echoes through the hall over the sound system, triggering a loving, responsive laugh from the crowd.

Such a casual, friendly manner confounds any image of him as the mystical God-king so zealously sought by Westerners for centuries. Indeed, this reputed incarnation of Avalokiteshvara seems bent on thwarting all efforts by believers to deify him. With a thermos of tea lodged beside him and the fan churning in the warm southern California air, he seems premeditatedly of this world.

When Christians go to church or visit great cathedrals, they are used to manifesting their religious devotion with a hushed and somber reverence. Many are surprised and confused by Tibetan monasteries where ceremonies are often conducted in what seems like an atmosphere of casual impiety bordering on sacrilege. It is almost impossible to imagine a Western priest or minister winking and then chortling at his subalterns during a service. But such gestures of the Dalai Lama are comfortably within Tibetan tradition and the Dalai Lama's own character, suggesting his urge to banish all pretense of solemnity and somberness from his worship.

Indeed, Tibetan monasteries are not so much hushed houses of God as places where monks perform their spiritual practice as they mingle with ordinary people carrying out their own devotions. In this sense, the monasteries are more like spiritual workshops than sites of reverential worship. In a largely nomadic society, monasteries also traditionally served as crucial meeting places for civil and secular society. In fact, it is not uncommon to find merchants hawking goods, beggars asking for alms, and idlers simply hanging out in the environs without anyone's feeling that apostasy is being committed.

When the Dalai Lama rings a little bell and begins speaking, the simultaneous translation into Mandarin echoing behind his own words, a hush falls over the audience.

"This is the first time in my life that I have given a teaching primarily for a Chinese audience," he begins, trying from the first to establish the historic nature of this Sino-Tibetan event. "But in doing so, I am just continuing the process of those lamas who throughout history have done such teachings."

After receiving a ceremonial scarf from a Chinese representing the Compassion and Wisdom Buddhist Association, the Dalai Lama recites several prayers. Then he begins discussing how, even though the mind is related to the body, it also has its own independent qualities that can be refined and cultivated through spiritual practice. "It is because of craving and strong attachment that we are kept bound to the cycle of existence, and it is only by renouncing these attachments that we attain enlightenment," he says matter-of-factly. "It would be senseless not to see your own ill deeds as the factors that harm you. . . . By thinking about the positive aspects of human life's preciousness, you should come to the conclusion that you must give it meaning by doing dharma practice in this life. One must not miss the opportunity, because the time of death is uncertain. We cannot decide this time for ourselves in terms of health and age. Even though we are all gathered here today for this teaching, it is not sure that we can all come back tomorrow."

I look around the hall. The audience is already in his thrall. For this brief interval, he seems truly to have cast off his many other roles and become simply a religious leader.

"When we encounter death, not even our friends and relatives can help us," he continues. "We cannot go to a court. Wealth cannot help you, because you cannot take it with you. Neither can your intelligence help you. You may be very powerful like Stalin and Mao, but at the time of death, they, too, went alone just the way wild animals do. Finally, we have to discard and leave behind our physical bodies. It is only dharma practice, the practice of purifying your mind, that will help you at the time of death.

"The first part of Buddhist cultivation of the self is to realize that all living beings are equal in not wanting unhappiness and suffering and equal in the right to rid themselves of suffering. You learn that your happiness is very much related to that of other living beings and that, while your own happiness is important, it is insignificant in comparison to that of others." He pauses and looks out across the silent audience as if he wanted to gauge our reaction. Then he smiles. With the butter lamps flickering in front of the *thangka*s, it is not easy to remember that, just outside, palm trees sway in the warm Santa Ana winds and that, across town, scientists at Cal Tech University and

NASA's Jet Propulsion Labratory are laboring over questions of outer, not inner, space.

"To practice loving kindness and compassion does not mean bowing down to others," he says, his guttural, deep voice reverberating through the darkened hall. "It can also mean taking a strong stand. One can use love and compassion as techniques to deal with the negative actions of others. The point of meditation is to view each sentient being just like your mother or your closest friend. We need to create a sense of equality between all beings by reflecting on the fact that [through reincarnation] everyone could have been a close friend at one time and shown kindness and compassion."

The first thrill of simply being in the presence of the Dalai Lama soon wears off. The audience begins to relax and settle in almost as if they were at a vocational training program. Children brought by their parents quickly lose their fascination with the novelty of what is happening onstage. After a while, two young boys sitting near me plow into a pile of Batman and Spider-Man comics. Other children wander up and down the aisles as their parents listen or even nap.

"A self-cherishing attitude is at the root of all negatives," the Dalai Lama is saying. "By taking the self and switching places with others, we turn things around and center concern on others. Cherishing others is the source of all happiness. As our love and compassion get stronger and stronger, they will induce the attitude of wanting to bring about the well-being of others. Out of compassion we take to ourselves the suffering of others. That's the point of meditating. The altruistic urge toward enlightenment is something that brings benefit all the time without stopping."

As the teaching progresses, one of the Dalai Lama's aides spots me. Knowing something of the book I'm working on, he motions solicitously for me to come onstage. It is a thoughtful gesture but also a reminder of how vigilant and astute the Dalai Lama's aides have had to become to deal with members of the media. Through much hard work, several have learned who's who in the media power structure and they are increasingly aware of how important proper homage and attention toward influential people can be in winning good press and financial support. Indeed, the Dalai Lama's best aides have had to take on the roles of informal press secretary, lobbyist, social host, fund-raiser, political spin doctor, and keeper of patrons all at once.

I find a place to sit between Melissa Mathison and Dennis Quaid just as a question-and-answer period begins. The way the Dalai Lama wears his robe and cranes his neck as he respectfully listens to one earnest question after another makes him look a little like a wise old tortoise, its head extended from its shell. When asked a theologically involved question calculated to display the erudition of the questioner, he answers with a disarming but not condescending or wounding humor.

One questioner wants to know "if he smells sweetness" when he does his spiritual practice. The Dalai Lama smiles naughtily, and replies that what he smells is not sweetness but sweat. Then he pulls the edge of his robe up to his nose for a sniff and laughs.

Sitting on his throne, bathed in orange light, the Dalai Lama emanates the sort of reassuring sense of security conveyed by a skilled pilot, in his case one who seems to understand the complexities of life. After all, one thing we humans want is to be able to place our trust in someone who can shepherd us safely, whether physically or spiritually.

When the teaching and ceremony finally come to an end, I leave the auditorium through a stage door with the Dalai Lama's entourage of aides and a flock of security guards equipped with telltale earpieces and walkie-talkies. As we step into the heat and bright ozone light of Pasadena, it is as if we had stepped into a blast furnace. Squinting against the blinding glare, I think about the light in Tibet. Especially when reflected off mountain snow, it, too, is blinding and strong. But rather than this blurry, fluorescent white sky, its cobalt blue has a unique sharpness; the high-altitude sun is piercing and intense. Tibet seems worlds away.

Although over the course of three days the Dalai Lama would gently but persistently admonish his Pasadena followers to guard against the delusions of the ego, Hollywood is not easily dissuaded from the kinds of self-aggrandizement and extravagant projects that have been its stock-in-trade for so long. Indeed, just then the two elaborate film productions were just gearing up to re-create the lost world of Tibet and Lhasa, in the Atlas Mountains of Morocco and the Argentine Andes, with Tibetans and their yaks flown in for the occasion like so much mail-order furniture.

But getting to *Seven Years in Tibet*'s or *Kundun*'s version of the sacred city was to prove hardly less daunting than reaching Lhasa in the nineteenth century, when it had been so resolutely closed to outside intruders. For a journalist to visit either mock Tibet meant not only getting to North Africa or South America but obtaining permission from the production companies to go on-location. Like the Chinese *amban*s, Tibetan officials, and armed nomads of yore who so zealously guarded every mountain pass leading to Lhasa, the public relations teams assigned to these film productions defended their closed sets—and that even more closely held property, "access" to the stars—with the corporate equivalent of religious zeal. Months of phones calls and faxes to those responsible yielded little but vague promises that they would let me know if a visit could be approved.

In the case of *Kundun,* I was reminded by scriptwriter Melissa Mathison that, a recent *Tonight Show* appearance notwithstanding, director Scorsese was "a very private person," and intrusions on his sets by members of the media were rarely well received. Still, she graciously offered to do what she could. I also learned that some involved with *Kundun* feared that I might trivialize what they were undertaking by making the film seem as if it were just another part of a new rage for Tibet. Scorsese's publicist, Marion Billings, was not optimistic about my chances of meeting with the director.

The fact that I was writing a book rather than a magazine or newspaper piece seemed to dampen everyone's ardor. It was not that film executives did not want journalists to see what they were doing—after all, they thrive on publicity—but that what they wanted were reporters connected to large, influential newspapers, magazines, or television networks who would help do publicity for them in a timely manner. They did not relish the idea of wasting time on a writer whose book would come out long after the film had left the multiplexes of America.

I was encountering similar resistance from those in charge of *Seven Years in Tibet*. The film's public relations watchdogs tirelessly told me that their sets, too, were going to be unusually tightly restricted, lest the multitude of curious journalists who had expressed interest in the unusual convergence of Hollywood, Tibet, Brad Pitt, and the Dalai Lama disturb the task at hand. Not even Peter Guber, whose Mandalay production company had helped bankroll the film and to whom I had been given an introduction by a friend, seemed capable of paving my way to Uspayatta, Argentina, where much of the film was to be shot. When a former Sony-TriStar executive faxed a plea to Argentina on my behalf, the production unit's publicist, Susan d'Arcy, replied, "You, I know, will appreciate the balancing act we go through dealing with the sensitivities of our players. We just have to keep faith with Brad. . . . What we can't do is jeopardize his goodwill at this crucial stage."

The seemingly insurmountable resistance on both fronts left me feeling increasingly dispirited, indeed on the verge of giving up. Then one day I awoke filled with an unexpectedly bullish explorer's impulse, an irrepressible, headstrong determination to proceed to one or the other of Hollywood's Lhasas in exactly the manner of all those earlier Western adventurers who had so willfully pushed on to the holy city despite lack of permission and impediments of every sort. And since *Seven Years in Tibet* was the bigger-budget Hollywood production—twice the size of *Kundun*—I decided to set my sights on Argentina.

— 6 —

THE EXPLORER

It was perhaps natural that Hollywood filmmakers eager to bring Tibet to screen life in the 1990s would reach back forty-plus years to a young Austrian mountain climber's classic tale of his two-year trek from a British prisoner of war camp to the palace of the spiritual ruler of Tibet. No book of real-life adventure had ever brought such Western attention to Tibet before and no such book could ever do so again, for that Tibet—the one that had existed in the blank space on a map of mountains so high that only the imagination could vault over them—was already ceasing to exist at the very moment Heinrich Harrer sat down in India in 1950 to pen his extraordinary story.

For Jean-Jacques Annaud or Martin Scorsese to make a film about modern Tibet would, of course, have been about as romantic as making a film about modern Iraq or Albania. With Chinese oppressors and

Tibetan victims, ruined monasteries and tortured monks, hydroelectric projects and Chinese-run karaoke bars, plus a whole host of intractable ethnic and national questions, where would the romance be? Who would Brad Pitt play? Films like Roland Joffe's *The Killing Fields* (1984), about the Cambodian genocide; Peter Weir's *The Year of Living Dangerously* (1983), about the Indonesian military coup of 1965; and John Boorman's *Beyond Rangoon* (1995); about Burma under the SLORC military junta are few and far between. While sometimes winning critical acclaim, films on such international political topics seldom prove box office bonanzas and cannot justify Hollywood-sized budgets.

Film scripts about Tibet—about the Tibet, at least, that has always attracted Westerners—have little choice but to stop in the 1950s at a time when it was still possible to ground our Western fantasies in an evocative but real land. Even Steven Seagal in his prospective film on guerrilla warfare on the Tibetan Plateau (which as of the beginning of 2000 showed no sign of getting made) was planning to stay as close as the story of Tibetan resistance would allow to that older Tibet where monks, monasteries, and yaks, rather than Party cadres, cement plants, and Mao posters, predominated. For Hollywood, it was necessary to recapture and "preserve" an older Tibet that could more comfortably contain our yearnings for an exotic traditional society that worked. And so it was logical that Hollywood should seek to breathe new life into the memories of Heinrich Harrer, a distinctly flawed man who had had a larger-than-life adventure and finally retired to the Austrian Alps to monumentalize it.

There is no question that Harrer's story is remarkable. On July 24, 1938, he and three colleagues became the first team to make the dangerous ascent of the north face, "the murder wall," of the 18,000-foot-high Eiger in Switzerland. Because it was the tallest and most treacherous unconquered peak in the Alps and because it had claimed so many lives—the president of the British Alpine Club had described the urge to scale it as "an obsession for the mentally deranged"—the Swiss government had forbidden all attempts. Harrer's 1938 ascent despite the Swiss prohibition, then, bespoke the kind of triumph of the will revered by the Nazis. So when his team's assault succeeded, he and his climbing partners were feted by the Nazi leadership and quickly became German folk heroes. Indeed, Harrer was awarded a special prize by Hitler himself at a huge sports festival in Breslau organized by the Führer to honor the four climbers.

In 1939 Harrer was chosen as part of a prestigious German-Austrian team dispatched to climb the 26,000-foot Nanga Parbat, a Kashmiri peak that earlier Western expeditions had repeatedly failed to summit. As it was situated in Central Asia, where according to Nazi racial lore the sacred Aryan race had arisen, such a mountain had a special mystical allure for the Nazis. It was on this expedition that Harrer remembers "succumb[ing] to the magic of the Himalayas." As he later wrote, they "worked on my mind like a spell."

Still in India in 1939 when war broke out between Germany and Britain, Harrer and his fellow climbers, who had not succeeded in summiting Nanga Parbat, were interned as POWs by the British colonial government. After five failed breakout attempts from several different camps, in April 1944 Harrer, fellow climber Peter Aufschnaiter, and several other inmates from Axis countries succeeded in escaping from a camp at Dehra Dun disguised as Indians. Since Tibet was neutral territory and Harrer and Aufschnaiter were skilled mountaineers, the two of them headed north with the vague hope of ultimately reaching Lhasa and then some part of China controlled by Japan, Germany's ally.

It was not until almost two years later that the ragged, starved, and nearly spent mountaineers finally, and incredibly, approached the forbidden city. "So near to Lhasa!" wrote Harrer. "The name had always given us a thrill. On our painful marches and during icy nights, we had clung to it and drawn new strength from it. No pilgrim from the most distant province could ever have yearned for the Holy City more than we did."

On a cold January day in 1946, disguised as destitute nomads on a pilgrimage, Harrer and Aufschnaiter passed through the West Gate that then guarded the entryway to Lhasa in the shadow of the Potala. "Almost every book about Lhasa says that sentries are posted here to guard the Holy City," Harrer later wrote. "We approached with beating hearts. But there was nothing. No soldiers, no control post—only a few beggars holding out their hands for alms. . . . Nobody stopped or bothered us. We could not understand it, but finally realized that no one, not even a European, was suspect, because no one had ever come to Lhasa without a pass."

Although it was not quite true that nobody without a pass had preceded them, it was generally true that the city had succeeded in remaining virtually isolated from, and unaffected by, events taking place throughout the rest of the globe. In this refuge from the war-stricken world, Harrer would not only live for almost five years but learn Tibetan, work for the Tibetan government, and become acquainted with the Dalai Lama, then a lonely fifteen-year-old boy. Soon this blond-haired *inji,* or "Westerner," and the young boy, who called him *gopa,* "yellow-head," would actually become friends.

As a tutor of sorts, Harrer helped the Dalai Lama understand something of science, English, and world geography. He even built him a small movie theater by hooking an old projector up to a generator run by one of the only automobile engines in Tibet. "I was a small link between his medieval world and his future life in the West," Harrer would recall. The young Dalai Lama, in turn, became Harrer's most important link to Tibet. "My life in Lhasa had now begun a new phase," Harrer wrote of the burgeoning friendship. "My existence had an aim. I no longer felt unsatisfied or incomplete." Indeed, he felt well rid of the outside world. "Often as we sat and listened to the radio bringing reports from our country, we shook our heads at the depressing news. There seemed no inducement to go home."

Although in his writings Harrer would emphasize Tibet's isolation and the uniqueness of his position as a Westerner who had penetrated the protective barriers that the country's theocracy threw up around the city and the Dalai Lama, by the time he arrived Lhasa had in fact already been linked, however tenuously, to the rest of the world. A telegraph line from India to the trading center of Gyantse had been in use since the 1920s. In 1923 an English school had opened in Gyantse, and by 1937 a permanent British mission had been established in Lhasa. Although Tibet had no roads, the thirteenth Dalai Lama, who had introduced modest reforms in the 1920s, bought himself a Baby Austin motorcar that ended up parked unused in a special garage. Despite the primitiveness of Tibet's transportation system, all kinds of foreign goods were available in local markets, Lhasa had a diesel-powered generator, and many among the aristocratic elite owned radios and phonographs. By Harrer's time, the Dalai Lama even had access to a telephone.

Nonetheless, Harrer was enchanted by the idea of Tibet as a spiritually pure, if primitive civilization—a counterweight to the modern but decadent West. "One cannot close one's heart to the religious fervor that radiates from everyone. It is a question whether the Tibetan culture and way of life do not more than balance the advantages of modern techniques," he wrote in a typical passage in his book. "Where in the West is there anything to equal the perfect courtesy of these people?"

In 1949, CBS radio broadcaster Lowell Thomas and his son were invited to Lhasa by the Tibetan government, which had become increasingly fearful of the postwar intentions of China's new Communist government and wanted to begin building some bridges abroad. Meeting Harrer and Aufschnaiter, the younger Thomas observed that "the two wear purple robes, eat Tibetan food and speak the language like natives. The Tibetans are fond of them. They in turn like the Tibetans. It seems to be an exceedingly satisfactory combination, so much so that Peter and Henry [Heinrich] plan to remain residents of Tibet for the rest of their lives." Asked whether they would not prefer to return with the Thomas caravan to rejoin their families in Austria, Aufschnaiter shook his head disparagingly. "When you look at the aftermath of the war in Europe," he responded, "do you wonder why Henry and I choose to remain here with our good and faithful friends in Tibet?"

Only a year later, however, both fled Lhasa before the approaching People's Liberation Army troops bent on reintegrating Tibet into the "Chinese motherland." Soon thereafter they reached India, where Harrer wrote the first lines of his book: "All our dreams begin in youth. As a child I found the achievements of the heroes of our day far more inspiring than book learning. The men who went out to explore new lands or with toil and self-sacrifice fitted themselves to become champions in the field of sport, the conquerors of great peaks—to imitate such men was the goal of my ambition."

When published in 1952, *Seven Years in Tibet* became an instant best-seller and was ultimately translated into forty-eight languages. The book perfectly embodied the Western fantasy of escape to a Tibetan Shangri-La. The dust jacket blurb of the Book-of-the-Month Club edition identified Harrer as "a destitute vagabond [who] gradually becomes the confidant of the youthful Dalai Lama, the fabulous religious leader of the Tibetans," and described the book itself as "a modern fairy story." A rising tide of Cold War fears and animosities gave Harrer's story of an evil Communist army invading the last utopian fantasyland on earth—a veritable paradise lost—a special persuasiveness.

Harrer called his Tibet a "beautiful and strange land" and offered entranced readers, of whom I was one, vivid and spellbinding proof of this judgment: "As we marched forward, we caught sight, after a while, of the gleaming golden towers of a monastery in the far distance. Above them, shining superbly in the morning sun, were tremendous walls of ice, and we gradually realized that we were looking at the trio Dhaulagiri, Annapurna, and Manaslu."

Of the Tibetans, he admiringly wrote, "Is there any people so uniformly attached to their religion and so obedient to it in their daily lives? I have always envied the Tibetans their simple faith, for all my life I have been a seeker." Then somewhat wistfully he continued, "Though I learned while in Asia the way to meditate, the final answer to the riddle of life has not been vouchsafed to me." But, he added, "I have at least learned to contemplate the events of life with tranquility and not let myself be flung to and fro by circumstances in a sea of doubt."

The fact that Harrer was, in effect, expelled from his Himalayan paradise and that its Communist occupiers soon set about destroying its feudal theocratic society and culture meant that his experience could never be duplicated. His Tibet would remain frozen in his book like some ancient insect in amber, the last mythologized chapter in the West's long narrative fantasy, impervious to the real events that began to besiege Tibet.

In the summer of 1996, before the film version of *Seven Years in Tibet* began to be shot, I went to Austria to speak with Harrer, by then eighty-four years old. Driving from the airport at Klagenfurt to Hütten-berg, near where Harrer was born in 1912 and still keeps a house, one passes through the beautiful and reassuringly well-ordered Norische Alps. The landscape, part of the Carinthian region of the old Austro-Hungarian Empire, is a patchwork of tidy family farms spread out over rolling mountains and quaint towns populated by burghers in Tyrolean hats and plump women in aprons tirelessly beating rugs on balconies festooned with perfectly kept window boxes of geraniums and begonias. Old churches and castles suddenly appear on hilltops and mountain-sides as if out of a Brothers Grimm fairy tale.

In the 1930s, Carinthia was considered something of a Nazi fiefdom in Austria. With its perfectly manicured and blindingly green pastures, dense pine forests, and spotlessly neat towns, Carinthia is visually the antithesis of unkempt Lhasa and the vast, arid wastelands of the Tibetan hinterland. It was here that Harrer was born into a large family presided over by a stern Seventh-Day Adventist mother and a father who served as a railroad postal worker. The young Harrer grew up in a house high on a mountain near the tiny town of Knappenberg. To escape from the strictness of family life, he became interested in sports, especially moun-tain climbing and skiing. Indeed, after attending university at Graz, he qualified for the Austrian ski team in the 1936 Winter Olympic Games, held in Garmisch-Partenkirchen, Germany. At the games, Hitler pledged a gold medal, ultimately won by Harrer and his team, to the first mountaineers to climb the north face of the Eiger, where ten climbers had already died during unsuccessful attempts.

Just beyond a hairpin turn outside Hüttenberg, a bright red banner hangs over the narrow road, announcing "Harrer Welt," or Harrer World. Pulling into town, one sees a giant Tibetan *thangka* inscribed with a Buddha image that materializes like an apparition on the face of a sheer cliff. Below it, there is a white stupa, a copse of prayer flags, a *mani* wall of prayer stones, and even a bank of prayer wheels made out of fifty-gallon oil drums.

Across the road by a roaring creek is the Heinrich Harrer Museum, opened by the Dalai Lama himself in 1992 in a tastefully remodeled old school building. It is filled not only with Harrer's exceptional collection of Tibetan artifacts but with ethnographic displays from expeditions he made to Borneo, the Congo, Brazil, Ladakh, and New Guinea. The museum also houses troves of miscellaneous knickknacks and hagiographic Harrer memorabilia that look as if they had been curated directly from his attic. The museum's glass cases are filled with his old golf clubs, expired passports, obsolete cameras, assorted pieces of antiquated mountain climbing gear, tarnished sports trophies, even admiring letters from the likes of Wernher von Braun, Thor Heyerdahl, King Leopold III of Belgium, and Bing Crosby. There is even a photo of Harrer with Adolf Hitler, taken at a reception on July 31, 1938, just after his Eiger triumph.

Harrer's chalet-style home sits on a bluff overlooking fields of grazing cows and Alpine peaks in the distance. When I knock, the man who greets me is not the young blond Aryan in the photos from *Seven Years in Tibet* but an elderly, slightly stooped gentleman whose snow-white hair puffs out around his head in the fashion of Albert Einstein. In the businesslike manner of someone who is well acquainted with being interviewed, Harrer ushers me out onto a deck. As birds dive for insects overhead and strings of prayer flags flutter in a gentle breeze, he begins by telling me about his first encounter with Tibet.

"When I was in school in Graz, I started reading works by the Swedish explorer Sven Hedin. And then one day in 1933 or 1934, Hedin came to Graz and I went to his lecture. Afterward I even asked him for his autograph. He was one of those role models, someone who had the idea to go up and explore the source region where the big Asian rivers arise. And he did it! But because he couldn't get permission, he never made it to Lhasa. Nonetheless, I have always adored people who have an idea, an exceptional idea, and then carry it out, even if they have to risk their lives. Although I then read and admired Hedin and his popular books, I had no idea of going to Tibet, but who knows? Maybe it was way back in my brain somewhere."

Another hero claimed by Harrer was Alfred Waggoner, who died exploring Greenland. "He was one of my role models, too," says Harrer. In fact, in 1939 after he climbed the north face of the Eiger, Harrer married Waggoner's granddaughter, Lotte. "But whether I married

Waggoner or his granddaughter, I don't know," he says, laughing. Soon after, he was selected to go to Nanga Parbat and went off, leaving his pregnant new wife behind. "More than thirty people had already died on that one peak's rugged face and we were supposed to find a new route that was not as dangerous," he says. "Now people just take helicopters, but back then we had to walk all the way to the mountain, which took months. Then after doing our reconnaissance, we had to walk all the way back again. But, oh, the people we met! For me, it was an unforgettable experience." But by the time the team arrived back in Karachi to await their freighter home, war was breaking out. "We had heard that there were some maharajas who did not like the British in the north," he continues, "so we went to seek refuge up there. We were immediately surrounded by British soldiers, however, and put behind barbed wire. It was in the camp that I got a message that my wife had given birth to a boy. Ultimately, she sent a letter requesting that I give her a divorce, because she had met another fellow. I tried to convince her not to get a divorce, but she insisted." He recounts all this in an unemotional tone of voice.

"And what became of your son?"

"My son is fifty-six and now works in Swiss television in Zurich." I don't immediately follow with another question, curious to see if Harrer has more to say about his son, but he says nothing. We go back to his experiences in the British camp.

"It turned out that we were very lucky. We had a Tibetan vocabulary and grammar book with us, but nobody in the camp cared about it, which turned out to be crucial for us later on. Now, had we been two thousand miles farther east in the foothills of the Himalayas nearer Central Tibet, the British never would have let such a book through. So we had this book and a few maps that we had copied by hand. And I kept drawing maps, studying Tibetan vocabulary, keeping fit, and planning. We had excursion rights that allowed us to walk outside the camp for eight hours once a month. In those hours, I was able to make incredible trips into the mountains. I was so fit, sometimes I went fifty miles crossing two passes! I could have won any long-distance run, just like the Kenyans! From behind the barbed wire we could see snow-capped mountains and they were for me an invitation to fly to the Himalayas and cross into neutral Tibet, which was only 150 to 200 miles away.

"I was ambitious, no doubt about it. With ambition you can surpass what's normal. You see, I never wanted to be just a normal person. I admit it. Others who were prisoners now say, 'You were so lucky that you weren't in the camp during the last year of the war. There was killing, bad things happened there.' But it wasn't luck—it was will!"

The tremendous challenge of reaching Lhasa spurred Harrer on. "There was a British officer whose reports I had read on the region and he said that the whole world had now been explored and that since the airplane had been invented nothing was left undiscovered. But there was still *one* mystery left in the world, a country on the roof of the world with a lama who was the head, with hundreds of thousands of monks. And in that country people were supposed to be able to do things like mysteriously fly through the air!

"Ah, we were great romantics reading all those exotic books. We had it in our imaginations that Tibet was 'out of this world.' Being a prisoner one had the right to try to escape. That was the invitation to me. They could try to prevent you from getting out, even shoot you, but I was incredibly fit." Like a compass needle that keeps swinging to magnetic north, Harrer has a way of returning over and over to his physical prowess and accomplishments.

In Harrer's memory, his trek to Lhasa, scavenging scraps of food along the way from nomads, was wonderful. Rhapsodically, he tells me of crossing one of the most remote and uninhabited parts of the Tibetan Plateau. "We came over a pass and were breaking through the ice where it was swampy and it was forty below zero. That evening we had blue-and-brown feet. We thought, 'Better give up now.' But we massaged our feet and I was able to make soup because I had learned how to make a fire with yak dung. In the morning, after we had rested, we decided to keep walking. In the Himalayas, if you start saying, 'I want to go home to my wife and family, this is too strenuous!' then, of course, you are not the sort of person who will be capable of crossing Central Asia. When we left the POW camp, we were originally seven, but the other five gave up after a while. Only Peter Aufschnaiter and I were able to sustain ourselves and keep going."

Even during their worst times trekking toward Lhasa, Harrer and Aufschnaiter found the mountains beautiful. "For us, it was like going to church," he says. "The mountains were something that you had all to yourself. You climbed for the love of it, not because people were watching and admiring you like now, when there are sponsors and people climb for money."

When they finally approached Lhasa, it proved to be everything Harrer had dreamed of. "Of course I knew what Lhasa looked like from drawings," he continues. "But when you actually see it from a distance, nobody could be unimpressed. There is nothing to compare with the Potala—no skyscrapers, no opera houses! There is no other building as beautiful and incredible! There are so many unforgettable things that are still alive within me. Riding through the town on horseback. That lovely life in Lhasa!"

Harrer still speaks lyrically of his friendship with the young Dalai Lama. "The Tibetans have two unique things: one is the Potala and the other the Dalai Lama. I would walk through that yellow door into the Norbulinka, the Summer Palace, and there was the Dalai Lama waiting impatiently for me inside. I remember his mother scolding me when I was not punctual. Ah, the moments when the two of us were alone together!"

I wonder if His Holiness was different as a boy. "He has not changed at all. His charisma is still there. In audiences with him, of course, I am serious. But when we are alone, I can tell him things that make him laugh. When I tell him silly things, he hits my thigh and says, 'Don't pull my leg, Heinrich!' "

There is a strange disembodied quality to the way Harrer discusses the Dalai Lama, as if he had been over the territory so many times for so many interviewers that he can no longer summon up true feeling. Indeed, much of what Harrer tells interviewers appears to come directly from the book, as if after all these years of retelling the text had become more real to him than the actual experience.

In any event, Harrer is deeply nostalgic about the past, and his nostalgia is infectious. "Tibet was this other-worldly country," he tells me somewhat wistfully. "All these mystical things that we feel are missing from life in the West we project onto this country on the roof of the world. It's a longing that grows out of our feeling that things are not satisfactory in our own lives. The Tibetans were absolutely content and their religious beliefs were all-encompassing. They lived in the midst of their own Shangri-La, so why did they need to search for something else? They accepted things as they were. I was a witness to the end of the old system that gave rise to the outside world's dreams. Now it's all gone. It's a pity that place is gone now and with it the whole lure of Tibet." He says these words with a mixture of disappointment and irritation.

"Oh, the Tibetans were such happy-go-lucky, fun-loving people!" he continues, regaining a little cheerfulness. "We could laugh there. We could dance and sing and drink! We were always so gay and it was all so easy. The women were a great temptation! They were very pretty and very happy. We danced and drank beer with them and had great fun."

When I inquire whether he had any girlfriends the way his colleague Peter Aufschnaiter did—indeed, Aufschnaiter ultimately married a Tibertan woman—Harrer is insistent that he didn't.

"It was well known that they all had venereal diseases, and I grew up with a real fear of syphilis," he tells me. "I was afraid, that's why I abstained. The Tibetans said, 'We have a virgin and we will bring her to you and she will take you to bed,' and so on. Of course they were wondering about me, because in Asian monasteries homosexuality was popular. They often said, 'If you don't want a woman, why not at least have a boy?' "

He pauses for a moment, as if some distant memory was just returning. "You know, there was a Frenchman who happened to pass through Lhasa and he kept asking me, 'What can I do for you? What do you need?' So finally I told him, 'If you insist, send me some Kodak film and some condoms.' "

"And what happened?" I ask.

"Well, when I finally fled to India and talked with the American ambassador, he said, 'Oh, by the way. There is a parcel waiting for you.' And there, at last, were my condoms and film!"

Harrer is also a realist about Tibet. "It's true," he tells me, "that it was a feudal system. You had to observe local rules, which I did. Sometimes there was a flogging or something. But nobody was starving. When I built the dam [for the city of Lhasa], we couldn't find workers because there were no unemployed people. But there were about a thousand professional beggars. So I said, 'Let's round up five hundred of them and work with them.' I insisted that every day we give them a piece of silver—which was my pay, too—that we feed them soup and tea in the afternoon, and that after eight hours' work they could leave. Well, initially we got several hundred of them signed up, but after three days, there were only fifty or sixty left. And then only ten after another three days. Soon, nobody came to work at all!" He chuckles at the memory. "They didn't see the point of continuing to work after they got three pieces of silver. These beggars had leather bags, and every Monday they went around door to door to get a spoonful of *tsampa* [roasted ground barley] or a piece of yak butter. After only half an hour, their bags would be full. In their view there was no point making more than you needed. It was sufficient to make enough to survive, and that was very easy to do in Tibet. People never starved and they never froze because they had *lokbar*s [sheepskin robes] over their naked bodies.

"After living in Tibet, I learned to take everything much easier. I learned from Tibet that when you are slow and patient things will gradually come to you. When you are in haste, they run away from you. Ours is a neediness that can never be satisfied. When I gave the Tibetans the news in 1949 that an airplane had crossed the Atlantic Ocean in seven hours, someone asked, 'Why?' I couldn't explain why, because to them, if a plane took a month, a week, or an hour, it was all the same. There was no admiration for speed. Tibetans had other life ambitions. Tibet *was* the last place!" Harrer says emphatically. "What was amazing was that it was a two-thousand-year-old living culture. Now nothing is left of that culture except the Potala."

As we have been talking, the sun has made an arc overhead and now bathes the picnic table between us. Harrer's wife activates an electric motor that unfurls a canopy over the deck area. Then she pointedly suggests that perhaps the interview has gone on long enough. But before I leave, I ask Harrer for his views of the many Westerners, including the growing complement of celebrities, now flocking to see the Dalai Lama.

"For my taste, there's too much Richard Gere," he replies, a note of churlishness entering his voice. "I know Richard Gere is doing a lot of good, that he's financed Tibet House in New York, and that he's wonderful. But it's too much," Harrer says. "He can't be a real Buddhist like Alexandra David-Neel, the Frenchwoman who spent years living up there in the mountains with a nice little monk to attend her. This is all pretense," concludes the man who has inspired a juggernaut of Hollywood interest in Tibet.

7

GATEWAY TO VIRTUAL TIBET

It had taken almost half a century for Harrer's story to make it to the screen. Although many people had been interested over the years in making a film about Harrer's extraordinary adventures, the logistics such a project posed deterred everyone before the era of global films, global financing, and global-sized budgets that allow for the kinds of expensive special effects that technological breakthroughs have now made possible. As the time now approached for *Seven Years in Tibet* to begin shooting, I still had not received permission to go on-location. Although I had met with numerous representatives from the film, had continued to phone, fax, and e-mail the public relations people responsible for coordinating media requests, and had even asked numerous friends who knew people involved in the production to offer entreaties on my behalf, my quest for access remained at a dead end. In my case, however, it was not a suspicious theocracy, tribes of fierce nomads, or snowbound mountain passes that barred my way but concentric circles of ferociously protective public relations agents. The more I was denied, the more fevered my imagination grew and so the more urgently I felt the need to ignore the obstructions blocking my pilgrim's route and defiantly press on.

Where the determined explorers of old, however, typically made their first way-station a bazaar in an Indian border town like Darjeeling to engage a caravansary of yaks, I started my pilgrimage at the Sony-TriStar studio in Culver City, California, where a production office for *Seven Years in Tibet* had been opened. The studio's lot is a massive, self-contained universe sequestered from the world behind baronial walls and grand gateways guarded by uniformed security police. From the parking area just inside the main gate, the first thing that catches one's eye is a giant reproduction of a billboard for the original 1937 Frank Capra film of *Lost Horizon.* The actor Ronald Colman gazes out over the parked cars, having just escaped in a dress suit from a plane crash in Tibet with Isabel Jewell in tow. The two stars stand silhouetted against towering snow-capped peaks, an armed nomad beside them, next to a bold headline proclaiming: "Frank Capra's Greatest Achievement."

On the studio's Main Street, rows of vintage shop facades—The Creamery, Better Way Dry Cleaners, Gower Café—harken back to a time when Capra was a master at creating another kind of virtual reality—on-screen idealizations of small-town life for Depression-era Americans. Even today, these relics of 1930s movie fantasy confer a time-warped feeling of virtuous civic and family values on the busy main thoroughfare of this massive modern movie lot in the middle of cutthroat Hollywood. In a series of films that stretched from *It Happened One Night* in 1934 to *Mr. Smith Goes to Washington* in 1939, Capra created what film writer Robert Sklar calls an "integrated pre-packaged network of myths and dreams" about this country in which the essential goodness of the ordinary citizen led by "good" leaders triumphs again and again over the duplicitous and greedy. Capra's identification with such movie-made idealizations fused perfectly with the utopianism of James Hilton's novel to implant the notion of Shangri-La forever in the popular mind.

The nondescript David Lean Building just off the studio's Main Street is occupied by a variety of production companies allied one way or another with Sony. A black felt board in the lobby announces *Seven Years in Tibet* and *Married . . . with Children* as co-tenants. As soon as I open the door to the film production's third-floor office, an unseen person in a back room sings out, "Hi! Have a seat. On the phone! Be right there."

The office has the feel of an inexpensive residential hotel suite that a temporary guest has tried to customize with a few passing decorative touches. Next to a copy machine, a collection of black-and-white photos of Tibetans in traditional dress are arranged on a peg board in such a way that they have the uncanny look of a small shrine. A cluster of *khata*s (ceremonial Tibetan scarfs), several reproductions of *thangka*s, Tibetan wall paintings, and a color poster of the Potala are pinned on the walls.

Finally, associate producer Alisa Tager, an energetic, friendly young woman, emerges to greet me. When I express surprise at finding her all alone in the office of such a large film, she ticks off a list of countries from India and France to Argentina and Canada where other members of the production team are scouting locations, designing sets, buying fabric for costumes, polishing the script, doing casting, or working on production logistics.

When I inquire about the possibility of meeting with some of the principal cast members before shooting begins, in order to follow how their views about Tibet evolve as the project progresses, Tager suddenly becomes noticeably more tentative. And when I raise the question of actually going down to Argentina, she becomes positively standoffish.

"Because of Brad, it's going to have to be a closed set," she warns me. "In any event, such important decisions will not be made by people on the creative side but by the public relations types."

Thirty-three-year-old Brad Pitt, in whose name this high level of security is continually invoked, was born in 1963 in Shawnee, Oklahoma, and raised in Springfield, Missouri, in a fundamentalist Christian family. He studied journalism at the University of Missouri at Columbia, tried his hand at advertising, and finally moved to Hollywood, where in 1991 he played the buff drifter in *Thelma and Louise.* Thanks to his later roles in box office successes like *A River Runs Through It* (1992), *Legends of the Fall* (1994), and *12 Monkeys* (1995), he quickly gained megastar status. Commanding salaries of more than ten million dollars a film, Pitt became one of Hollywood's demigods, protected from the starstruck world by teams of personal handlers, bodyguards, production company and studio spin doctors, and privately engaged public relations managers. Access to his presence, it turns out, is more closely controlled than access to the Dalai Lama.

Tager does give me the name of Francine Maisler, "one of the young, new, really hot casting directors around town." Her company, Francine Maisler Casting, has been working on *Seven Years in Tibet* and her office happens to be just down the hall. Tager thinks that she, at least, will see me.

When I stick my head in the door, Maisler is on the phone, but as I wait, a talkative receptionist is glad to tell me something about the casting of the film.

"We just had an open call for Asian actresses to play the female lead and over 150 people turned out. We've been simultaneously casting *Seven Years in Tibet* and Oliver Stone's *The People vs. Larry Flynt,* so we've been getting a pretty weird mix of monks and strippers in here at the same time." She gives a little chuckle of delight.

Just then, Maisler appears at the door. A funny, gum-popping young woman from New Jersey who, as she puts it, has "gone Hollywood," she looks uncannily like TV talk show host Rosie O'Donnell.

"I had no real knowledge of Tibet when I began work on the film," she tells me. "But when I tried to imagine Tibet, I saw a beautiful place with mountains where all life's questions were just answered. Since then, we've been going around meeting all these Tibetans who have had to resettle here in the States, and talking to them has been heart wrenching. I was in New York when all the hunger strikes were going on at the United Nations to protest the visit by the Chinese Communist Party secretary-general, and the Tibetans just seemed so pure of heart. It made me want to cast real Tibetans for the roles rather than use actors and actresses of Chinese descent. I thought that putting Chinese in a movie about Tibet's tragedy would be too much. So I started going to all these Tibetan exile meetings, gatherings, and marches. My relationship with the Tibetans just grew as I heard their stories of broken families. Their plight overwhelmed me. It's hard not to get emotionally involved.

"For instance, in Santa Fe we met about sixty Tibetan exiles, most of whom were just doing menial things like house cleaning. But still they had such a wonderful spirit! And then I met these Tibetan monks in Minnesota during an audition. Even though they didn't speak English, there was a kind of joyous feeling about them, so that . . ." She falters as if she might be on the verge of tears. "I don't know how to describe it in words." From the top of her desk she picks up a stack of Polaroid photos taken at auditions and, as if dealing a hand of cards, begins to peel off a series of radiantly smiling Tibetan faces.

"But working on *Seven Years in Tibet* and *The People vs. Larry Flynt* at the same time is a challenge," Maisler says, suddenly changing her mood and giving a raucous snort of laughter. "It's a real challenge not to mix up my Larry Flynt life with my Tibet life! I mean, in the mornings we're looking at miniature Dalai Lamas and in the afternoons we're doing sexy strippers! Talk about mind-bending!"

As for Buddhism's appeal, Maisler feels so caught up in the Hollywood world that she hasn't had time to really explore what she calls "this whole spiritual thing."

From Maisler, I slowly make my way up the film's production food chain, until several weeks later I return to the *Seven Years in Tibet* office to talk to the fifty-three-year-old director, Jean-Jacques Annaud. Born into a working-class family in suburban Paris in 1943, he went on to study at the Institut des Hautes Études Cinématographiques and the Sorbonne. By 1977 he had abandoned a lucrative career making commercials, joined the French army, and been sent to West Africa as an army film director. There he made *Black and White in Color,* shot on a shoestring in the Ivory Coast, which won an Academy Award for best foreign film. Bigger films like *Quest for Fire* (1982), *The Name of the Rose* (1986), *The Bear* (1988), and *The Lover* (1992) followed. When he came upon a script of S*even Years in Tibet* that had been drifting around Hollywood for years, he was so enthralled by the story that he took the project up as his own.

Annaud greets me warmly at the door to his temporary office with a complete lack of Gallic hauteur. He is dressed unassumingly in loafers, faded blue jeans, and an open-necked white shirt. A genial man who wears wire-rimmed glasses and has an amused twinkle in his eyes, Annaud's hallmark is an unruly coiffure of gray curls that billow up from his head like so much foam on a tankard of ale.

Having recently shot a 3-D IMAX film, *Wings of Courage,* in the Argentine Andes, Annaud insists that nothing will be lost by having to re-create Lhasa in a Latin environment. "It looks just like Tibet," he tells me emphatically. Anyway, even if China had allowed him to shoot in Tibet, he feels he would have been constrained by a "Chinese image" of Lhasa, whereas what he wants is the image of the city before the Chinese occupation. But yes, he admits, China's extreme sensitivity to the Tibetan issue did cause him repeated trouble. "The Chinese even convinced the Indian government to kick us out of Ladakh, where I wanted to shoot. Then when we decided to move to the Andes, they went to see the Argentinian authorities to frighten them into denying us permission. They've been very tough. For instance, the person in charge of French foreign affairs with the Chinese is a friend of mine. When he heard I couldn't shoot in China, he said, 'Hey, Li Peng, China's premier, is coming to Paris. We'll invite you for dinner.' But then when he realized what my movie was about, I got a call from his secretary postponing the invitation. He was basically saying, 'Wait until we have the Airbus jetliner deal signed.' But even when they signed the deal, I never got the dinner."

When he began work on *The Name of the Rose,* Annaud tells me, he could find no existing medieval monastery that quite "captured the right emotions" for the film version of Umberto Eco's monastic murder mystery set in the fourteenth century, so he had a full-scale monastery re-created from scratch. It turned out to be the largest set built in Europe since Hollywood's epic 1963 flop, *Cleopatra.* Now Annaud is confronted with an even greater challenge—building Lhasa from scratch in Argentina.

Annaud is taking great pains to steep himself in his subject. He has read the historical literature and traveled to Nepal, Bhutan, India, and Tibet, where he took thousands of still photographs as ethnographic guides for his film's sets, costumes, and props. As he told a reporter for the British newspaper the *Guardian,* "When you dig into a country like that, it is not only about landscapes [and] architecture. It's about a people. I look at their costumes, their shoes, the way they braid their hair. It's not only getting to understand the behavioral aspect but the mind of a people . . . their soul."

Annaud delights in re-creating worlds that no longer exist. "When I studied Latin and Greek I became passionate about pre-Hellenic cultures. When I had a girlfriend whose mother was interested in Neanderthal man, I got interested, too, which led to *Quest for Fire.* I'm instinctively drawn to old societies and cultures. I identify very much with Harrer, a man of Western values who realizes the limits of material goods, fame, success, and the modern Western world and looks for something else. All my movies are about culture shock. *Black and White in Color* was about the shock of being white in black Africa. *The Lover* was about East versus West in Indochina. I've always had a fascination with Asian cultures, but culture clashes are my favorite. Tibet poses the ultimate encounter with a different culture. The appeal of Tibet comes from our need to know that there are other sets of values in the world that give human satisfaction."

And why, I ask, do we care about other cultures that are strange and exotic?

"We want options. If there are no other solutions, life is bound to be disastrous. In the 1930s, for instance, communism was viewed as an alternative, something that offered another way that was vital so that we could maintain hope. Of course, although it was a lovely idea, it didn't work. Tibetan culture provides another alternative and hope, especially for our own material culture."

Annaud, who has given countless interviews as a director, nonetheless conveys the impression of someone who is actually interested in conversing with you, someone who is genuinely trying to glean from any discussion new ways of looking at the world. Indeed, thoughts and questions spill out of him with an effusiveness that makes an interviewer feel both included and superfluous.

"The abbot of a Tibetan Buddhist monastery in Darjeeling, India, recently gave me a book by the Dalai Lama, and the title was *What Is the Meaning of Life from a Buddhist Perspective?*" A bemused look registers on Annaud's face as he considers this Monty Pythonesque question. "The fact is that we Westerners have a constant sense that we don't have what we want. Even though my friends here in L.A. have big houses, they aren't making movies they like. They are rich, famous, and unhappy. They have everything but respect. Why don't they take chances and do what they want? I guess they lack confidence in their own opinions and, of course, they fear the box office dictum. Why is everyone in L.A. always so upset and so fragile?" As Annaud's excitement grows, his gray curls tremble like springs. "Because they don't have dignity. They want to be taken seriously and to have done something that they can be proud of, and yet they keep doing things that embarrass themselves. They suffer from this very much."

"And you?" I ask.

"Oh yes," he says quickly, raising his hands as if in surrender. "In the early stages of my life I was a director of commercials. I was like a whore! And I had a nervous breakdown before I was twenty-eight." He makes a clucking sound of disapprobation and shakes his head. "When I went into movies, I resolved that henceforth I would only go upstairs for love, not money." He smiles. "Everyone is so stuck on commercial success, but then if one's movie does well, one is trapped into having to be successful again. What I hope to show are my passions and convictions. If I fail, then at least I've done the movie I wanted to do and I'll have no shame. Obviously, the search for self-respect and inner peace is a theme that also lies very much at the root of *Seven Years in Tibet*. Finally, I don't want just this one set of Western values in the world. That's why I don't live here in L.A. That's why I'm making this movie—

to remind people that there's another way to get people to question their values. If I can help people understand the transformation that takes place in *Seven Years in Tibet* from a quest for success to a quest for happiness, that generosity and compassion are good words because they make one happier than anything else, then . . ."

To Annaud, the word Tibet is like "a brand name" for another way of being, for something that most people ignore about their spirit. "People have a deep fund of unconscious yearning for mystery. For Westerners, Tibet taps into this unconscious reservoir of yearning. And Tibet represents one of the most extreme alternative ways of structuring a society. If that disappears, then our own lives become something like a highway with no exits. I loved Harrer's book. After all, it is one of the century's great adventure stories in one of the great spiritual lands."

As a book is transformed into a Hollywood movie, there is an almost automatic impulse to enhance the story in ways that producers, directors, scriptwriters, and actors imagine will make the resulting film better satisfy the viewing public's current yearnings. Many involved in the production of the movie version of Harrer's book, director Annaud included, felt that his matter-of-fact account was also distinctly in need of certain embellishments. As the official film biography, *The Seven Years in Tibet Screenplay and Story behind the Film,* explains, the script had to find a way to fill in "what had been missing from Harrer's book." For example, the book is distinctly unrevealing about his private life, not to speak of his inner feelings. And about his political life back in Austria in those years when Nazism was on the rise, it is completely silent. By the time the script was ready for shooting, a whole new human dimension, not even hinted at in the book or anywhere else in Harrer's life, had materialized.

Upon seeing an early version of the script, Annaud, too, remembered feeling that "there was something essential missing." Harrer kept talking about "the cold in his feet but not what was in his heart. He was not a very nice person in the beginning. So in the script we invented what was not in the book—an emotional arc involving a wife and a son that he had left behind in Austria. Then, when I told Harrer that we had invented a wife for him and that we had made her pregnant when he left on his climbing expedition, he calmly said, 'Well, actually, I did have a wife and she *was* pregnant!' When I heard that, I just screamed! I was so pleased. That was a great moment of discovery. You know, so often books are not about what they say but about what they don't say. They are about the missing sentence."

It was left to Becky Johnston, the scriptwriter, to breathe life into that "missing sentence" and so to turn Harrer's saga of mountaineering and adventure into the journey of emotional self-awakening, discovery, and spiritual transformation that Annaud hoped would speak to audiences who were as fascinated with the human-potential movement as with Tibet itself.

Although Harrer's book never hints that he communicated in any way with the son who was born after his departure for Nanga Parbat, Johnston's script has him penning heartfelt missives to the boy from Lhasa. "Dear Rolf," the Hollywood Harrer writes. "If you can imagine a hidden place, tucked away from the world . . . concealed by walls of high snow-capped mountains . . . a place with all the strange beauty of your nighttime dreams . . . then, you know where I am."

Johnston, in fact, ended up conceiving of the script as a kind of love story between "two lonely people," Harrer and the young Dalai Lama, who "meet and find each other." As a synopsis of the film issued by the production company puts it, "Through their relationship, Harrer experiences the kind of selfless love a father feels for a child and the emotional transformation which began on his way to Lhasa is completed in his friendship with the Dalai Lama. And he finally realizes the steps he should take to be united with his own son."

All this may indeed provide emotional heft for a Hollywood film but, of course, *Seven Years in Tibet* is not fiction but the story of a man still in this world. And the unvarnished facts suggest that Harrer rather callously left his pregnant wife to go mountain climbing and then essentially forgot about her and his son. Moreover, when he finally returned to Austria in 1953, far from "getting in touch with his feelings" and embracing his abandoned child (as the film script has it), Harrer allowed the boy to be shipped off to a series of boarding schools. By the time Peter Harrer was eighteen, he had attended close to a dozen schools, hardly a testimonial to a doting and loving father. "He became a famous person, so he had no time," the younger Harrer told a *Vanity Fair* reporter. "We didn't have much of a relationship. . . . I would have liked to have a family. I never had one."

While I continued to plot my illicit trip to "Tibet" in Argentina, I contacted the person to whom the task had fallen of transforming Harrer from a cold-hearted, calculating egoist fixated on physical culture into an acceptably warm and fuzzy Hollywood hero with an "emotional arc" to his life. Becky Johnston agreed to meet me at her home in Clearlake, a residential area just north of downtown L.A. where many younger movie people now live. Although the neighborhood is not as fancy as Bel Air or Beverly Hills, I am greeted by the quintessential L.A. soundscape—Hispanic gardeners calling to one another over the roar of leaf blowers and hedge trimmers. Johnston herself lives in an unpretentious 1930s-style house with a small swimming pool. Her screenwriting credentials include *Under the Cherry Moon* for the rock singer Prince and *The Prince of Tides* with that novel's author, Pat Conroy, for Barbra Streisand, which earned her an Academy Award nomination.

Johnston greets me in a sweatsuit and sneakers at the door of a living room filled with books. Indeed, after taking on the assignment to write the Harrer script, her library began to acquire a new complexion. In among the volumes of Chekhov, Freud, and Austen, an upstart collection of works on Tibet now occupies a shelf. The research she did for the project left her with an abiding fascination for both Tibet and Buddhism.

"It's not hard to understand why Hollywood likes this subject," she begins, fiddling with several red strings on her wrist, "friendship bracelets" often worn by Tibetans and other Buddhists. "After all, it's epic and huge in scope but kinder and gentler in message. I admit I was drawn to the subject because I hoped to find paradise. I had a fairly romanticized vision of old Tibet as an idealized theocracy based on spiritual principles. I was completely unwilling to see anything negative, like the Chinese argument about a feudal society." She laughs self-deprecatingly. "I think my need, and other people's need, to idealize Tibet stems from some latent, ancient dream of an earthly paradise, a place where human goodness or perfection has been fully realized. Needless to say, that dream exists only in the mind and at its core is the desire to re-create oneself, to be made pure, or better, or more complete by touching that place. Tibet was probably the last holdout of that dream."

As she talks, there is no doubt that the subject has affected her deeply. "I knew there would be no way to attempt writing this script without studying Buddhism," she tells me. "So I looked for someone who could work one-on-one with me for several months. I was lucky to find a brilliant teacher, Tenzin Dorjee. He's a wonderful, brilliant man who used to be one of the Dalai Lama's translators in Dharamsala. With me, he was extremely patient, able to make the core concepts of Tibetan Buddhism understandable. For many months, Tenzin and I worked nearly every day, going through a lot of different texts, different teachings, and talking, talking. It quickly became very intense and unsettling. Often I would find myself railing against everything I was learning. But Tenzin never forced anything or pushed me. He just very gently led me in a direction I had never been before. The experience was earth-shattering. It became much, much more than research."

Johnston's studies culminated in a one-month trip to Tibet. She spent three weeks of it with a Wisdom Publications group led by Stephen Batchelor and Nick Ribush, two prominent American Buddhists. When finally confronted with the reality of Tibet, Johnston felt as if "a bomb had gone off" in her head. "I went with all my mythological ideas firmly intact. But there was nothing you could read about this place to prepare you for the sheer magnitude of emotion it generates. Firstly, it's the most singular landscape on earth. It's completely unique, with a scale and scope that reduces you to a mere speck. You can't believe the beauty of its vistas; the sky is so blue, the colors so intense. And then there are people who are so profoundly, deeply alive—even under the state of occupation in which they live—that you can't help but feel humbled. The combination of such a rare landscape and an even rarer kind of human being inhabiting it is very, very moving.

"But even so, being with a group going through the countryside in a relatively comfortable bus, staying at the Lhasa Holiday Inn, was like seeing Tibet through a fishbowl, a Disneyland kind of tour that in many ways only heightened my preconceived notions of exotica. I wanted to get inside the soul of Tibet, understand it in a much deeper, more intimate way. So, one evening I went to the Jokhang [the sacred shrine in the center of Lhasa] and did the circumambulation for a long, long time with all the Tibetans, hoping for that 'hit' I'm talking about. The truth was, as I got swept up in the current of bodies, I became afraid. I realized that as much as I wanted to be a part of them, of their deep devotion, there was a huge, unbridgeable gap. I would always be the *other* to them, as they were the *other* to me. It just completely freaked me out! I came back to my hotel room and cried, because I felt resigned to being shut out, to feeling that I'd never understand these people or open up to that kind of profound experience."

Johnston returned a year later, alone. She had by then largely given up the notion that Tibet would trigger a transformation or provide "transcendental experiences." It was a "clearer trip," she says. "I saw it without trying to project myself onto everything. And like a love affair, my feelings were more powerful when these projections stopped. Tibet is so isolated, so removed from the world, so remote and separate. For an American, this remoteness fits with our own personal mythology of the pioneer spirit. Even though in Tibet the individual is not so much esteemed, the landscape forces an almost melancholy sense of your individuality on you.

"My original faith really got shaken by my study of Buddhism," continues Johnston. "I was a Protestant from Michigan who went to obligatory Sunday school as a kid and never questioned the existence of God. Like all baby boomers, I went through a spiritual crisis and then a period of supermarket spiritual shopping, but I never lost my central, unshakable belief in God. By the time I was deeply into the script for *Seven Years in Tibet,* the dharma had pretty much taken over my life, and one of the most personally difficult things I had to deal with was where to fit in God. Where does this belief have a place in Buddhism, which assiduously denies the existence of a creative being, higher power, whatever you want to name it? I would say this was one of the biggest traumas I faced with Tenzin. And I still don't know quite how to make it work, but I try. What I love so much about Buddhism is that it has helped to take me out of the Western mode of overrationalizing, of needing a reason for everything. So I try to apply the same open-endedness to this matter of God."

After Johnston's first trip to Tibet, she went on to Dharamsala to the Dalai Lama. In her mind, the entire journey took on the air of a mountain ascent, the summit being her encounter with the Dalai Lama in person.

"The Dalai Lama is a huge human magnet for the dharma. People are drawn to Buddhism because of or through him, myself included. And his draw is his total humanity. I mean, someone like me can't conceive how it's possible for an enlightened person, a realized being, to be so completely and powerfully present as he is. And you want to get near that presence. So the same need to be transformed by an experience came into play. It's a combination of vain delusion and naïveté, but I wanted to make some kind of connection. I imagined when I shook the hand of the Dalai Lama that the Shakti, the female energy of the god Shiva, would rise up my spine from the contact.

"I was totally unprepared for what actually happened. First of all, I was so incredibly nervous. They took me into a room where he was standing, waiting for me. And I presented a *khata* to him. He took it and kind of tossed it on the table, as if saying to himself, 'Oh please, not another *khata*!' I was kind of floored. He was so businesslike, so perfunctory. He acted as if the interview were a responsibility, which of course it was, but I was too wrapped up in what I wanted it to be to understand this.

"Throughout the interview, I was aware that I was comparing my preconceived image of His Holiness with the real person sitting in front of me. One of the most startling incongruities between the image and the reality was seeing how masculine a man he is. I know it sounds crazy, but I kept looking at his hands. He has beautiful, powerful, manly hands. Because His Holiness is celibate, I expected to encounter a eunuch. And I was shocked by how earthy he is, how manly he is. And I was moved, too, because his level of spiritual attainment comes after much renunciation. You realize what he has given up to gain so much.

"The interview was quite short, only about forty-five minutes. About halfway into it, as he began to talk about his relationship with Heinrich Harrer, he became extremely animated and began to laugh and enjoy himself. And when you see him laugh you say, 'This is the Dalai Lama whose image I've had fixed in my mind all this time.' The fact that I couldn't process other parts of his personality only tells you about my limitations, not his. What I saw was that a person in his position carries a terrible burden, the weight of everyone's needs as they project them onto him."

For Johnston, the appeal of *Seven Years in Tibet* is that it's an old-fashioned epic that glimpses a world very few people know or have ever seen. "It's also possible," she believes, "that these films could make millions of people feel that if they could just get this instant fix—get to Tibet or talk to the Dalai Lama—everything would be okay. *Seven Years in Tibet* may especially promote this because in the film Harrer *is* transformed. The movie shows Tibet having power over him by planting a sense of love and compassion in him. On the other hand, I would rather be accused of writing a movie that gave people a naive hope of transcendence than of writing a movie that inspired people to stand in the middle of a highway and see if they get hit by a car.

"Hollywood is one big altar to artifice and greed," she says, explaining the persistent dysfunctionality of movie types. "Basically, I think the lavish excesses of Hollywood make everyone here pretty sick. We live in a jaded nonculture where we've hit a wall, so we look to another, legitimate culture for new values. I think what's drawing people to Tibetan Buddhism is a yearning to reduce the self and a desire to escape the vulgarities of commercialization. But like everything else in L.A., people can overdo it, even the dharma. It becomes the answer to everything."

ˈ   ˈ   ˈ

By the fall of 1996, the shooting of *Seven Years in Tibet* was in full swing, and everyone was in Argentina, with only a lowly assistant left behind in Los Angeles to man the phones. When I called the offices of PMK, the well-known New York–based public relations firm hired by the studio to manage the film's publicity, I was told that my request was still "in process"—or as Tibetans might say, in *bardo,* the limbo stage into which one's spiritual consciousness moves between death and reincarnation. PMK's Leslee Dart regaled me with tales of Brad Pitt's difficulties with obsessed fans and the press since arriving in Argentina. In fact, in one phone call she told me how just a few days before he had been hounded from a quiet dinner at a restaurant in Uspayatta, where the film was being shot, by an ambush of paparazzi and local admirers. She seemed to imply that such unseemly deportment by fellow travelers of the lower estates had only compromised my own chances of being granted access. And as the days went by and permission seemed an ever more remote possibility, I found myself feeling more and more as I imagined those adventurers of old must have felt as they waited helplessly in Darjeeling or Shigatse for a permit to travel on to the holy but forbidden city of Lhasa. As I reread some of their accounts, I was reminded that my pre-cursors had hardly waited politely for official approval before dyeing their hair, putting on the rags of pilgrims, insinuating themselves into yak caravans, and setting off against all odds for the real Lhasa. Was it not precisely the fact that their trips were unauthorized that made their accounts so exciting? Of course, I was no Heinrich Harrer and would not need to march for almost two years over a barren, mountainous wasteland in subzero temperatures, wear uncured sheepskins, smear my face with rancid yak butter to protect against the scorching high-altitude sun, or beg raw yak meat off hostile nomads. Mine would be a covert journey, too, but a latter-day pilgrimage via jetliner, hopefully upgraded to business class.

Never mind the speed, ease, or mundanity of the conveyance, the idea of stealing into "Lhasa" uninvited was still intoxicating! I began plotting my confidential route: from San Francisco to Miami there was an afternoon nonstop flight on United Airlines that conveniently connected with an overnight United flight to Santiago de Chile. From there I would cross the Andes to Mendoza, Argentina, in a small Lan Air Chile plane and then make my way by rental car up into the mountains to Uspayatta. There, in imitation of all those headstrong seekers of bygone days, I would somehow elude whatever security might be on watch and penetrate Hollywood's ersatz Tibetan kingdom.

As my departure neared, my excitement as well as nervousness grew, fed both by the anticipation of seeing this miraculous re-creation and by the thought that I would also be something of an outlaw. Indeed, I felt much the same exhilaration that I recalled upon setting out on my first trip to the actual Lhasa. Now, however, I found myself confronting a perplexing, if unique, problem: what books should I take—guide books for Argentina or Tibet? How, I wondered, did a conscientious journalist prepare to visit an illusion?

Then, just two days before my furtive departure, the phone rang. When I picked it up, I heard Leslee Dart's crisp, no-nonsense voice on the line. PMK was confirming that my petition to visit Uspayatta had been officially granted. She proudly informed me that I should plan to depart almost immediately.

Her announcement was so anticlimactic, so unexpectedly disappointing that I was utterly unable to offer up any of the requisite expressions of gratitude that the moment seemed to call for. After all, Dart had presumably worked hard to prepare my way to this forbidden city, and how was she to know that she had only ended up snatching my adventure away from me?

When I somewhat dispiritedly called associate producer Alisa Tager on her cell phone in Argentina to announce my pending preapproved arrival, she was somewhere out on the Andean high desert. "It's magnificent down here!" she reported breathlessly through the crackle of static. "It's freezing at night and the sun scorches you by day. There are dust storms and endless problems! But on the set, it's like a dream!"

I immediately felt better.

PART II

— 8 —

MY ARGENTINE HAJJ

Lugging a duffle bag crammed with books about all those travelers who long ago tried to reach Lhasa, I board my night flight for Santiago de Chile in the warm tropical heat of Miami. When the dinner trays are finally removed and the cabin lights dimmed, I pile the books I had selected for this hybrid pilgrimage onto my folding table and begin to leaf almost randomly through them. I know most of them well, old friends unearthed over the years in used bookstores. Their tattered fabric bindings, thick vellumlike pages, and musty smell have no place on this sleek jet aircraft with its plastic-paneled cabin and glossy in-flight magazines. My seatmate, a businessman armed with a luridly colored Robert Ludlum paperback, glances uneasily at the pile of antiquated tomes that has arisen beside him and then turns to a spreadsheet on his laptop. Before me are: *To Lhasa in Disguise,* by William Montgomery McGovern; *India and Tibet,* by Sir Francis Younghusband; *A Conquest of Tibet,* by Sven Hedin; *Lhasa and Its Mysteries,* by L. Austine Waddell; *Travel and Adventure in Tibet,* by William Carey; *My Journey to Lhasa,* by Alexandra David-Neel; *Tibet, the Mysterious,* by Sir Thomas Holdich; and, of course, Harrer's classic account. Almost all these volumes have been with me for so long that they now seem part of me. I have carried some of them around the world more than once, indeed several have ridden on the backs of yaks for weeks at a time and now have broken spines and mangled bindings to prove it.

As the other passengers nod off to sleep in the darkened cabin, I begin to lose myself in the dreamlike descriptions that lie within these old volumes. I read that Marco Polo was the first European ever to pass through or near a Tibetan ethnic border region. He did so during his thirteenth-century journey across Central Asia to China, and in his *Description of the World* (published in English as *The Travels of Marco Polo*), he was not impressed by what he heard and saw. He referred to Tibet as a "desolate country" of "immense size" that was "infested by dangerous wild beasts." About the Tibetans themselves, he bluntly noted that "their customs are disagreeable" and "they have Mastiffs as big as donkeys."

The first European known to have made the arduous trek into Central Tibet itself was an Italian Franciscan friar, Odorico de Pordenone. He had been sent to Asia by the Holy See in the early part of the fourteenth century to search for a "lost" Christian kingdom of medieval legend said to be ruled with benevolence by the mythic Prester John. Upon returning home sometime in the 1330s, Friar Odorico wrote what evidently was the earliest description of Tibet by a European, never mind that some modern scholars have come to believe it was largely constructed from hearsay rather than from firsthand observation. "I came to a certain kingdom called Tibet, which is on the confines of India proper and is subject to the Great Khan," recounted the friar. "The chief and royal city, Lhasa, is built with walls of black and white and all its streets are well paved. In this city, no one shall dare shed the blood of any, whether man or beast, for the reverence they bear a certain idol [Buddha] which is worshipped there."

Five centuries later, surprisingly little more was known of Tibet in Europe. Picking up British Tibetologist L. Austine Waddell's magisterial *Tibetan Buddhism, or Lamaism,* published in 1895, I alight upon a passage in which Waddell describes Tibet as "the most impenetrable country in the world. Behind its icy barriers, reared round it by Nature herself, and almost insurmountable, its priests guard its passes jealously against foreigners." And here in his later *Lhasa and Its Mysteries* I find British viceroy to India Lord Curzon, who dispatched the Younghusband expedition to Lhasa in 1904, marveling at how "in the heart of Asia there lasts to this day one mystery which the nineteenth century has still left to the twentieth to explore—the Tibetan oracle of Lhasa." A few years later, the adventurer William Carey was moved to pronounce Tibet "the least known, the most mysterious area on the surface of the earth."

When in 1922 the British scholar and adventurer William McGovern succeeded in secretly making his way to Lhasa disguised as a caravan porter, he romantically wrote of Tibet as "a mysterious and unknown country" and of Lhasa as "the Forbidden City of the Buddhas into which entrance by many adventurous explorers has been sought in vain."

In *Tibet, the Mysterious,* a long-out-of-print book by Sir Thomas Holdich (K.C.M.G., K.C.I.E., C.B.), the surveyor-general of India, who visited Tibet in the 1930s, that land is almost lovingly described as having "held herself so far apart from the meddling interference of the busy commercial world, as to provoke the enterprise of generations of speculative geographers, who, accepting 'omne ignotum pro magnificum,' have startled the world with small instalments of truth surrounded by wide embroideries of decorative fancy."

And then, of course, there is Heinrich Harrer, whose battered volume is now always with me. He wrote of being a youth who "devoured" many of the books on the tray table before me until there "grew in my mind, out of a complex of vague desires, the ambition to realize the dream of all climbers—to take part in an expedition to the Himalayas."

Lost in my books, I read on until the wing of our plane slowly turns silver in the breaking dawn. As the sun appears over the horizon, I look down and see that we are flying over a seemingly endless spine of towering, jagged, snow-streaked peaks that make my Tibetan dreams seem all too real. Then, as the plane dips its wing, unexpectedly the blue of the Pacific Ocean limns a coastline below, jolting me from my Himalayan reverie and reminding me of where I am—over the Peruvian Andes.

Only hours later, I am at the Mendoza airport, expelled from my Tibetan time capsule into Argentina, struggling to communicate with a taxi driver who speaks only Spanish.

9

BRINGING THE GOSPELS
TO LHASA

When in the middle of the seventeenth century Lhasa was first reached by Europeans who stayed long enough to leave behind verifiable accounts of what they saw and experienced, living in this remote city must, indeed, have been like living in a dream.

It was in 1661 that an Austrian Jesuit, Johann Grueber, who had been working as a mathematician in the observatory of the Jesuit mission in Beijing, teamed up with the Belgian priest Albert d'Orville to make the long overland journey back to Europe via Tibet.

Before leaving Venice for Beijing, Grueber had promised another Jesuit scholar at the Roman College, Athanasius Kircher, that he would keep a record of his travels for an encyclopedia that Kircher was planning to compile. It was to be written in Latin and was to bear the elaborate title *China Monumentis Qua Sacris Qua Profanis Nec Vadiis Naturae et Artis Spectaculis, Aliarum Rerum Memorabilium Argumentis Illus-trata,* or *China Illustrata,* as it came to be known when it finally appeared in 1667, to be expanded and translated into French in 1670.

On their return trip to Europe after two years in Beijing, Grueber and d'Orville's route took them westward on the ancient Silk Road through Amdo—today's Gansu and Qinghai provinces—up onto the Tibetan Plateau, and finally south to Lhasa. There they spent a month and recorded for Western readers the first reliable, but tantalizingly brief, descriptions of the city and of Tibetan life.

The two Jesuit fathers were impressed by the elaborate dress of the nobility, but found ordinary Tibetans uncouth and primitive. "Neither men nor women wear shirts nor lie in beds, but sleep on the ground," commented Grueber. "They eat their meat raw and never wash their hands or faces." He also noted that Tibetans were ruled by a lama, whom he referred to as the "Pope of the Chinese and Tartars" and who turned out to be the fifth Dalai Lama.

Not surprisingly, what most interested these Catholic clerics was Tibet's curious religion. "Whence do the Christians call the Roman High-Priest Father of Fathers, so these Barbarians term their false Deity the Great Lama, that is, the Great High-Priest, and the Lama of Lamas, that is, the High-Priest of High-Priests," Athanasius Kircher, relying on Grueber's notes, explained in his encyclopedia. This lama of lamas was so revered, said Kircher, that in his presence all "fall prostrate with their heads to the ground and kiss him with incredible veneration." Tibetans believed in this great lama, he reported, because "from him, as from a certain fountain, floweth the whole form and mode of their religion," never mind if the Jesuits viewed this religion as a "rather mad and brain-sick idolatry." Grueber himself was quoted describing the fifth Dalai Lama as a "devilish god the father, who puts to death such as refuse to adore him."

An audience with the Dalai Lama was never arranged for the two itinerant Jesuits, perhaps because Grueber made it indelibly clear that, had such a meeting been offered, he and d'Orville would have refused it. For Catholics to have prostrated themselves before a pagan religious leader would, of course, have been an abomination before God. It went without saying that their sense of Christian universalism was offended by what they took to be evidence of heresy at work. Thus, ventured Grueber, "hath the Devil, through his innate malignity, transferred to the worship of this people that veneration which is due only to the Pope of Rome, Christ's vicar."

Grueber was groping to describe that unique form of Buddhism whose ferocious-looking protective deities and shamanistic practices must have given it a frightening countenance to the good Catholic friars. Indeed, they evidently found almost every Buddhist practice they observed strange and offensive. Grueber was particularly repulsed by the custom of the laity's eating "curative pills" containing the Dalai Lama's excrement.

Alas, Grueber never got around to writing a book of his own, and so we are left to rely on the truncated account in Kircher's encyclopedia for the first tantalizing bits of Tibetiana of any consequence to appear in the West, including a sketch of the Potala that remained the West's only image of the palace until the twentieth century. In fact, there is evidence that Grueber was not entirely satisfied with Kircher's repackaging of his notes, verbal accounts that, in any event, Sven Hedin called "as dry as the rocks of the Tiber." In 1667, he wrote Kircher complaining that "I wish you had, at least, sent me headings of the chapters before going to press; I should have certainly supplied you with several data of no small importance. . . . There are certain points in *China Illustrata* that need correction."

It was not until the next century, when a new generation of Catholic missionaries were able to spend longer periods of residency in Lhasa, that more thorough and accurate accounts of life there were finally penned. The first Europeans to live in Lhasa for any length of time were a group of Capuchin friars who set out from Kathmandu, Nepal, on the Indian side of the Himalayas in 1708. This dangerous journey was led by the mission's prefect, Father Domenico da Fano, and included Fathers Giuseppe da Ascoli, Francis Maria da Tours, and Francesco Olivero Orazio della Penna di Billi. After working in Lhasa for less than three years, they were forced to leave in 1711, not because of Tibetan inhospitality but because, given the paucity of souls they had succeeded in harvesting for Jesus, the Vatican was unwilling to continue providing the large outlays of funds needed to keep the mission in the field.

In 1716, however, the mission was reestablished by Fathers Orazio della Penna di Billi and Giovanni Francesco, who were to labor in Lhasa for many years thereafter. "We on our part, will not fail incessantly to entreat the King of Kings and Lord of Lords to look down with favor upon your kingdom from above, to pour out His blessing upon it, and visit it with His grace and heavenly influences; and, above all, to let the bright light of His truth and Gospel shine upon your own heart and mind," they wrote to the regent of the Dalai Lama's government in hopes of a conversion. Unlike later European pilgrims eager to explore new kinds of spiritual salvation, the Capuchins were consumed only with the task of bringing the gospel of Jesus to the Tibetans, whom they naturally viewed as godless souls lost in apostasy.

The presence of the Capuchins in Lhasa had aroused the competitive instincts of that other Catholic order the Society of Jesus, or the Jesuits, who, thanks to the earlier efforts of Fathers Grueber and d'Orville, viewed Tibet as something of their own special preserve. "On the fifteenth of August, 1712, I at last obtained permission from our General, the Very Reverend Father Michelangelo Tamburini, to go to the East Indies, and was ordered to open and start missions in the kingdoms of Thibet," wrote Father Ippolito Desideri, an Italian Jesuit priest whose ambitions ran to making an outpost in Lhasa in the name of the Society of Jesus's founder, Saint Ignatius Loyola. Accordingly, in 1714 he and Father Emanuel Freyre, a Portuguese Jesuit, set out across the Himalayas. To reach the holy city, however, the two clerics first had to traverse much of Tibet on a journey that led to terrible privation. For three months, they struggled across the uncharted wastes of the Changtang plateau's high, mountainous plains without encountering so much as a single village at which they could reprovision. Fierce cold, blizzards, loneliness, avalanches, snow blindness, and frostbite were their constant companions. Desideri wrote of being exposed to weather so bitterly cold that one ran the almost constant "risk of losing noses, fingers, toes and even your life."

As Father Freyre was to later write of their frightful passage, "One day it happened that my horse began to bleed from the nostrils and stagger from hunger, and at last toward night sank dead in the snow. . . . All I could do was to lie against the horse's belly for the sake of warmth and wait for the morning."

Arriving in Lhasa in March of 1716, the two Jesuits soon found themselves in direct competition with the Capuchins, who reappeared three months later. Indeed, part of Desideri's official duties consisted of keeping watch on the other order's successes and failures. A somewhat disappointed Desideri reported that "the earth is arid and sterile" in Tibet and "only becomes productive after great labor and much sweat." The trying circumstances of Lhasa were evidently all too much for the dispirited Father Freyre, who described the city as "little suited to Europeans on account of the extreme cold and poverty of food." He soon abandoned the mission and returned to India. Fortunately for Father Desideri, Tibetan authorities allowed him not only to remain in Lhasa alone but to carry out his evangelical work without obstruction.

In fact, Desideri was welcomed at an official audience by the Qoshot Mongol king, Lhabsang Khan, who then ruled Tibet. So receptive was he to Desideri's presence that he even gave him permission to enter the venerable Ramoche monastery in Lhasa to study the differences between Buddhism and Christianity. Father Desideri's fortunes changed suddenly, however, when Lhabsang Khan was overthrown and murdered by a rival Mongol tribe from Dzungeria in the fall of 1717. It was a bloody event, which Desideri vividly chronicled in his notes, and it precipitated a dizzying series of intrigues that finally led the emperor Kangxi to dispatch imperial Chinese troops to Tibet. In 1720, Qing soldiers entered Lhasa in alliance with the seventh Dalai Lama, establishing for the first time the basis for considering Tibet as a protectorate of China.

Through all this upheaval, Desideri kept a record of everything he saw and heard. Even though Tibetans were viewed by Desideri as pagans and much of his work involved pointing out the "false and peculiar religion prevailing in Tibet" as well as the erroneousness of Buddhist doctrine, he managed to write with a certain objectivity about what he observed. He spoke with a sympathetic tolerance of ordinary people. "Tibetans have a vivacious intellect and are ingenious and clever ... kindly, courteous by nature, good craftsmen, active and extremely industrious." He was even impressed by "the reverence shown by all Tibetans" to the grand lama. Indeed, such was his admiration for their devotion that he admitted being "ashamed to have a heart so hard that I did not honor my Master as this people did their deceiver."

But Desideri's Catholic faith made it impossible for him to reconcile Christian dogma with the beliefs of such "pagans and idolaters." He could hardly accept the common practice of polyandry, the belief in the transmigration of the soul, mortuary practices that involved the flaying of the dead and the feeding of their flesh to wild raptors, and, above all, the refusal of Tibetans to acknowledge a Supreme Being as a divine creator. So, despite his considerable interest in Tibet and sympathy for Tibetans, Desideri could not help but see the devil's hand at work in Buddhism.

When in 1718 the Vatican's Congregation for the Propagation of the Faith decided to turn the entire missionary franchise in Lhasa over to the Capuchins, Ippolito Desideri was reluctantly forced to close his outpost. He left in 1721, a discouraged man. After all, he had saved few Tibetan souls. His copious writings, however, provided the first comprehensive and accurate Western account of the geography of Tibet and the life of its people. Indeed, what strikes a reader today about Desideri's writing is its matter-of-factness. Sven Hedin called his three-volume, 633-page journal a "classic work" providing "the first reliable description of Tibet given by a European." Unfortunately, it remained lost to the world until 1875, when it was discovered in Pistoia, Italy, among the papers of an Italian nobleman.

Tellingly, even in 1904, the year the Italian edition of Desideri's notes was finally published under the title of *Relazione,* they still comprised one of the most detailed and informative records of Tibetan life to that time. In comparing Desideri's reports with accounts written since, Filippo de Filippi, the editor of the 1931 English-language version, wrote that none of the later works could measure up "for completeness, precision, for sureness of judgement, for objective serenity." De Filippi went on to extol Desideri's work as "the first accurate general description of Tibet . . . made possible by his perfect knowledge of the Tibetan language."

In 1733, the Capuchins, too, were forced out of Lhasa by an increasingly restive Tibetan theocracy. But the tenacious Orazio della Penna di Billi refused to give up so easily. In 1740, he set off once again from India at the head of yet a third Capuchin mission, this time carrying a small printing press among his impedimenta. Surprisingly, Tibetan authorities allowed this renewed band of friars to resettle in their old mission. In fact, they were again received in a hospitable manner by Tibetan officials and the Chinese *ambans*, the Qing dynasty emissaries now stationed in Lhasa. Father Cassiano Beligatti da Macerata, who returned with the friars and had a penchant for recording almost everything he saw in his journal, noted that "the King"—that is, the Chinese-appointed administrator—"admitted us to his presence and received us with the greatest affability, appearing to be pleased at our arrival."

Soon enough, however, the Capuchins, who had even been allowed to build a church, were confronted by suspicious monks from Lhasa's great monasteries, who took a more jaundiced view of evangelizing outsiders than had Lhabsang Khan, the former Mongol king. "Several hundred of Buddhist priests, gathered from the different convents of Lhasa and the neighborhood, invaded the royal palace and upbraided the King for his partiality," wrote Beligatti. "The latter, being terrified and dreading to meet the fate of his three predecessors, declared forthwith that the fathers had fallen from his favor; he enjoined them to preach no more in Tibet," and the friars left Lhasa in 1745.

What was surprising was not that the Capuchins were finally asked to leave but that, given their raison d'être, they had been permitted to stay as long as they were. "Considering that the logical purpose of their sojourn was to overturn Buddhism in this its main centre and stronghold, they could hardly expect Tibetan authorities, who derived their position solely from their religion, to continue their patronage," observed historian Graham Sandberg over a century and a half later in his 1904 book, *The Exploration of Tibet.*

In religious terms, the departing Capuchins had accomplished little more than Desideri and the Jesuits. As dedicated as he was, Orazio della

Penna di Billi won only thirteen Tibetan souls for Christ during all his years in Lhasa and, sadly, discovered few other pleasures toiling in this difficult, faraway vineyard. As is evident from his writings, he took little joy in the spectacle of ordinary Tibetans' lives. "They are . . . dirty and nasty and without refinement," he wrote tersely. In his records, one finds not a drop of the sort of romantic fascination for the spiritual side of this otherwise primitive people that would so grip Europeans of a later time. In 1745 he, too, left Lhasa, having failed to establish a real Capuchin presence. Brokenhearted, he died several months later in Patan, Nepal, and not long thereafter the Tibetans razed the Capuchin mission.

The departure of the Capuchins ended an interlude of surprisingly friendly contact between European Catholics and Tibetan Buddhists. Mongol kings, Tibetan authorities, and Chinese *amban*s had, for a while, all exhibited a remarkable level of tolerance for these doctrinaire foreign evangelists. The idea of Tibet as an emblem of resistance to incursion and of Lhasa as a forbidden or mysterious city had yet to be born in the West. Indeed, what makes the journals that the early clerics left behind so interesting is the matter-of-fact way these men recorded what they heard and saw—Father Beligatti even did watercolors and sketches—without romanticizing Tibet.

Although his journal was not uncovered until over a century later, in Macerata, Italy, the records of the Capuchin mission to Lhasa were summarized in 1762 in one of the few basic works on Tibet to appear in the eighteenth century, Antonio Agostino Giorgi's *Alphabetum Tibetanum*. A massive 820-page compendium written in scholarly Latin and tracing the Capuchin experience in Lhasa since 1708, it was meant as a kind of handbook for future missionaries to Tibet. Embedded in an elaborate and somewhat forced argument that tried to explain Tibetan Buddhism as an offshoot of Manichean Christian heresy was a wealth of detail about Tibetan culture, festivals, history, religion, and geography, including the first floor plan of the Jokhang ever published in Europe.

These relatively laconic, meager written beginnings ultimately became informational building blocks out of which Western notions of Tibet would slowly be fashioned. And it was not hard to see how Tibet's colorful pageantry and exotic rituals would come to fascinate Westerners, whose world was undergoing a dreary industrial revolution. For example, in describing the annual Dawa Dangbo festival that ends each year with a fabulous cavalcade through Lhasa, Father Desideri wrote the following: "First come a number of . . . monks of a lower grade, not in their ordinary costume, but clothed in silk made in various fashion, and each monk carries a banner or something appertaining to the treasure of the temple of Lhabrang [the Jokhang]. They are followed by other monks . . . on horseback, clothed in damasks and brocades from China, very beautiful and curious to behold. After them, also on horseback, come . . . the nobles, the governors of provinces, and the feudal vassals, most richly dressed with many jewels. They are followed by many important Lamas on horseback with their emblems and many ornaments, and by several of the Grand Lama's ministers, monks on horseback with banners . . . bearing rich vessels with burning incense and perfumes in front of the Grand Lama, who is carried in a rich palanquin."

It was from just such vivid accounts of this distant culture that the West would later begin to spin its web of romantic fantasies.

10

HACIENDA BRAD

Mendoza is an orderly, European-looking provincial outpost at the edge of the eastern foothills of the Andes. It is here that the indoor scenes for *Seven Years in Tibet* will be shot in a studio that was once a garlic warehouse. What is immediately obvious upon my arrival is that Mendoza is very much aflutter over "Bread Peet." His recent movie *Seven* has just been released in central Argentina and so "Bread's" arrival has had the same kind of almost magical impact as would the Dalai Lama's unexpected reappearance in downtown Lhasa.

At the Buenos Aires airport, Pitt and costar David Thewlis were virtually chased across the tarmac by a crowd of teenage girls tipped off about their arrival by loose-lipped security guards. And when Pitt finally made it to Mendoza, reportedly aboard the president of Argentina's own jet, there was another teenage mob scene. "The whole place is going crazy over Bread!" a young woman waiting on tables in a downtown café tells me enthusiastically. She also tells me that she has never heard of Tibet.

When Pitt is not on the set in Uspayatta some ninety miles to the west, he retires to the relative civilization of Mendoza, holing up in a hacienda-style mansion called El Cortijo on the outskirts of the city. Here, he whiles away his weekends in the company of his makeup person, two bodyguards, and his soon-to-be fiancée, actress Gwyneth Paltrow, whom he met while playing the role of her husband in *Seven*.

When news of Pitt's arrival hit the local press, thousands of people started gathering outside El Cortijo, taking photos of nothing in particular and chanting over and over, "Olé! Olé! Olé! Bread Peet!" Ultimately, at Pitt's urging, the film production company erected a thirty-thousand-dollar security wall to protect his privacy. Even in deepest provincial Argentina, it seems, Brad Pitt is infinitely more familiar and entrancing to ordinary people than any head of state.

My first stop in Mendoza is at El Cortijo. Several weeks into filming, Pitt's retreat looks something like a prison. Atop its encircling stucco wall rises a new tier of shiny sheets of corrugated tin roofing meant to discourage even the most agile potential voyeur or intruder. This tin shield gives the otherwise elegant estate the look of a space-based solar collector that has crash-landed back on earth. Even though iron bars have been secured over all the doors and windows, some determined fan has still managed to chalk WE LOVE YOU, BRAD! on a side door.

I leave Mendoza in my rented Ford Fiesta to head up into the Andes to the set in Uspayatta without even the most fleeting sighting of Brad Pitt. As I gain altitude, the arid and desolate terrain of rocky snow-capped peaks punctuated by occasional oases of green poplars along riverbeds indeed resembles the landscape of Tibet; the air, moreover, has the same feel of extreme dryness, the sky the same azure clarity, the wind the same relentless and penetrating power. It is as if, having blown unobstructed across so much open space, the wind acquires a unique, cutting sharpness. As I drive away from Mendoza, I know in my rational mind that at journey's end there will be no Potala floating over the scene as I approach, but nonetheless I almost believe that I am truly winding my way toward the holy city.

For anyone approaching Lhasa, the Potala is the visual centerpiece of the moment of arrival. Even though so much has been written about it and so many stunning photos of it have been published, it still takes you by surprise when you first see it sitting like a fairy-tale fortress on Red Hill. With its imposing red-and-white ramparts, gold-leafed roofs, and elaborate ornamentation, it conveys the feeling of an Oriental dream palace. Lhasa without the Potala would be as unimaginable as Athens without the Acropolis or Beijing without the Forbidden City. It is the emblem of the city, the essential icon from which much of the mystique of Lhasa and Tibet derives. From afar, wrote Alexandra David-Neel, the French Tibetologist and adventurer who traveled across Tibet in disguise during the early part of the twentieth century, the Potala appears to be "a tiny castle suspended . . . in the air like a mirage."

How this extraordinary structure was built without the benefit of modern engineering, steel, or reinforced concrete remains something of a mystery. Construction was begun in 1645 by the fifth Dalai Lama and carried on after his death in 1682 by his regent, Desi Sangye Gyatso, who was so eager to finish this magnificent edifice that he kept news of the Great Fifth's death secret from the public for fourteen years so that construction would not be derailed. Even though the Potala is three hundred yards long and almost as high, it seems to grow organically out of the cliff face of Red Hill. As Lowell Thomas Jr., son of the famed CBS radio broadcaster of the same name, observed after seeing the Potala for the first time in 1949, "It is hard to tell where the hill ends and the building begins."

Besides its rooftop winter quarters for the Dalai Lama, the Potala contains roughly a thousand rooms—including chapels, living quarters for hundreds of monks, kitchens, government offices, dungeons, storerooms, and the tombs of several deceased Dalai Lamas—all filled with an endless catalog of artworks and precious religious objects. But it is perhaps the Potala's gold-leafed roofs that cast the most powerful spell, especially when seen from afar shimmering in the sun under Tibet's cobalt blue sky.

The Potala "draws the eye like a magnet," wrote the *London Daily Mail* correspondent Edmund Candler, who first glimpsed it when he arrived on the outskirts of the city with the Younghusband expedition in 1904. Its golden roofs, he exclaimed, shine in the sun "like tongues of fire," and "its massive walls, its terraces and bastions stretch upwards from the plain to the crest, as if the great bluff rock were merely a foundation-stone planted there at the divinity's nod."

When F. Spencer Chapman arrived in 1936 with a British delegation, he abandoned his normal English reserve and described the Potala as partaking of a "divine excellence." In *Lhasa: The Holy City,* he extolled it as "one of the most astonishing buildings in the world," a "palace of the gods" possessed of an "indefinable quality of magic."

"Perched on the summit of the eminence which rises from the level plain of Lhasa, with the sun striking flame from the golden pavilions of its roofs, or whether riding out before dawn," wrote Chapman, "you see the moonlight thrown back with unearthly brilliance from the white-washed wall of the immense southern face." What Chapman loved most about the Potala was the "untamed dignity" that dwelt "in perfect harmony with the surrounding rugged country." For him, it conveyed a sense "not of having been built by man, but of having grown there, so perfectly does it fit in with its surroundings." The palace had about it a quality of "unchangeableness" that seemed to say, "Here I have been for hundreds of years, and here I intend to stay forever."

Some believe the Potala's name comes from a corruption of Potaraka, the legendary hilltop abode at Cape Comorin in southern India of the Buddha of compassion, Avalokiteshvara—or Chenrezig, as Tibetans know him—whose spiritual emanation the Dalai Lama is said to reincarnate. Others claim that the name is derived from the Sanskrit *Bodala,* meaning "Buddha's mountain."

And now Hollywood has attempted to replicate the Potala, or at least an illusion of the Potala, outside of Uspayatta in the shadow of 22,835-foot-high Mount Aconcagua, the tallest peak in the Western Hemisphere. But I know that even Hollywood is incapable of duplicating the way the real palace's golden roofs shimmer from afar in the sun or the moonlight. Moreover, I know that there will be no Dalai Lama in residence to impart a sense of divine mystery and that no other monastery complexes filled with thousands of monks focused on enlightenment will dot the surrounding mountains.

What is more, the loss at having had my unauthorized trip snatched away at the last moment and replaced by one to be conducted under the aegis of the film's public relations apparatus leaves me feeling all the more deflated. Nonetheless, as I near my destination, I feel a reassuring sense of excitement rising within me. After all, is not Brad Pitt—a modern God-king in his own right—ensconced in Uspayatta? And despite the unshakable recognition that nothing will be "real" about this Lhasa, the many months of rebuke and thwarted effort in getting here have imbued my journey with enough of a residual forbidden air that I nonetheless feel a lingering sense of kinship with my nonvirtual predecessors.

— 11 —

FIRST AMONG FEW

Toward the end of the eighteenth century, Western interest in Tibet, modest as it was, began to shift from saving heathen souls to trading with them. It was then that the British in India began to look northward and to probe the Himalayas in hopes of learning something about the lands beyond the barrier of mountains that divided the Indian subcontinent from the rest of Asia. What interested them initially was the possibility of finding overland trade routes to Central Asia and the interior of China.

In 1774, the British East India Company, which had been chartered by Queen Elizabeth I to begin England's corporate colonialization of India in Moghul-ruled Bengal, was asked by Warren Hastings, the governor-general of all British East India territory, for permission to send "an English gentleman" to "explore an unknown region for the purpose of discovering . . . [by] what means it might be most effectively converted to advantage." When approval was given, George Bogle, a twenty-eight-year-old Scot, was dispatched to find out about the "countries [which] lie between Lhasa and Siberia" and to "open mutual and equal communications of trade between the inhabitants of Bhutan [including Tibet] and Bengal." Bogle was also urged to explore whether a British "resident" might be permanently stationed in Tibet, to plumb Tibet's relationship with China, to quietly assess rumors that Lhasa was the repository of huge quantities of gold, and "to keep a diary, inserting whatever passes before your observation."

Entreated by Tibetan border officials to give up the very idea of such a trip, Bogle nonetheless set out in November 1774 and stayed in Tibet for six months, mostly at Tashilhunpo monastery in Shigatse, which lies approximately halfway between the Indian border and Lhasa. The monastery is the seat of the Tashi (Teshu) Lama—currently known as the Panchen Lama—then as now Tibet's second-most-revered reincarnation.

When Bogle reached Shigatse, he took up residence in quarters near those of the Panchen Lama and soon their relationship blossomed into what seems to have become a real friendship. Being not only a careful observer and a good listener but an able writer, Bogle kept a meticulous journal. In their discussions, which took place in Hindustani, Bogle learned how the Panchen Lama's own advisers, as well as the regent then ruling in Lhasa in the name of the underaged Dalai Lama, were all determined to steer Tibet clear of further contact with foreigners, a change in attitude since the days of the Capuchins and Jesuits. As Bogle learned from his new friend, much of Lhasa's wariness about the outside world, and especially the East India Company, emanated from Beijing through the Manchu-appointed *amban*s, who were by now opposed to allowing Westerners into Tibet at all and to whom, according to Bogle, the Tibetans "had a dread of giving offence." After all, by this time the Qing dynasty had some one thousand soldiers posted to Lhasa.

Bogle also learned something of how Tibetans tended to view the outside world. The Panchen Lama told him he had heard that the "Fringies" (evidently a mistransliteration of the Tibetan word for

"English," or *Injies*) had extraordinary power and that the East India Company was "fond of war and conquest." He went on to explain that "as my business . . . is to pray to God, I was thus afraid to admit any Fringies into the country."

Despite his hardly irrational wariness of British imperial ambitions, the Panchen Lama impressed Bogle as "open, candid and generous," "extremely merry and entertaining in conversations," and able to tell "a pleasant story with a great deal of humor and action." As Bogle got to know his unlikely new friend better through wide-ranging conversations, he became increasingly impressed with the Panchen Lama's intelligence and decency. "From his pacific character, and from the turn of his mind, naturally gentle and humane, he is averse to war and bloodshed, and in all quarrels, endeavors by his mediation to bring about reconciliation," he wrote. "In conversation, he is plain and candid, using no flattery or compliments himself, and receiving them badly if made to him. He is charitable and universally beloved and venerated."

Since Bogle was not an unskeptical man and certainly did not want to sound uncritical in his reports to his East India Company superiors, he wrote that he assiduously endeavored "to discern those defects which are inseparable from humanity" in the Panchen Lama's character. Bogle discovered, however, that "not a man could find it in his heart to speak ill of him."

"Although venerated as God's vice-regent through all the eastern countries of Asia, endowed with a portion of omniscience, and with many other Divine attributes," wrote Bogle, "he throws aside, in conversation, all the awful part of his character, accommodates himself to the weakness of mortals, endeavors to make himself loved rather than feared, and behaves with the greatest affability to everybody, particularly strangers."

In describing a mass audience the Panchen Lama held for the faithful, Bogle was deeply impressed by their respect for him. "First came the lay folk. Everyone according to his circumstances brought some offering; one gave a horse, another a cow; some gave dried sheep's carcasses, sacks of flour, pieces of cloth, etc; and those who had nothing else presented a white Pelong handkerchief. . . . After this, they advanced up to the [Panchen] Lama, who sat cross-legged upon a throne formed with seven cushions, and he touched their heads with his hands, or with a tassel hung from a stick, according to their rank and character."

Life in Tashilhunpo monastery was so consecrated to religion, however, that even Bogle complained there was "nothing but priests; nothing from morning to night but the chant of prayers and the sound of cymbals and tabors," and he candidly admitted that he often found the repetitive quality of life there "joyless and uninteresting." He described Tibetan Buddhism as having adopted "the humane maxims of the Hindu faith," but when it came to grasping the intricacies of it, he acknowledged that he was not up to the task. "The religion of the lamas is somehow connected with that of the Hindus, though I will not pretend to say how," he wrote dismissively.

"In order to fulfill the purpose of my commission, I had to gain confidence and to conciliate good will," Bogle explained. "With this view, I assumed the dress of the country, endeavored to acquire a little of the language and manners, drank a deluge of tea and salt and butter . . . and would never allow myself to be out of humor." Indeed, so friendly with the Panchen Lama did Bogle become in the process, that he is even reported to have "married" one of the holy man's sisters, with whom he is said to have sired two daughters.

If Bogle's interest in Tibet's culture did much to color his positive disposition toward its people, it also allowed him a platform from which to look back somewhat wryly on the foibles of his own society, an inclination that would only become more pronounced among Western visitors in the years to come. "The Tibetans have great faith in fortune telling which indeed seems common to all mankind, except our European philosophers, who are too wise to believe in anything," observed Bogle sardonically.

Where his Catholic precursors had seen mainly filth and heathen superstition, Bogle saw noble savages whose simple, earnest ways had much to recommend them. Indeed, on his departure from Shigatse, he wrote a letter to his sister extolling the Tibetans for their fundamental goodness and generosity. "Farewell, ye honest simple people! May ye long enjoy that happiness which is denied to more polished nations; and while they are engaged in endless pursuits of avarice and ambition, defended by your barren mountains, may ye continue to live in peace and contentment, and know no wants but those of nature." Although he had no way of realizing it, Bogle was planting the first modest seeds of worship that would grow into the Occident's later romance with Tibet and become one of the most characteristic leitmotifs in Western writing about its people.

During his stay at Tashilhunpo, Bogle was ever hopeful of reaching Lhasa and having an audience with the young Dalai Lama himself. Unfortunately, the Chinese *amban*s and the regent were so suspicious of British motives that they refused all his requests. When Bogle inquired about their grounds for denying him permission to visit Lhasa, the regent's deputies replied that "much conversation was not the custom of their country." Then they wished Bogle a felicitous journey back to India.

Nor did Bogle ever extract a trade agreement from the Tibetans. But he did end up compiling an extremely informative set of diaries, which languished for a century until the Geographical Department of Britain's India Office rediscovered and published them in 1876 as the *Narratives of the Mission of George Bogle to Tibet.*

But this is to skip ahead of our story. Nine years after George Bogle's mission, he was followed to Tashilhunpo monastery by another British emissary, an officer in the army of the British East India Company, Lieutenant Samuel Turner. In the spring of 1783, Turner set off from Calcutta for the Tibetan Plateau, also delegated to explore trade routes from India to China. Since the Panchen Lama of Bogle's acquaintance had died of smallpox while visiting Beijing in 1780, Turner was deputized to pay the East India Company's official respects to his newest reincarnation, a young boy about to be enthroned as the seventh Panchen Lama.

Although Turner was not inclined to romanticize Tibet, he could not help but be deeply impressed when at sunrise he and his expedition saw Tashilhunpo from afar for the first time. "If the magnificence of the place was to be increased by any external cause, none could have more superbly adorned its numerous gilded canopies and turrets than the sun rising in full splendor directly opposite. It presented a view wonderfully beautiful and brilliant; the effect was a little short of magic."

Turner's observations about Tibetan society were otherwise quite matter-of-fact. He described Tibetans as "divided into two distinct and separate classes, those who carry on the business of the world, and those who hold intercourse with heaven." Although the East India Company was more interested in the former, Turner himself was curious about Tibetan Buddhism. Tashilhunpo monastery proved a perfect vantage point for observing how Tibet's highly ritualized, theocratic society— where one in four males became a monk—actually functioned. In his reports, he described the rituals he saw in great and sometimes lurid detail. Turner was particularly intrigued by Tibetan mortuary practices, indeed by all rituals that centered around dying and death. In this land where burial in rocky, often frozen ground was difficult and cremation impractical due to a paucity of wood, Tibetans had devised a custom for speeding the release of a being's "consciousness" on its transmigratory journey that was both expedient and appropriate. The body of the deceased was taken to a designated hilltop and dismembered with knives by a special undercaste of scavenger-morticians known as *rogya-ba*s. The flayed flesh, and ultimately the crushed bones as well, were then fed to the flocks of raptors that inevitably congregated around such places.

Of an October ceremony for the dead, Turner wrote: "As soon as the evening drew on and it became dark, a general illumination was displayed upon the summits of all buildings in the monastery. . . . The darkness of the night, the profound tranquility and silence, interrupted only by the deep and slowly repeated tones of the bowbut, trumpet, gong and cymbal, at different intervals; the tolling of bells and the loud monotonous repetition of sentences of prayer, sometimes heard when the instruments were silent; were all so calculated by their solemnity, to produce a serious reflection, that I really believe no human ceremony could possibly have been contrived more effectively to impress the mind with sentiments of awe."

Turner, like Bogle, was denied permission to visit Lhasa, a prohibition that he also attributed to the fears of the *amban*s. "The influence of the Chinese overawes the Tibetans in all their proceedings, and produces a timidity and caution in their conduct more suited to the character of subjects than allies," he observed.

Like the reports of Desideri, Beligatti, and Bogle, Turner's vivid descriptions of Tibetan ceremonial life were read only by his superiors at the time and thus had little immediate effect on European perceptions of this still largely opaque land. Tibet was viewed, when viewed at all, as an unknown and forbidding place largely extraneous to Britain's imperial designs in Asia. Few Europeans gave it a thought.

Only when the industrial revolution began to radically change the way Westerners regarded their own societies and colonial expansionism spurred a fascination first with geographic and then with spiritual exploration were these dormant accounts exhumed from file drawers, attics, and closets to influence Westerners searching for a sense of adventure, enchantment, and mystery. A century later, the observations of Bogle and Turner would do much to help fill in the blank place occupied by Tibet on Western maps—and in the Western mind.

Bogle and Turner were the first and last official British emissaries to spend significant time in Tibet for over a century. With no other first-hand English-language accounts, the *idea* of Tibet was left to incubate in the British imagination unencumbered by reality, until it became as much an imagined dream as a geographic place.

Unlike Europe, the Asian lands surrounding Tibet had a long, rich, and complex history of relations with it, and their perennial jockeying for power and influence increased in the years when Britain was largely shut out. In the 1760s Nepal, which lies between India and Tibet, began to consolidate its various Himalayan fiefdoms into an organized and expansionist new state under Prince Prithvi Narayan Shah. In 1788 a series of invasions by the Gurkhas, an aggressive hill tribe that successfully dominated other weaker neighbors and established its own dynasty in Nepal, menaced Tibet's isolation and independence. An alarmed China came militarily to Lhasa's aid and in the process gained an even stronger foothold in Tibet by elevating its *amban*s from mere imperial representatives to the status of governor-generals.

At the same time, increasing numbers of Europeans had also begun arriving on the South China coast demanding more access to Chinese markets and equal diplomatic representation in Beijing. Anxious that they might also avail themselves of the "back door" into China through Tibet, in 1792 China's Qianlong emperor took virtually complete control over Tibet's foreign affairs and ordered its borders closed to the outside world. Indeed, only one Briton would manage to reach Lhasa during the whole of the nineteenth century.

Thomas Manning was an eccentric Cantabrigian scholar with a love of Chaucer, a wanderlust, and an almost obsessive interest in China, the Chinese language, and Central Asia who ended up in the Chinese branch of the British East India Company in Canton in 1808. His long flowing beard, quasi-Chinese garb, and faithful Chinese retainers ever by his side made one historian remember him as "a queer fellow" with an "unconventionality of aspect."

Accompanied by one of these retainers, Manning arrived in Calcutta in 1811 determined to slip into Lhasa unnoticed. In trying to dissuade him, the well-known essayist Charles Lamb urged him by letter to abandon his "foolish" quest. "Believe me, 'tis all poet's invention," wrote Lamb. "Pray, try and cure yourself. . . . Pray to avoid the fiend! Read no more books of voyages, they are nothing but lies!" Paying no heed to Lamb's entreaties, Manning set out for the border disguised as a Bengali pilgrim. Once across the frontier, he ran into the caravan of a Chinese general on his way to Lhasa. After he had plied the general with "two bottles of cherry brandy and a wine glass," Manning wrote in his journal, his "new friend" became "very civil and promised to write immediately the Lhasa Mandarin [*amban*] for permission . . . to proceed." It certainly helped that Manning spoke Chinese and knew the rudiments of medicine, which enabled him to minister to the medical needs of some of the general's men. Although Manning cursed the general as "no better than an old woman," it is unlikely that he would ever have reached Lhasa without his patronage.

Unfortunately, Manning's diary is disappointingly mundane and filled with trivia: accounts of how a vicious horse bit and kicked him, of being "eaten up by little insects," and of endless personal struggles with his eternally sulky and combative Chinese servant. Even though he was in Tibet on the adventure of his life, Manning devoted much time to writing a bizarre essay about the clothing worn by the British in India. Passing through the slovenly caravan stop of Phari, he did, however, immortalize himself with his banal and since oft-quoted haiku-like judgment: "Dirt, dirt, grease, smoke. Misery, but good mutton."

Upon arriving in Lhasa, Manning was admittedly impressed by the Potala, reporting that his "eye was almost perpetually fixed on the palace." If the palace exceeded his expectations, however, the city fell far short. "There is nothing striking, nothing pleasing, in its appearance. The habitations are begrimed with smut and dirt. The avenues are full of dogs, some growling and gnawing bits of hide which lie about and emit a charnel-house smell; others limping and looking livid; others starved and dying and pecked at by the ravens; some dead and preyed upon. In short, everything seems mean and gloomy, and excites the idea of something unreal."

Like Turner, Manning had few flattering things to say about the Chinese *amban*s, describing them as disturbingly disrespectful of Tibetans. "It is very bad policy thus perpetually to send men of bad character to govern Tibet," he presciently wrote. "It no doubt displeases the Grand Lama and Tibetans in general, and tends to prevent their affections from settling in favor of the Chinese government. I cannot help thinking from what I have seen and heard, that they would view the Chinese influence in Tibet overthrown without many emotions of regret; especially if the rulers under the new influence were to greet the Great Lama with respect, for this is a point in which these haughty mandarins are somewhat deficient, to the no small dissatisfaction of the good people of Lhasa." The *amban*s evidently viewed Manning with equal lack of enthusiasm. "They detested Europeans," Manning wrote. Their attitude was "now [that] one man has come to spy [on] the country—he will inform others—numbers will come, and at last, they will be taking the country from us."

It is difficult to say what Manning was searching for in Tibet. Whatever it was, his descriptions of Lhasa, where he spent four months, were hardly the stuff from which future dreams of Shangri-La would be fashioned. His main distinction was that he had not only made it to Lhasa but had become the first British citizen ever to be given an audience with a Dalai Lama. It was one Tibetan experience that left Manning deeply impressed. "The Lama's beautiful and interesting face and manner engrossed almost all my attention. He was at the time about seven years old and had the simple and unaffected manners of a well-educated, princely child. His face was, I thought, poetically and affectingly beautiful. He was of a gay and cheerful disposition; his beautiful mouth perpetually unbending into a gracious smile, which illuminated his whole countenance." Manning described himself as being "extremely affected" by the encounter. "I could have wept through the strangeness of sensation," he wrote.

Although Manning's account of the first meeting between a Westerner and a Dalai Lama would for a while also slip from history unnoticed, from his and similar later accounts would ultimately be spun the notion of a God-king wrapped in an aura of enigma and transcendent spiritual magnetism, hidden in a golden-roofed aerie protected by thousands of enigmatic monks and a majestic mountain barrier. As Australian cultural historian Peter Bishop has written in his fascinating book *The Myth of Shangri-La,* what Manning did was to make "contact with an image of divine perfection." When this image began to merge with reports of devoted pilgrims prostrating themselves inchworm fashion as they endlessly circumambulated religious shrines and spirit mountains, of spiritual ascetics and hermits sequestering themselves in caves for years at a time, of lamas astrally projecting themselves, of monks withstanding subzero temperatures in flimsy open robes through mental discipline, of shamans raising the dead, and of oracles foretelling the future, it was not hard to see how Tibet might ultimately turn into a fabulous fantasyland in the Western imagination.

So effective was Tibet's closed-door policy that the only other Europeans to reach Lhasa during the nineteenth century were two wandering Lazarist priests, Abbé Evariste-Régis Huc and Joseph Gabet. After trekking across China and Mongolia, they paused at the great Kumbum monastery in Amdo. Then, dressed as lamas and living like nomads, they set out for the holy city. By seeking to reach Lhasa in disguise, they, too, helped launch the image of a romantic and mysterious world that could be plumbed only by stealth and guile. Their example would serve as a stimulus to scores of other Westerners who read the popular book that resulted from their trip and would themselves try to steal into this peculiarly reluctant place in years to come.

The two camouflaged French priests reached Lhasa in January 1846. Despite the city's closure to outsiders, they were welcomed by the regent, Pishipa. During the brief months they spent there, Huc kept copious notes, which were later published as *Souvenirs d'un Voyage dans La Tartarie, le Thibet et la Chine pendant les Années 1844, 1845, et 1846* (*Travels in Tartary, Thibet, and China: 1844–1846*). It was a vivid work but again one in which hearsay was alleged to have entered the narrative as fact. Huc was said to have unskeptically reported stories he heard along the trail as if he had witnessed them himself, particularly tales involving mystical or supernatural phenomena and occult practices associated with Tibet's shamanistic Bon religion.

"When the appointed day is come, the multitude of pilgrims assemble in the great court of the Lamasery, where an altar is raised in front of the Temple-gate," he wrote of one such occurrence he evidently heard about while trekking around an ethnically Tibetan border region. "At length the Bokte [presiding priest] appears. He advances gravely, amid the acclamations of the crowd, seats himself upon the altar, and takes from his girdle a large knife which he places upon his knees. At his feet, numerous lamas, ranged in a circle, commence the terrible invocations of this frightful ceremony. As the recitation of the prayers proceeds, you see the Bokte trembling in every limb, and gradually working himself up into phrenetic convulsions. . . . Then, the Bokte suddenly throws aside the scarf which envelopes him, unfastens his girdle, and seizing the sacred knife, slits open his stomach in one long cut. While the blood flows in every direction, the multitude prostrate themselves before the terrible spectacle, and the enthusiast is interrogated about all sorts of hidden things, as to future events, as to the destiny of certain personages. The replies of the Bokte to all these questions are regarded by everybody as oracles."

Then, according to Huc, as the recitation of prayers continues, the

Bokte "takes, in his right hand, blood from his wound, raises it to his mouth, breathes thrice upon it, and then throws it into the air with loud cries. He next passes his hand rapidly over his wound, closes it, and everything, after a while, resumes its pristine condition [with] no trace remaining of the diabolical operation, except extreme prostration."

After only two months in residence, Huc and Gabet were forced by suspicious *ambans* to leave what they called these "dismal regions." The book they jointly wrote, however, would help spark a new fascination with Tibet as a place to quest not for souls to save or wares to trade but for the good of one's own soul. Though not yet apparent, the time for imagining Tibet as a primitive land of "begrimed" towns ruled over by a theocracy of un-Christian and autocratic bent was about to be challenged by a purer and more spiritual vision.

As the age of global exploration and conquest reached its climax in the nineteenth century, the fact that "the roof of the world," as Tibet came to be called in the Victorian era, remained closed would give it an irresistible magnetism and cachet, particularly to the British encamped so close at hand in India. The Trans-Himalayan barrier would become a symbolic demarcation line between the known (hence boring) and the unknown (hence thrilling). It became a line whose impermeability aroused rather than stilled the interest of those it excluded. As Tibetologist Donald Lopez puts it in his thoughtful book *Prisoners of Shangri-La,* "The failure of the European powers to dominate [Tibet] politically only increased European longing and fed the fantasy about the land beyond the Snowy Range." There was, indeed, something seductively perverse about this Promethean and very Western impulse to trespass where not welcomed.

"One might think devout Buddhists had excluded strangers in order to preserve the myth of the city's beauty and mystery and wealth," wrote Edmund Candler of the *London Daily Mail* before he got to Lhasa in 1904. Of course, Tibetans and Chinese had no understanding of the paradoxical urge for Westerners to go where they were not wanted. In fact, a regent of the Panchen Lama had admitted to Samuel Turner a century earlier his puzzlement as to why so many "Fringies" were willing to leave their countries for the "inclement climates and rude, inhospitable men" of distant lands. It was a good question. But the answer, had it been given, would have been enigmatic to Tibetans. As one British captain in the Royal Fusiliers noted after a hunting trip in the Himalayas during the 1870s, "I was curious to see a place which was so studiously shut out from European eyes."

The urge of coming generations of soldiers, explorers, and seekers of all sorts to transgress forbidden places, added to the new geopolitical concerns of the major powers, would soon turn Central Asia into an object of intense imperial competition. The Tibetans soon found themselves at the center of an international whirlpool that they little understood and certainly could not control.

During the middle of the nineteenth century, the British in India grew increasingly suspicious of czarist Russian intentions in Central Asia. The ensuing rivalry—the "Great Game," as it came to be known—made filling in the "huge white blank on our maps," as British explorer Captain Hamilton Bower put it, a matter of sudden urgency. The British began to view Tibet not as a terra incognita of no strategic significance but—should it ever fall under Russian influence, much less suzerainty—as a potential threat to India. It was now deemed a necessity that British subjects map Tibet's uncharted wastes and clarify Tibet's murky allegiances.

European attention was also being drawn to Tibet's unique landscape for another reason. As Peter Bishop observes, George Bogle made his way to Tibet just when "the European—and in particular the British—relationship to mountain landscape was changing and reaching a new pitch of intensity." Suddenly mountains, which had previously been viewed as forbidding obstacles to human intercourse, were coming to be seen as inspirational—of stark but compelling beauty. What is more, as recreational travel grew in popularity among Europe's upper classes and the Grand Tour of the Continent turned into a rite of passage for young English gentlemen, so, too, the relationship of the traveler to mountains, especially the Alps, began to change.

In 1646, the British traveler John Evelyn had described the Swiss

Alps as "horrid mountains" filled with "ugly, shrivelled and deformed" people. In his view, they were obstructing landforms—"as if Nature had here swept up the rubbish of the earth"—through which it was difficult and dangerous to travel. And when in 1715, while journeying from Kashmir to Lhasa, Father Desideri passed through Western Tibet and saw Mount Kailash, the most sacred of all mountains for Hindus and Tibetan Buddhists, he described it unappetizingly as "covered with snow and ice, and most horrible, barren, steep and bitterly cold."

Little more than a generation later, however, mountain peaks would be transformed in the European imagination from frigid and fearful climes to be avoided into majestic heights possessing a beauty and allure that beckoned romantics tired of civilization and its discontents. It zwas not long before the idea of communing with such wilderness was viewed as balm for the soul rather than unwelcomed exile from civilization; in other words, as an ennobling, and certainly fashionable, experience. Alpine vistas were no longer dismissed as "savage," but exhalted as "mysterious" and "grand beyond description." Smitten by a new naturalism, writers began extolling the mountains in increasingly religious terms.

As early as 1851, the Reverend Karl Gützlaff, a Prussian sinologist, wrote of Tibet as a "magic land . . . encompassed by the most stupendous mountains of the globe . . . a wonderful country . . . a territory where extremes meet and where everything is extraordinary." It was logical, then, that Tibetans, too, should be "wonderful" and "extraordinary." In fact, Gützlaff, a German missionary with many years' experience in China but only a few days in a Tibetan border area, was moved to describe Tibetans much as he did their landscape, as having "strongly contributed to enhance the 'wonderful' by their curious mode of life and creed."

Similarly, arriving in California in 1868 and falling under the thrall of the "divine wildness" of the Sierra Nevada's "Godful solitude," Scotsman John Muir described the mountains surrounding Yosemite's valley as being "like immense halls or temples lighted from above." Walking among these towering peaks was, for him, a profoundly sacred experience during which he could view glaciers as being "on errands of divine love." To see these mountains, admittedly "awful in [their] stern majesty" in the "divine light" of evening, was for Muir "one of the most impressive of all terrestrial manifestations of God." The American painter Marsden Hartley's search for transcendence also led him into the mountains of North America, where, after one camping trip, he rhapsodically proclaimed, "I know I have seen God now."

By 1869, Elizabeth Sarah Mazuchelli, whose British husband had been posted by the colonial service to a hill station in the foothills of the Himalayas, could speak of "the longing I had felt ever since my eyes first rested on that stupendous amphitheater of snow-capped mountains" and wax on about how this "longing" soon "ripened" into an irrepressibly "strong determination to have a near view of them." It was certainly a sign of the times when, that same year, she became the first Western woman to trek to the base of Everest and described herself as transfixed by the "almost fierce majesty and barren grandeur of Nature in this great lonely land." She had visited "most of the mountainous districts of Europe," she said, but in her view they "give not the faintest idea of the wild desolation of these regions." For her, the experience was, indeed, a religious one. "As I stand in these vast solitudes, I do so with bent knee and bowed head, as becomes one who is in the *felt* presence of the Invisible."

Much of the new reverence for mountain solitude grew out of a gathering disenchantment with modernity. "Solitude is a true balm, which heals," wrote the Frenchman Gabriel Bonvalot after he had trekked through Northern Tibet with the duc de Chartres's son, Prince Henri d'Orléans, in 1889. The barren landscape impressed him as "a very fascinating place of sojourn for one who has lived in large cities, and has been put out of humor by the petty miseries of civilization."

In the latter half of the nineteenth century, as Europeans began to feel challenged rather than intimidated by the grandness of snow-capped peaks, mountaineering also came of age as a sport. Now, instead of steering around imposing mountains, men—and a few women—began to head right up them, to launch elaborate expeditions to "conquer" and "subdue" them. "I was driven by those mysterious impulses which cause men to peer into the unknown," wrote Sir Edward

Whymper, who in 1865 became the first man to reach the top of the Matterhorn.

The new appreciation of mountains soon resonated among Europeans stationed abroad. The British Alpine Club was founded in 1857. Since the British had no significant mountains of their own, they naturally turned not only to the Alps but to the Himalayas, which bordered their colonial domains and boasted the world's highest peak, the 29,028-foot-high Mount Everest, or Chomolungma, "The Goddess Mother of the World," as it was known in Tibetan.

By the late 1800s, the way Westerners looked at the Himalayas had so changed that L. Austine Waddell, who wrote one of the first comprehensive geographies of the region, could gaze up at them not with revulsion but with unalloyed awe and reverence. "We now could see looming high above the quivering haze that smothered the dusty plains, the soaring peaks of the cool 'hills,' as the Anglo-Indians are wont to call these loftiest summits of the earth," he wrote in 1898 in *Among the Himalayas.* "In the distance they looked as if they belonged to another world."

As the very act of approaching mountains acquired religious significance, climbing them often came to be seen as a physical analogue to the process of spiritual uplifting and enlightenment. Typically, Rudyard Kipling, Britain's most popular writer at the turn of the century, set his young hero in his 1901 novel *Kim* climbing into the Himalayas with his lama and crying out almost ecstatically, "Surely the Gods live here!"

Even the barren and desolate Mount Kailash now evoked a different European response. Captain C. G. Rawling, a member of a 1903 British military expedition, referred to it as "a vast cathedral" and "this most beautiful mountain." And as the Asianist Amaury de Riencourt climbed into the Himalayas and thence onto the Tibetan Plateau, he seemed to sum up this new sentiment: "I had the extraordinary impression that I was rising, through layers of cloud, from hell to heaven, leaving behind and below me this scientifically technical world which has done so much to increase man's misery." And these sentiments were seconded by Sven Hedin, who in 1905, after three years' absence from Tibet, wrote, "My study began to be too small for me; at eventide, when all was quiet, I seemed to hear the sough of the wind, a voice admonishing me to 'come back again to the silence of the wilderness.' I must return to the freedom of the desert and hie away to the broad plains between the snow-clad mountains of Tibet."

Two decades later, during his 1921 reconnaissance mission to Everest, the famed mountaineer George Leigh Mallory stood before this "prodigious white fang—an excrescence from the jaw of the world" and wrote to his wife: "In the evening light the country can be beautiful, snow mountains and all: the harshness becomes subdued; shadows soften the hillside; there is a blending of lines and folds until the last light, so that one comes to bless the absolute barrenness, feeling that here is pure beauty of form, a kind of ultimate harmony." As Peter Bishop succinctly puts it, "The emergence of a genuine wilderness aesthetic and an appreciation of these previously rejected regions was vital to the eventual creation of Tibet as a sacred place in the Western psyche."

Given that Everest was visibly the ne plus ultra of sacred symbolic mountains, it was a simple leap to the anointing of Lhasa as the Vatican of this mountain-locked Asian spiritualism. "The eyes of millions look with longing to Lhasa," wrote William Carey in his 1902 *Travel and Adventure in Tibet.* "As far north as the Volga, and over the whole of Mongolia and Tibet, the mysterious city has cast its spiritual spell."

The growing fascination with Tibet as a celestial kingdom and the relative absence of information about it combined to make it a magnet for all manner of fantastic projections and fantasies. Indeed, by the 1870s a veritable stampede of Westerners, fired by the tantalizingly incomplete tales of earlier sojourners, had begun to compete to be "the first" to breach its sacred heart.

Lhasa, as one turn-of-the-century writer put it, had become "the El Dorado of all modern travellers." If one could only reach it, perhaps its spiritual power or its magic might somehow rub off. Western pilgrims from many lands—"trespassers on the roof of the world," as historian Peter Hopkirk has called them—were prepared to endure unspeakable hardships, even death, to reach the holy city. And the fact that, one after another, they failed only increased the ardor of those who followed.

Some sought to reach Lhasa via Amdo through the present-day Chinese provinces of Gansu and Qinghai and the homeland of the Goloks. Others came from the southeast through the present-day provinces of Sichuan and Yunnan and the ethnically Tibetan region of Kham. Most, however, started in India and came through Ladakh or Sikkim and then on to Gyantse and Shigatse. Whatever the route, whatever their motives, whatever fantasies about Tibet propelled them onward, almost every one of these passionate pilgrims left a record, and each of their accounts only added further fuel to the increasingly Tibet-inflamed imagination of the West.

From Russia came a czarist emissary, Colonel Nikolai Mikhailovich Przhevalsky, a young soldier of Cossack origin from the General Staff Academy in Saint Petersburg. Przhevalsky was a larger-than-life explorer of great notoriety in Russia whom a biographer, Donald Rayfield, calls a "Byronic romantic." But he was also a man of "ruthless determination" who described his own position in the Imperial Army as that of "a diamond, but in a pile of dung."

Working with the Imperial Geographical Society, Przhevalsky was intent on reaching Lhasa. Despite the fact that he was repelled by Asians as a race, he set off on a series of expeditions to explore Central Asia, a land about which he disdainfully viewed the Western world as being "almost totally ignorant." In 1870 he undertook his first trip, but after three years before he ever got near Lhasa, was forced to turn back by harsh conditions, failing pack animals, and vigilant Tibetans. "The privation is terrible," Przhevalsky wrote along the way.

He refused, though, to give up. Filled with visions of Shambhala, which he had heard from a lama was "an island lying far away in the northern sea" where gold abounded, crops grew to "enormous heights," and poverty was "unknown," he started out again in 1876, this time with a Chinese passport. He bragged that, if necessary, he would shoot his way into Lhasa with the huge arsenal of weapons and ammunition accompanying him, which he described as "the best of all Chinese passports." But after falling sick and running short of supplies, he was forced to eat his bravado and once again turn back.

In 1879, again armed with a Chinese passport, a new contingent of

Cossack marksmen, and another huge cache of weapons and ammunition, Przhevalsky tried once more. Heading across Siberia, he brought with him a Buryat Mongol adviser, Agvan Dorzhiev, who had studied Tibetan Buddhism at Drepung monastery in Lhasa and had become a confidant of the thirteenth Dalai Lama. However, because of his close connections with the Russians he was suspected by the British of being a czarist agent. Przhevalsky also brought a caravan of twenty-three camels loaded with sacks of sugar, crates of brandy and sherry, dried fruit, and a collection of tinted photos of Russian stage stars—all gifts for the natives. For the Dalai Lama, Przhevalsky planned something more personal—wild-strawberry jam that he himself had made. Just in case his gifts did not do the trick, however, he also packed enough powder to blow up a good chunk of the Potala.

Always impressed by a nicely done preserve, the British were perhaps fearful lest Przhevalsky's cache of strawberry jam turn the Dalai Lama's head toward Saint Petersburg. They need not have worried. As it turned out, Przhevalsky never had a chance to proffer his gifts. A hundred and seventy miles from Lhasa, he was halted by angry Tibetan officials exercised by rumors drifting through the capital that the Russians were coming to kidnap the Dalai Lama.

Back home in Russia, Przhevalsky was feted by high and low but could not get exploration out of his system. In Karl E. Meyer and Shareen Blair Brysac's marvelous book on the Great Game, *Tournament of Shadows,* he is quoted as having longingly written: "A sad yearning feeling always comes over me as soon as the bursts of joy on returning home have passed. The further time flies amid ordinary life, the more this yearning grows, as if something unforgettable, precious had been abandoned in the wilderness of Asia which could not be found in Europe . . . an exceptional bliss—freedom—which may be savage but is infringed by nothing, almost absolute."

In 1883 Przhevalsky was at it again. And once again he failed. Undeterred and by now an ardent advocate of Russia's annexing most of Central Asia, the persistent Przhevalsky launched a fifth exploration in 1888. While still in the foothills of the Tianshan Mountains in Xinjiang, far from Lhasa, he died of typhus. Back home, his exploits as one of the great explorers of the nineteenth century were memorialized by none other than Anton Chekhov, who insisted that explorers such as Przhevalsky were "heroes who personify a higher moral force" and were "worth ten institutes and a hundred books."

"He can hardly be said to have been very successful as a traveler in Tibet," British historian Graham Sandberg commented snidely a few years later. Nonetheless, word of Przhevalsky's ceaseless efforts and militance about the appropriateness of imperial Russia's annexing Central Asia helped excite British fears that they were being outmaneuvered by the czar and that if the British Raj (the word *raj* is derived from the Sanskrit, meaning "rule") failed to take forceful measures a geopolitical debacle would ensue.

The year of Przhevalsky's final expedition, a young attaché at the American legation in Beijing, William Woodville Rockhill, a noted linguist, ethnographer, Sinologist, and Tibet scholar and the man who later drafted the United States' 1899 Open Door policy toward China, made a valiant and typical try to reach Lhasa. As a student in France, Rockhill had read Evariste-Régis Huc and Joseph Gabet's diary of traveling through China and Tibet during the 1840s and had been enchanted by it. And since arriving at the American legation in Beijing in 1884, he had conceived the ambition of visiting Tibet. In 1888, with a commission from the Smithsonian Institution, Rockhill entered Tibet from China on the route taken by Huc and Gabet. His only companion was a Chinese, who, as it turned out, had accompanied Francis Younghusband (about whom we shall hear more shortly) on a trip he had made two years earlier across China and Central Asia. In hopes of fooling people along the way, Rockhill disguised himself by "dressing and living like a Chinaman."At Kumbum monastery near Xining in what is today the province of Qinghai, however, he abandoned his Chinese companion and his disguise, shaved his head, donned a monk's robe, and set off alone with a dog for Lhasa.

But with his money, food, and pack animals exhausted, a disappointed Rockhill was forced to give up his quest four hundred miles from his goal. "I nearly starved to death," he wrote. "Time and again I was snow-blind; I had to run for my life before the hostile lamas of Eastern Tibet; and I vowed I would never go on another such fool's errand."

But in less than two years Rockhill, too, was trying again. Approaching this time from the northeast and led by a Golok guide, he came within 110 miles of the holy city before dwindling provisions and the threats of local tribesmen under strict orders to bar the entry of all foreigners forced him once again to turn back toward Beijing, where in 1905 he was appointed the U.S. envoy to China by President Theodore Roosevelt.

In 1893, Jules Dutreuil de Rhins set out with Fernand Grenard on another ill-fated expedition to Lhasa, this one supported by the French government's Academy of Inscriptions and Letters. These audacious Frenchmen, too, were animated by hopes of being the first Europeans to reach Lhasa. Alas, as Grenard despondently reported, "Who foresaw then, that a day would come when the entire mission would be dispersed, sacked and almost annihilated without a trace?"

Approaching Tibet through Ladakh, they spent four harrowing months of privation on the trail. "It was a rough experience," wrote Grenard, "and this journey in the midst of such desolate and infinite solitudes was one of inexpressible melancholy." Despite the hardships that his journal recounts in painful detail—the "pitiless wind, which was accompanied by a cold of thirty-five degrees below freezing point, penetrated into us even to the marrow and peeled the skin from our face and hands"—Grenard was able to see beauty in his surroundings. He could extol the "white mountains displaying their majestic and icy masses" and the natural landscape "robed in silence," which made him feel not just lost but "transported to some olden world that had lain dead for centuries."

After making daily forced marches to advance as far as they could before being detected, they arrived at a place only six days' walk from the capital. *"Nous avions touché le but,"* wrote a hopeful Grenard. It was at this point, however, that the pair was halted on the trail by a messenger sent from Lhasa ordering them to proceed no further. Dispirited and low on supplies, they regretfully turned back.

Even in retreat, however, there was to be no relief. After taking a wrong trail, they were robbed of several of their horses. On June 5, 1894, they happened on a small settlement of Goloks called Thom Bundo, not far from Mount Amnemachen. Stopping to take shelter from a storm, de Rhins got into an altercation over two horses that he claimed Goloks had stolen. The angry nomads began firing on his small band, wounding him and driving his confreres away. They then reportedly seized the injured explorer, bound his hands and feet, and threw him to his death in the freezing waters of a tributary of the Yellow River.

"They bring terror to the hearts of all their neighbors and travellers," Joseph Rock, the great Viennese-born explorer of the Tibetan border regions, could still write several decades later. "One must take for granted that every Tibetan, at least in this part of the world, was a robber sometime in his life," he sardonically observed of the Goloks. "Even the lamas are not averse to cutting one's throat, although they would be horrified at killing a dog, or perhaps even a vermin."

"What was left to do with this life? Had I not lost all that which I prized?" asked a despondent Grenard. "And if the hate of man spared me, had I not yet vast deserts to be traversed, where cold and hunger and wolves lay waiting for me?" In July 1894, Grenard returned alone to Xining, currently the capital of Qinghai province.

Because of India's proximity to Tibet, British trespassers on the roof of the world outnumbered all others. Some of their expeditions, if they can be called that, were bizarre indeed. Take for instance that of Mr. and Mrs. St. George Littledale, who set off in 1894 from Kashgar with a pack train of a hundred animals to cross the wastes of the Changtang with their nephew from Oxford and their fox terrier, Tanny. Although they traveled only by night to avoid detection, the results were by now expectable. "It was heartbreaking, having to turn back when so near our goal," Mr. Littledale lamented as his wife's health began to fail and supplies grew short. As consolation, it could be said that he and his family had come within seventy miles of their quest, closer than any Occidental traveler since Abbé Huc and his companion.

And then there was Henry Savage Landor, lured on like so many others of his generation by the idea of being an "explorer." Having become "deeply entranced" by an account of Sir Samuel Baker's expedition up the Nile, Landor wrote, "Oh, how I was longing to be a man and do like Sir Samuel, and go and see countries and meet savages and wild beasts."

The mystique of Lhasa proved irresistible. Tales then circulating that a "white man going into that country had no chance of coming back alive" only whetted him with "an all the more invincible desire to visit that strange country." So in 1897, Landor left for India to swagger his way into Tibet disguised as "a Hindoo doctor." The aptly named Savage Landor was neither an aesthete nor a mystic but a blustering gate-crasher looking for trouble and a good yarn to tell when he got home. And given the growing fascination with Tibet in the West, he was undoubtedly dreaming of a successful book as well. Indeed, he seemed to have little trouble writing about things he never saw, including allusions to the Potala, upon which he never laid eyes.

When finally caught by Tibetan militiamen, he evidently began remonstrating with them in an arrogant and hostile but predictable manner. They, in turn, treated him with the very savagery for which he seemed to be in search. He reported that one of his captors told him that "before the sun goes down, you will be flogged, both your legs will be broken, they will burn out both your eyes, and then they will cut off your head."

His response to such indignities was, according to him, utter defiance. "I had on many previous occasions found that nothing carries one further with Asiatics than to keep calm and cool," he wrote complacently. For his impertinence, one of his retainers was flogged almost to death, and then he—if his account is fully to be believed—was sequentially tied up, thrown into a dung heap, lashed to a saddle bristling with iron spikes and shot at, threatened with blinding by a red-hot iron bar, and subjected to a mock beheading. Needless to say, all these indignities, whether actual acts or fantasies incubated in Landor's overheated brain, ended up being luridly described in his controversial book *In the Forbidden Land: An Account of a Journey in Tibet, Capture*

by the Tibetan Authorities, Imprisonment, Torture, and Ultimate Release,
a work that the *New York Times* described as "a book that thrilled
the world."

Savage Landor's account was certainly not of the genre that extolled
Tibetan spiritualism or waxed romantic about mountain landscapes. It
did, however, add to the air of strangeness—if also, in this case, of
barbarity—that had become part of the Western idea of Tibet.

So great was the lure of Lhasa that such tales of hardship, despair,
and failure only goaded others on. Now Sven Hedin entered the race to
be the first Westerner to Lhasa. As a child, he, too, had come under
Tibet's spell. "Even as a boy," he wrote, "I devoured Abbé Huc's and
Przhevalsky's descriptions of journeys in Tibet, and dreamed about the
opportunity of seeing that country."

After two efforts, Hedin set off again in 1901 disguised as a Buryat
Mongol pilgrim but was turned back a little more than a hundred miles
from Lhasa by armed militia led by a provincial governor who bluntly
warned Hedin, "No, not one step further to Lhasa. That would cost
your head—and mine, too. I do my duty. I get orders from the Dalai
Lama." Hedin, not unsympathetic to Tibetans' wishes to remain undisturbed, obeyed. "The Tibetans had asked for nothing but to be left in
peace," he commented. "I had the satisfaction of going to the limit of
adventure without capitulating until the opposition proved absolutely
unconquerable."

In 1905, Hedin began a final Central Asian exploration. After a
journey during which almost all one hundred of his pack animals perished, he at least managed to reach Shigatse, where, like George Bogle,
he was welcomed by the Panchen Lama. Although Hedin failed to get
to Lhasa itself, he did succeed in visiting sacred Mount Kailash, exploring much of the remote Changtang region of Western Tibet, and mapping the sources of the Brahmaputra and Indus Rivers. His book, *A
Conquest of Tibet,* did much to infuse the area with a romantic sense of
unconquerability.

Not only was Hedin one of Heinrich Harrer's main inspirations,
but while Harrer was still in Lhasa, the two famed explorers actually
began a personal correspondence. After all, Harrer had succeeded in

accomplishing Hedin's lifelong dream. "With admiration and enthusiasm I read your letter in which you describe your marvelous fairy-tale-like wanderings and adventures," Hedin wrote Harrer. "It is quite simply fantastic that two Europeans have been living for years in that otherwise so hermetically closed capital of Tibet, that Mecca of the Lamaist world. . . . I read your letters like novels, for they are reports from the destinations of my old dreams."

Despite often Herculean efforts, none of the dauntless nineteenth-century Western adventurers ever reached the Mecca of Tibetan Buddhism. Instead, they were left to vie with one another for a far less lustrous consolation prize: who had gotten closest.

12

LHASA AT LAST

Uspayatta is a mountain-locked truck stop on the remote road from Santiago de Chile to Buenos Aires. But instead of the gold-leafed roofs of the Potala gleaming under azure skies, what first catches a visitor's eye at the center of town is the huge plastic sign of a modern gas station filled with big rigs. Just across the road lies the entrance to the Hotel Uspayatta, one of the two hotels being used as mustering grounds for the cast and crew of *Seven Years in Tibet*.

As I pull into the hotel parking lot, there is evidence everywhere of the presence of the $65-million production. Fleets of trucks, cars, jeeps, buses, vans, and RVs with *Seven Years in Tibet* windshield placards fill the parking areas. Because the film's makeup, hairdressing, and costume departments are located inside the Hotel Uspayatta's dark, cavernous lobby, scores of extras dressed up as Tibetan nomads, monks, noblemen, and Chinese People's Liberation Army soldiers mill around in the foyer drinking Cokes, sit on couches snoozing, or eat while chatting in the dining room. A group dressed in ragged sheepskin *chuba*s are asleep in one corner of the lobby, looking every bit like real Tibetan nomads. The congregation of young men dressed as if from the PLA turn out to be Japanese-Argentine extras with mind-warping names like Leonardo Yoshida, Marcello Fujioka and Sebastian Takahara. They are eating breakfast and discussing soccer in Spanish with a group of robed monks who turn out to be real-life Mataco and Jujuy Indians imported from Bolivia and northern Argentina because of their swarthy, Tibetan-looking features.

At a nearby table a little boy with a shaven head and wearing a miniature monk's robes—one of the three child actors who will portray the young Dalai Lama at various ages—is drinking Sprite and manipulating a beeping Game Boy while his bored mother stares off into space. In the bar by a bowling alley a complement of potbellied Caucasian crew members sip coffee and eat croissants as a TV suspended from the ceiling blares a Spanish-language variety show featuring a Charro-like chanteuse in tight toreador pants dancing to cha-cha music. Back in the lobby, a phalanx of Laotians dressed as Buddhist pilgrims stream past, chattering away in Hmong.

Many of the extras are speaking Tibetan, however, because the production has flown in some 140 native Tibetans, including many practicing Buddhist monks, from India, Nepal, the United States, and Europe. A small army of young American, English, and Latin women in jeans and T-shirts, armed with clipboards, preside over this cinematic melting pot.

In the hair room, which occupies the hotel's reception area, hundreds of different styles of Tibetan headdresses are trussed up on mannequin heads arrayed around the walls like so many Buddha statues festooning a temple. As I walk in, stylist Maria Teresa Corridoni, who has done hair for the best of them—including Pier Paolo Pasolini, Luchino Visconti, and Bernardo Bertolucci—is putting the finishing touches on an elaborate traditional hairdo for a young Tibetan exile from Simla, India, who is playing a government minister's guard. (In the

Tibet of the 1940s, secular officials wore their hair piled up on their heads, while monks were clean-shaven, and ordinary people wore pigtails.)

In an adjoining room two Bolivian Indians and the head of an Argentine army detachment posted in Uspayatta are getting their heads shaved to play monks. Next to them, a young Tibetan is being done up as a nobleman by a British hairdresser with a white beard and a Mongolian-style hat—one of many exotic forms of millinery worn by the traditional aristocracy and officialdom—parked comically on his bald pate.

Another young Tibetan, also being made up, tells me that his father is a nomadic yak herder from Amdo. He himself fled his homeland in 1989 after getting in trouble with the Chinese police. "Ever since leaving seven years ago, I've wanted to go home and see my parents," he says. "Of course, I can't call them because they're nomads living in a tent and only stay in one place for a month at a time. I do write, but the Chinese always open the letters.

"Being here is so odd," he continues. "Yesterday on the set we shot a scene where we Tibetans signed the so-called Seventeen-Point Agreement on the 'peaceful liberation of Tibet' with the Chinese—the initial agreement signed between Tibet and the Chinese Communist Party in May 1951—and lots of us just broke down and cried. That was when we really lost it all. Acting it out was such a nostalgic experience. It's so strange for us to be here in this movie reliving our history. Sometimes I'm not sure where I am."

Over a cup of coffee in the hotel dining room, Jimmy Chow, the film's Chinese-Canadian prop master, tells me about the problems that arose when the Indian government refused to give the production permission to shoot in Ladakh. "When we switched locations, we had to send all this stuff here from India," he sighs. "Then the Tibetans would tell us, 'Well, this thing is not quite right.' So we had to try to make it all over. We had to satisfy the experts—who are our own cast. Every day we struggle to get the sets, costumes, and props correct. But finally it's so gratifying when these Tibetan exiles look around and tell you that they feel like they're really home."

"The line between the film and life is so blurred,"adds one of Jimmy Chow's assistants. "When the Tibetans get all dressed up in their costumes and get into it, they seem to fall into a different reality. Before we shot a scene at an old bazaar, the more elderly monks were all walking around the booths examining props and pointing to things for sale in the movie that they hadn't seen since leaving home. It seemed so right and familiar to them that they were quite thrilled and very nostalgic."

"We foreigners get so engrossed in getting things done that there's little time for reflection," interjects Chow. "But you know, when all this is shot, I think there is going to be a lingering pain for these Tibetans." He fingers the prayer beads he has around his wrist. When he sees me looking at them, he says, "I wear them to remember where I am," as if he were in fact in Tibet, not Argentina.

What I want to do as soon as possible is, of course, to see the sets for this Tibet *español*. The production unit publicist, Sue d'Arcy, has let me know that I will be able to go on-set only on certain days, lest I "disturb Brad." Her warning does not seem, however, to include visiting the sets after hours. So that evening after the crew has wrapped, I head off down a poorly paved road that shoots straight as an arrow into the alpine desert surrounding the oasislike town. Here, where rain is rarer than a solar eclipse, the air is as dry and clear as if it were outer space.

Turning off the road at a sentry shack, where during daytime hours a guard stands watch to turn back Argentine pilgrims in search of Brad Pitt, I follow two tire tracks that lance across the sand through tumbleweed and thorn bushes. Distant, snow-capped peaks cast gathering shadows across the plain. With a plume of dust billowing behind me like a jet trail, I have the humbling sensation of heading toward the very edge of nowhere through the same kind of infinite unoccupied space that so overwhelms one in Tibet.

Then, up against the crest of a low-lying, shale-strewn hill, my eye catches a fluttering flash of bright color. As I draw nearer, I spot prayer flags snapping in the wind over the desert scrub. At a turn in the dirt road, eight white *chorten*s, the traditional tiered Tibetan monuments containing sacred relics that represent the enlightenment of Buddha, miraculously appear on the barren landscape like so many oversized chess pieces. Behind them, rising from the sand like an apparition, is the Bargo Kani, the old West Gate. Itself a giant *chorten* with a portal through its middle, it sat for centuries beneath the Potala Palace guarding the road into Lhasa, the seldom-passed end point of so many perilous journeys by Western questers. Alas, the real gate is gone now, razed by the Chinese to make way for a modern avenue.

For the moment, as I stand on sand dotted with yak manure, the white *chorten*s silhouetted against a sun-streaked evening sky, the branches of willow trees rustling, and strings of prayer flags fluttering against a backdrop of snow-capped mountains, it is all too easy to feel that I am actually about to enter the Lhasa of Heinrich Harrer. But to the left and above, there is, of course, no Potala perched in all its magnificence. Indeed, there is not even a place for it to perch.

And what's this? A piece of chicken wire unexpectedly reveals itself in the brickwork plinth of this ancient, revered gate! As I look more closely, the perfection of the moment begins to crumble. Someone has carelessly left a Pepsi can on a wall. When I kick a piece of yak dung, it makes a clinking sound, being a ceramic reproduction and another emblem of the film's commitment to detailed authenticity. And when I yank at one of the willow trees, it proves to be nothing more than a branch stuck upright into a tub of gravel.

To step through the gate is to exit the illusion completely. On the other side I am suddenly standing amid an industrial jungle of electric cables and metal scaffolding supporting a rampart of cheap yellow plywood anchored against the wind by huge plastic vats filled with water. Then a parking area reveals itself, marked off in the desert by the kind of yellow plastic tape police use to cordon off urban crime scenes. It is filled with a flotilla of dressing-room trailers, mobile cranes, generators, equipment trucks, buses, and banks of the gaily colored chemical toilets that spring up around every Hollywood film set. A lone Argentine soldier, presumably a guard, is asleep on an aluminum deck chair in front of a khaki-colored pup tent, the pages of a girlie magazine perched on his chest riffling in the breeze.

When I circle the hill beside the West Gate, I find the film's Potala perched on the other side. But, alas, it consists only of a mock-up of the roof terrace that lies adjacent to the Dalai Lama's personal quarters, from which as a young boy he was able to look down longingly on the ordinary people of Lhasa through his beloved telescope. When the film goes into postproduction, this sliver of the palace will through computer magic be superimposed onto an image of the real Potala that is being shot by clandestine crews surreptitiously filming in Lhasa. In the finished print, it will, of course, look as if Brad Pitt/Heinrich Harrer and the young Dalai Lama are indeed standing together on the roof of the real Potala.

In the fading evening light, I walk up the long stairway constructed of pipe scaffolding and wooden treads that leads to this disembodied replicated slice of Lhasa. The scene for which it was built was shot several weeks ago and this Potala is already beginning to disintegrate. The paint is fading. A giant drum with a plastic head lies cracked and abandoned outside the Dalai Lama's sleeping quarters amid a clutter of soft-drink cans, mineral water bottles, Styrofoam cups, and soiled prayer flags.

Gazing down onto the valley floor, I spot the Jokhang, the ornate cathedral-like edifice built by King Songtsen Gampo, who introduced Buddhism to Tibet in the seventh century. Reassuringly, it is positioned very close to where it would be if this were Lhasa and I were standing atop the real Potala. Because it contains Tibet's most revered statue of Shakyamuni—given to Songtsen Gampo by his Chinese princess bride, Wencheng, as a marriage gift—it is considered the most holy shrine in Tibet. Like the Great Mosque in Mecca, or Saint Peter's in the Vatican, the Jokhang is the spiritual heart of Lhasa to which every devout Tibetan hopes to make at least one pilgrimage in his or her lifetime. Indeed, even today, pilgrims laboriously make their way across Tibet to the Jokhang, prostrating themselves while repeatedly reciting the prayer *Om mani padme hum.* All I can see from where I stand, however, is the back of the Jokhang's set—more plywood and steel bulwarks surrounded by another flotilla of tractor trailers, mobile homes, fire equipment, and white catering tents that make the set look as if it were being readied for some misplaced debutante ball.

' ' '

Beneath an imposing sign announcing "Grupo de Militaire Artillería de Montana 8," a sentry in combat fatigues, a beret, and an M-16 stands at attention beside two old howitzers. When I arrive on the tranquil outskirts of Uspayatta early one morning at the compound known as GAM 8 for short, a lackluster military marching band is just beginning to play. A complement of young soldiers in boots and fatigues appears and marches in a circular parking area around the bronze bust of a certain Colonel Placido Obligado, who boasts ramrod-straight posture, a very Latin mustache, and a bemedaled uniform with epaulets. It's hard not to think of the generals (and probably a few colonels, as well) who during the 1970s and 1980s successfully "disappeared" hundreds of Argentine dissidents.

As I watch, the scene begins to morph. A robed Tibetan monk unexpectedly wanders into the frame and pauses to gaze at the oompahing band. Then a contingent of Tibetan women in brightly colored native dress streams across the parking area and vanishes into a large warehouselike building. I'm reminded of one of those puzzle drawings in which children are challenged to identify the six things that are out of place.

The large building, usually the GAM 8 mess hall, has been converted into a canteen for the film's extras and crew members. At mealtimes it's a veritable Babel of mismatched people chattering away in a polyglot of languages. To provision and feed this seven-hundred-person multinational Hollywood army of men, women, and children from twenty-two countries (who speak Spanish, Hindi, Tibetan, English, Laotian, Italian, Chinese, and French), the producers have hired two separate catering services. Argentine chefs offer a Western menu, while Indian chefs provide an Asian menu.

Inside, hundreds of Tibetans and Tibetan look-alikes wolf down their meals of choice under the gaze of an agonized crucified Christ whom GAM 8 commanders have left hanging on one wall opposite an Argentine flag. I seat myself next to an elderly Tibetan monk.

"I am originally from Eastern Tibet, the region called Kham," he tells me in heavily accented English as he works on a Styrofoam plate heaped with lamb curry and roasted potatoes. "But now I am a monk in a Tibetan Buddhist monastery in Darjeeling, India."

The monk was young when he left Tibet in 1959. His mother died on the trek out and his father refused to return as long as the Chinese were there. "So now I have no country," the monk tells me, "but to be here is nice because it reminds us so much of our home." He flashes a surprisingly cheerful smile.

The monk speaks enthusiastically about the shoot. "We Tibetans hope that it is going to be an important political film, so we want to contribute to it." Nevertheless, he believes that the recent foreign interest in Tibet is sparked more by the country's religion and culture than by its political dilemma.

As for the film's cast, he cannot tell who is Laotian, Bolivian, Tibetan, or Argentine. "They just all look Tibetan to me," he says, "especially when they get suntanned and are standing out there in the desert. Sometimes the Argentinians think I am one of them and start speaking to me in Spanish. Or sometimes I start speaking Tibetan to a South American Indian or a Laotian. Everything is so mixed up here!" He points out the window to a sports field where several Tibetan monks in habit are playing soccer with Argentinian soldiers in fatigues. It is indeed a bizarre sight, quite a stretch from the days when it is said that the theocracy banned soccer in Lhasa because high lamas viewed the act of kicking a ball as symbolically akin to kicking the head of Buddha.

In an adjacent building, I stumble across a group of monks who have been working on one of the film's more elaborate props, a series of huge, intricate, elaborately colored butter sculptures that will be placed at the entrance to the Jokhang for some of the film's most important shots. Traditionally, such sculptures have been made at monasteries during the winter Monlam Festival, when the weather is cold. I can recall from my own trips to Tibet how, even in the chilly winter, these curious religious offerings emit the powerfully rank odor of rancid yak butter. But to accommodate the hot Andean sun and the many days of shooting to come, these Argentine replicas have been olfactorily neutralized by being constructed largely out of wax.

"If they melt, that's OK because it will prove that they are real," one of the monk sculptors tells me philosophically. "Anyway, the ritual of making these sculptures is actually meant as a reminder of the impermanence of all things." He chuckles with Buddhist satisfaction over the notion that something he has been working on for weeks is destined to vanish as the wheel of life keeps turning.

At the very back of the base, where the Grupa Militaire ordinarily maintains the pack mules and horses it uses to patrol this remote and mountainous region, there is now a new menagerie of animals: goats, dogs, ducks, pigeons, chickens, *and* a herd of yaks. Right behind a house occupied by a veterinarian attached to the Argentine army, twelve shaggy, lugubrious-looking black yaks stand near a rail fence. As I wander over to take a closer look at these exotic immigrants, one of the animals turns, plants its feet in the dust, and gives a long, baleful, existential moo.

Months earlier in Los Angeles, I had asked Alisa Tager how they could possibly make a film about Tibet without yaks. She had sighed and admitted, "Yeah, we have been having a real yak problem. We don't have any yaks yet, and we don't know where we are going to get them. We've been frantically scouring Latin American and even U.S. zoos. The problem is we've discovered that in order to import yaks into Argentina, they virtually need passports. They have a big beef industry down there and they're worried about mad-cow disease."

The idea of locating, training, and then airlifting a herd of these shaggy bovines from the Northern to the Southern Hemisphere with the proper immigration documents so that they could make a cameo appearance in a movie did strike me as far-fetched. But yaks are, after all, the quintessential animal of the Tibetan Plateau. Indeed, they provide almost all life's needs for the pastoral nomads who still make up most of Tibet's population of two million. Almost everything about nomadic Tibetan life relates in some way to the yak.

In Tibet's harsh and unique environment, its virtues are indeed numerous. First, the yak is itself miraculously able to survive bitter-cold temperatures, howling winds, and long blizzards through its ability to lick dry grass up from beneath even deep snow. What is more, in barren mountains where trees are rare and firewood almost nonexistent, dried yak dung is the standard fuel for cooking. Yak hair is woven into tents; yak hide is made into boots, saddles, and tack; and yak meat is a basic dietary staple. Even the printing of Tibetan Buddhist scriptures was once dependent on the polymorphous yak, because the ink used by monastic printing houses was made from the carbon found in the soot of burned yak dung.

By far, the animal's most important contribution to nomadic life, however, is its milk. Although it is commonly cultured to make yogurt and dried to make curds, most of it ends up being churned into butter, a product that is at the very hub of Tibetan life and culture. Easily stored inside sheepskin bags in such a cool climate, it is melted into Tibetans' tea (to which salt is also added), making a beverage few Westerners ever learn to love. The butter also provides a crucial source of fat, and is used as a religious offering at temples and monasteries, as oil for butter lamps, as barter for manufactured goods, as a skin emollient against sun- and windburn, and as a waterproofing compound on leather goods.

Making a Hollywood film about Tibet without yaks would be like . . . well, making a film about the Andes without using llamas, a notion that brings to mind the old Ogden Nash nonsense poem:

> The one-l lama,
> He's a priest.
> The two-l llama,
> He's a beast.
> And I will bet
> A silk pajama
> There isn't any
> Three-l lllama.

In any event, since *Seven Years in Tibet* is definitely a big budget production, yaks there must be. The task of finding yaks outside of Tibet, Nepal, or Ladakh fell to associate producer Richard Goodwin, a Brit who looked as far afield as Russia and Poland until he finally found a herd of refugee yaks in residence in Polson, Montana. They were owned by a man named Lawrence Richards, one of a small number of American ranchers who had somehow taken a fancy to yaks and started breeding them as if they were purebred poodles. Indeed, in recent years the yak diaspora has gained enough momentum for overseas breeders to establish an International Yak Association, also based in Polson, Montana.

It was after he managed to buy his expensive prop yaks from Richards that Goodwin's real problems began. He still had to get his unruly charges to Argentina. After much research on the care and feeding of yaks, he loaded his herd onto a Boeing 747 (and has the photos to prove it) for the flight to Buenos Aires.

First, however, Goodwin had to get his yaks the proper travel documents. Because the appropriate Argentine authorities accountable to their country's powerful beef industry feared that alien yaks might introduce dangerous diseases into indigenous cattle herds, they required that each yak have its own set of papers, accompanied by three photos (front view and both profiles).

The task of training and caring for the yaks, as well as all the other animals involved in the shoot, fell to Paul Ball and a staff of ten. I find Ball one day standing next to a couple of livestock trucks just behind the Jokhang set. He is watching over two cages of Lhasa apsos and mastiffs, who, while waiting to go on, are barking themselves hoarse. From the inside of one of the truck cabs, a voice crackles over the walkie-talkie system that serves as the communications network for the huge crew.

"Can we get the chickens in position for when Brad and David enter the market?"

"Roger. It's all systems go with the chickens," another voice responds.

Ball, a tall man with a neatly trimmed beard who wears jodhpurlike trousers accessorized with a bowie knife and a cell phone scabbard, needs no more than a whip to complete the image of the proverbial circus lion tamer. In fact, he was brought up in Kenya and now works as an "animal wrangler" for Critters Ltd., a London-based company that specializes in managing animals for movies, magazine ads, and TV commercials.

The yaks are not required on the set today, but Ball tells me that he still has his hands full.

"I've got 230 animals here on location, but the yaks are by far the most exotic," he says in a clipped English accent. "They were also the most difficult animals to get a hold of. We had to quarantine them for thirty days in the U.S., bring them by lorry from Montana to L.A., fly them by plane to Buenos Aires, and then put them in quarantine for another three to four weeks here, with access to everyone restricted.

"They arrived here healthy but wild. Only one of them was semi-docile, but you really had to keep clear of the others. They are bad-tempered animals who spook really easily, and if they run amuck they can cause a lot of trouble."

As anyone who has spent time climbing or trekking in Tibet knows, few animals in the world are more powerful or more ornery than the yak. An untrained yak is just about the last beast you'd want to let loose on an expensive movie set where almost everything has been constructed out of brittle plaster and cardboard-thin plywood. As one of Ball's assistants put it, "This set is hardly Pamplona."

"You have to be careful all the time," Ball continues. "When we go into the corrals, we have to take whips for our own protection. To get these Montana yaks used to being around chaps in Tibetan clothes was really something. And now my ten lads have to actually be in the film dressed up like nomads in order to keep them under control. I've even had to dress up myself in order to work them on the set." He gives a tug at his jodhpurs.

At the end of filming, Ball tells me, the yak herd will probably be donated to the Mendoza zoo here in Argentina. Perhaps a few will remain here in Uspayatta as keepsakes.

The yaks are not Ball's only headache. "I do everything from yaks to rats and mice," says Ball. Then, sotto voce, as if he were broaching a highly classified subject, he adds. "I also do flies. And to be frank, at the moment I'm having a bit of a problem. Because it's been cold, you see, so no new flies are hatching out in nature. However, I've managed to catch a few in my office, so now we have begun breeding flies ourselves." There is a note of triumph in his voice.

When I express curiosity about how he prevents his precious hatchlings from just flying away before the camera can immortalize them on film, he replies in a near whisper. "What you have to do is cool them down before you put them on the set. That way they get sluggish and can't get airborne right away, at least until they warm up." He looks back over his shoulder as if to see if anyone is listening. Then, with a certain urgency, he continues. "It's amazing how few other wranglers know the secrets of this fly technique."

If there is one sartorial feature in which traditional Tibetans excelled above all others, it must be millinery. Among the aristocracy, the various ranks all had their own unique styles of hat, many of which were borrowed from Mongolia during those periods when the Mongols controlled Tibet.

Michael Jones is this production's Minister of Funny Hats. An Englishman who has worked such previous films as Bernardo Bertolucci's *The Last Emperor,* he sits at a broad workbench in the recreation room of the Hotel Valle Andino, where most of the principal cast and crew members are staying. This room, near the hotel swimming pool, has become the costume factory presided over by the legendary designer Enrico Sabbatini. The billiard and Ping-Pong tables are now buried under bolts of brightly colored fabric, banks of sewing machines, and drifts of costumes. Jones sits to one side before a clutter of half-finished hats, mannequins, hat stretchers, irons, scissors, books of photographs, and piles of felt, fur, yak tails, and exotic tassels. With his gnomelike visage, wire-frame glasses, and tousled gray hair, he looks a bit like an elf employed in Santa's workshop. On the wall, three clocks like those that hang over check-in desks at international hotels are labeled Argentina, Italy, and Morocco, the three countries where he evidently has other milliners at work.

As he labors on a Tibetan nobleman's hat that boasts a flaming orange fringe, Jones tells me in his soft-spoken way how he got into the trade. After starting as an actor, he more or less fell into the costume business when a theater with which he was associated closed down and sold him all its costumes at a bargain rate. From there, he moved into making hats for the Royal Opera at Covent Garden and for various West End musicals in London.

"Ah, well, you always get the bit about 'the mad hatter,' " he says when I ask him about his craft. "But Tibetan hats are something really special." He takes down a series of bizarre creations from the shelf beside him—each with a daunting Tibetan name—and tells me a little about each. One exotic-looking number has a flat, round, crimson circumference hung with fringe—something like a Frisbee turned into a lamp shade. Another is bright yellow and has a round, cream-puff shape that leaves the impression that a flying saucer has accidentally landed on the wearer's head. Still another is a round, cymbal-shaped construction with a Bismarckian spike on top. Then, of course, there are the saffron-colored coxcomblike fringed bonnets worn by Gelugpa monks that some have described as resembling a blond Mohawk haircut. For women, there are elaborate trellis constructions affixed to their heads for putting up their hair.

"There should be an exhibit," says Jones admiringly as he surveys his creations. "When things are made as authentically as these are, they ought to be preserved and shown." For a moment he seems embarrassed by his unalloyed enthusiasm for his own work.

Jones has never been to Tibet. But ever since he was in China for *The Last Emperor,* he's wanted to go. "But here we have our own little Tibet and the old Tibetans who are advising us on this film get so fanatical about everything being just right, because they want things to be truly representative of the culture they have lost. For them, authenticity is a passion and it rubs off on us so that we, too, want to do our absolute best to make things appear real. This is what has made the experience of this film so utterly unique."

While Jones is proud of his hats, he takes particular pleasure in making things look old and broken-down. "Lots of people think you just take a hat, put it on the ground, and stamp on it to make it look old," he tells me. "But not at all! To really give the appearance of oldness, we have to singe, grate, file, spray, paint, dye, and bend it. Believe me, it's no easy task!"

❧ ❧ ❧

On Sunday, while Brad Pitt retreats to his corrugated-tin-enshielded fortress in Mendoza, the film crew takes its single weekly day of rest. Although I still have not so much as laid eyes on him, even in his absence his superstarness hangs over the small town of Uspayatta. Passengers on the buses that stop at the town's truck-stop restaurants talk about little else. After Pitt was driven from dinner by paparazzi and local rubberneckers here in Uspayatta, the particular restaurateur shrouded the floor-to-ceiling windows of one section of the dining room with new curtains. Unfortunately, though, Pitt never reappeared, rendering the expensive addition useless.

Pitt returns to Uspayatta on Sunday night, but he and Gwyneth Paltrow promptly withdraw unseen to his bungalow within the confines of yet another military compound. Only his two bodyguards and his makeup woman, Jean Black, show up at the Hotel Valle Andino, where the other cast members are eating dinner. They report on Pitt's weekend confinement in El Cortijo; the major activity was reportedly barbecuing and racing remote-control cars around the floors.

While the star was taking his ease in the relative splendor of Mendoza, I dropped in on several other members of the cast and crew.

B. D. Wong is an American-born Chinese actor who won a Tony Award for his role in the Broadway production of David Henry Hwang's *M. Butterfly*. He has since played in such films as *Family Business* (1989) with Sean Connery and Dustin Hoffman and *Father of the Bride* (1991) with Steve Martin and Martin Short. In *Seven Years in Tibet* he has been cast as a collaborator Tibetan nobleman, Ngawang Jigme, who signed the 1951 Seventeen-Point Agreement with Beijing. I meet him over breakfast in the dining room of the Valle Andino.

"Tibet occurs to people as an untouched mystery," he begins, "and for Jean-Jacques I suppose that the ultimate way to possess this elusive place was to re-create it in toto. He's a brand of filmmaker who is very special, who chooses to dissect and illuminate a culture or a place rather than a person or a relationship."

Wong is, in fact, a walking incarnation of the sort of cultural authenticity being emphasized in the film's costumes and on the set. He has been growing his hair for a year the better to be coiffed as a Tibetan nobleman, with two buns sitting on top of his head so that they look somewhat like large black Mickey Mouse ears. Since it takes hairdresser Corridoni three and a half hours to complete Wong's do, he is allowed to wash his hair only once a week. The rest of the time he walks around, sleeps, and eats with his mouse ears done up in a bandanna, looking for all the world like an Asian soul brother protecting his "process."

"It gets insanely itchy," says Wong cheerfully. "But I feel so Tibetan in it that it's worth putting up with it."

Two young boys with shaven heads arrive in the restaurant with their mother. They are eight-year-old Sonam Wangchuk and fourteen-year-old Jamyang Jamtsho Wangchuk, two ethnically Tibetan brothers living in Bhutan who are playing the Dalai Lama as a youth. "Yes, it's exciting to have two Dalai Lamas as sons," quips their mother as they dump vast quantities of sugar on bowls of Cheerios.

"Have you ever done Cheerios with His Holiness?" Wong asks impishly.

"One of the keys to this movie's catching on," he says, turning back to me, "is the Tibet mania, or lama mania, that's around." He gives his mouse ears a kind of trembling scratch with an outstretched pinky. "The movie is not 'pop' itself, but because there is so much interest in Tibet and His Holiness, it may dovetail with a lot of pop trends. And then, of course, there's Brad Pitt. He'll bring in young people who have not paid a lot of attention to Tibet, people who have had no understanding of the place."

Back at GAM 8 I run into Jim Erickson, a sardonic Canadian who is the production's set decorator. "So, here we are in Argentina when everything we needed to buy for costumes, props, and sets was in Tibet and India," says Erickson. Although it is dusk, he is still working, preparing for the next morning's scene in which PLA soldiers will force a young monk to shoot his teacher point-blank in the head as he kneels over a pile of burning Buddhist sutras.

"When the Chinese started pressuring India and we abandoned the idea of filming in Ladakh, we had to switch continents and move all this incredibly ornate stuff here." He gestures toward a large shed chock-full of prayer flags, gold Buddhas, butter churns, flamethrowers, ox yokes, saddles, and the like. "The Tibetans say that they feel at home here, and we take it as a great compliment. But anyone who was forced to leave his home is bound to have selective memory. After all, most of us think of our childhoods as idyllic. I know Jean-Jacques does not want to over-romanticize the film and we've really tried to show things as they were. But it's going to be a commercial film." He shrugs.

The next morning, I drive past GAM 8 and keep going beyond the turnoff to the Potala, the West Gate, and the Jokhang, until the narrow road turns to dirt. After half an hour or so, something ahead suddenly glints in the sunlight. Coming around a turn, I run headlong into a conglomeration of tents and trucks, even an ambulance. In the distance, far across the desert, is the spectacular vista of Mount Aconcagua.

Following a snarl of cables that snake up a hill, I crest a bluff to find an abandoned stone building, once part of an old copper mine, from which clouds of theatrical smoke are billowing and strings of Tibetan prayer flags snap in the crisp breeze. Hundreds of cast and crew members stand among piles of Halliburton luggage, props, lights, and tables loaded with mineral water, pastries, and plastic urns of coffee. To one side, a semicircle of folding canvas chairs inscribed with the names of the directors and producers are arranged as if ready for an on-the-air discussion group.

"Let's get this going!" a voice finally barks out. The Japanese-Argentine PLA soldiers who have been hobnobbing with a throng of robed monks with bloodstained faces snap to attention and gather around a fire where piles of wooden printing blocks for Buddhist sutras are smoldering, ready for the take.

Jean-Jacques Annaud paces to and fro, hands thrust into the back pockets of his camouflage fatigues like an anxious general about to go into battle.

"Number three on my cue!" a voice shouts. The soldiers gather around the fire as several robed monks kneel on the ground before them.

"Roll the camera!" barks another voice. Fire and smoke miraculously billow forth from the recesses of the old mine building. The hush that has descended on the set is suddenly broken by the command, "Action!"

With gut-wrenching realism, the soldiers begin to scream, kicking the kneeling monks and clubbing them with their rifle butts. "Fire! Shoot him! Open fire!" they command a young monk in Chinese. He is sobbing and aiming a wavering pistol at the temple of an elderly lama futilely clutching a string of prayer beads.

Finally, the young monk is hectored into pulling the trigger. As the elderly lama falls face-first into the dust, a blood-chilling wail of anguish rises over the hushed set from the horrified executioner. There is little doubt that he is not simply acting.

This grisly scene is part of a sequence dreamed by the young Dalai Lama in 1950 as he fears Tibet's days of independence are numbered. It is one of the scenes that scriptwriter Becky Johnston has added to Harrer's story to prefigure the Chinese atrocities that the time frame of *Seven Years in Tibet* would otherwise preclude. To blur fantasy and reality even further, the lama being executed in the film is, in fact, a real lama, Geshe Yeshi Gyatso, who is originally from Drepung monastery, outside Lhasa. As the scene is shot again, tears stream from his eyes. By its end, many crew members have also begun to weep.

"No, no. I don't mind the pain," Gyatso tells me as we walk to lunch afterward. "This is one of the most important scenes in the film. Because the Chinese forced so many monks to kill their students and teachers, I am happy to do this role. This company has invested so much money in this film, and it means that now the truth about Tibet will be revealed and the world will know." Still clutching his prayer beads, he looks up and gives a broad, toothy smile seemingly devoid of rancor. "When I tried to escape in 1959, the Chinese caught us three times, and six monks with me were injured and died," he continues as we walk down the dusty road to a huge catering tent. "Many others were put in prison, where they, too, died."

"If you woke up here in these mountains one morning, might you think you were home in Tibet?" I ask.

"Yes, perhaps in Western Tibet. It makes me feel very homesick and confused."

By the time we arrive at the tent, people are already heaping their plates with everything from fresh fruit, prosciutto, tomato salad, and spaghetti to hot slabs of ham and roast beef. Special freezers have even been trucked in to serve the cast and crew ice cream bars, as if the agony of the morning's shoot needed to be banished with a good meal.

In the afternoon the crew moves farther into the remote and arid hills to a site where the PLA will blow up a peasant family's house described in the script as being located near the birthplace of the Dalai Lama. It is another scene added for dramatic effect.

As cameras are positioned, I strike up a conversation with Lama Kyab, a Tibetan extra who is wearing a fox-skin hat, leather boots, and a traditional Tibetan tunic. A handsome young man in his early twenties, he tells me in Chinese about his life. Its general outline makes up a story shared by almost every Tibetan on this set.

Kyab comes from Amdo, the very part of Tibet in which this scene is supposedly set. Like many other promising young Tibetans, he was sent away as a boy to a Chinese-run boarding school where only Mandarin was spoken. But due to bad conditions there, he and several of his friends decided to flee. As a fifteen-year-old, he walked across much of Tibet from Amdo to Lhasa, then on to the Shakya monastery in Central Tibet, and finally to the Nepali border. It was a journey of hundreds of miles of dangerous mountains, a daunting proposition for anyone, much less a group of ill-prepared teenagers.

"We were running away from politics, and it was the thought that we might see His Holiness in India that kept us going," he tells me, offering proof that China's efforts to Sinicize a new Tibetan elite may not be working according to plan. "Along the way, we got arrested again and again, but we so much wanted to have a little freedom and to meet His Holiness that we somehow kept going. Without him, we Tibetans would not exist. He is our jewel."

As we watch the crew prepare a stone peasant house for detonation, I ask Kyab how he feels about the film. "Oh, it's great!" he beams. "This will be a big punch in the face for the Chinese government." He punches the air with a clenched fist like a boxer. "Those guys in Beijing never tell the truth and only know how to distort history."

"Isn't it hard to watch scenes where Tibetans are getting shot and blown up by Chinese?"

"Sure, it makes me sad. Even though I know that they're just Japanese Argentines dressed up like the PLA, whenever I see the soldiers, it really disturbs me."

Lama Kyab, who now lives in London, is married to an English wife whom he met in India. As we look out over the pseudo-Tibetan terrain, he says, "Oh, yes, I'm glad to be out of China, but I miss my parents. How I wish I could go back and see them!"

13

FILLING IN THE BLANK

Unknown to most of the Europeans competing to be the first to reach Lhasa in the latter half of the nineteenth century, a group of audacious colonial Indians, or "pundits," had in fact already won the race several times over. (The word *pundit* is derived from the Hindi *pandit,* meaning "a person of knowledge.") Pundits were native Indians whom British officials from the Great Trigonometrical Survey, which in 1808 began to chart the Indian subcontinent and came to be known as the Survey, disguised as pilgrims and then dispatched across the border to map Tibet.

After surveying the Himalayan range—a monumental task that owed much to Colonel Sir George Everest, the distinguished British geographer who became superintendent of the Survey in 1823 and after whom the world's tallest peak (previously named Peak XV) was renamed—the

Survey was ready to move on to the region beyond. As late as the 1860s, Tibet's geography was still largely obscure to Europeans; even the position of Lhasa had not been precisely fixed by cartographers. In fact, the best maps available continued to be those done by the Jesuits a century and a half earlier.

"Tibet remained simply a blank, or a blind eye, on the maps of the world," wrote the adventurer William Carey. That the czar had begun to make efforts to expand Russian influence into Central Asia lent a special urgency to Britain's felt need to map the regions of the Tibetan Plateau, despite the inability of even the most artfully disguised Caucasians to fully penetrate the region. Captain Thomas George Montgomerie, who arrived in India in 1852 with the Bengal Engineers and soon thereafter joined the Survey as a first assistant, came up with an interesting idea while mapping Kashmir and Ladakh. He noticed that, whereas British surveyors were often met with suspicion and hostility by local people, "natives of India passed freely backwards and forwards" as traders and pilgrims across even the most forbidden frontiers. It occurred to him that if "a sharp enough" Indian could be made proficient in exploration and cartography, "he would have no difficulty in carrying a few small instruments amongst his merchandise, and with their aid, good service might be rendered to geography." He turned to a clan called the Rawats who lived in the Johar Valley on the Tibetan border and spoke Tibetan.

The ultimate result of Montgomerie's idea was the establishment of a school at Dehra Dun (where Heinrich Harrer would later be interned) in which native Indians were trained in the arts of both surveying and geographic espionage. Secrecy was to be of the essence in this undertaking. "We are convinced," warned a Government of India Foreign Department report, "that, whether in the interest of the British Empire in India or in the interests of the intrepid explorers whose lives are endangered for our sake, it is essential that a veil should be drawn over the proceedings by means of which our intelligence in respect to the Trans-Himalayan countries is acquired."

In 1863, the first pundits, two Tibetan-speaking Hindu cousins, Nain and Mani Singh from the Kumaon Indian hill region, entered the school. Both had traveled extensively in Central Asia. They were taught to use a compass and a sextant, as well as to estimate altitudes according to the changing boiling points of water. They also learned to pace off distances—carefully calculated at two thousand strides per mile—while surreptitiously recording each step on specially altered Buddhist rosaries with 100 rather than the traditional 108 beads, to customize prayer wheels to serve as hiding places for their coded notes, to conceal compasses in the heads of walking sticks, and to hide other specially made surveyors' instruments in secret pockets and false bottoms of their luggage.

After the two cousins were turned back by wary Tibetans on their first attempt to cross the border, Nain Singh—referred to only as R.G.S. in Survey reports—set out alone once more in 1865, hooking up with a Ladakhi caravan and walking six hundred miles to Lhasa. It took him a year, but he managed to calculate every step of the way and took careful readings of his positions en route. In Lhasa, he confronted another problem, the risk of being discovered and severely punished. Nevertheless, he took up residence in a quarter adjacent to the Jokhang and continued his work. During his stay, he was able to calculate the exact altitude and position of the city, gather copious notes on the life, politics, and religious rituals of Lhasa's inhabitants, chart the course of the Tsangpo River before it flows into the Brahmaputra, and even get an audience with the twelfth Dalai Lama, then just a boy of thirteen.

"You can easily imagine his feelings when ushered into the Great Lama's presence with his prayer wheel stuffed with survey notes and an English compass in his sleeve," Montgomerie wrote admiringly of Singh to Roderick Murchison, president of the Royal Geographical Society in London.

In 1867, Nain and Mani Singh, accompanied by Nain's brother Kalian, set off for Western Tibet to investigate rumors of bountiful Tibetan gold fields—the ancient Greek historian Herodotus had written of "gold-digging ants" in what might have been this region—which the British feared the Russians might occupy. (The rumors had no basis in fact.) The Singh family was to undertake two more secret expeditions to Tibet before R.G.S. finally retired to train a new generation of pundit explorers. Only then was his real identity revealed.

On his retirement from fieldwork, Nain Singh was cited by Colonel Henry Yule of the Royal Geographical Society as "the Pundit of Pundits" and recommended for a gold medal. Referring to Singh's 1865 and 1867 expeditions, Yule insisted that "either of his great journeys in Tibet would have brought this reward to any European explorer. To have made *two* such journeys adding so enormously to accurate language, is what no European but the first rank of travellers like Livingstone or Grant have done."

In 1878, the first Geographical Society gold medal given to a "native" would indeed be conferred on Nain Singh by the viceroy of India. But the Singh family's exploits in Tibet were by no means over. That same year another of Nain's cousins, Kishen Singh, known as A.K. by the Survey, left with several retainers for Lhasa, then continued northward to the Dunhuang caves in northwest China before looping back to India. In four and a half years, he traveled some 2,800 miles on foot. Lieutenant General James T. Walker, the new superintendent of the Survey, remembered Singh's party as returning "in a condition bordering on destitution, their funds exhausted, their clothes in rags, and their bodies emaciated with the hardships and deprivations they had undergone."

In 1879, Sarat Chandra Das, or S.C.D., undertook the first of two more trips to Tibet. Unlike the Singhs, who were simple hill people, Das was a Bengali who had been well educated at British schools established to feed bright young native candidates into the Survey's Indian bureaucracy. It was at the Bhutia Boarding School that Das studied Tibetan under the Sikkimese Buddhist lama Ugyen Gyatso. In 1876 he stumbled across a book containing accounts of both Manning's and Bogle's trips to Tibet. "I read the book over and over again," reported Das. "It kindled in my mind a burning desire for visiting Tibet and exploring its unknown tracts."

The thirty-year-old Das's chance to go to Tibet came when the Panchen Lama granted travel permits to Ugyen Gyatso, allowing Das to go to the Tashilhunpo monastery with his tutor to study Buddhism. Nain Singh gave Das a refresher course on surveying techniques in preparation for the trip. But his trek into Tibet was not an easy one. He was stricken with a bad case of altitude sickness as he crossed the first pass near Mount Kanchenjunga on the border with Nepal and had to be dragged over the summit by a fellow traveler. "In this miserable fashion," he later wrote, "did I cross the Jon-sang La into Tibet, the very picture of desolation, horror and death, escaping the treacherous crevasses which abound in this dreadful region."

Approaching Shigatse, Das described Tashilhunpo monastery as "like a dazzling hill of polished gold." The rest of his trip turned out to be relatively peaceful and in November 1879 he returned without incident to Darjeeling, where the Survey praised his trip for having brought back "fruitful information" that was "of much value for the requirements of mapping."

In 1881, Das was ready to set out again with Ugyen Gyatso, this time dressed as a Tibetan lama and hoping to get all the way to Lhasa, where he was instructed not to risk mapmaking, which was "likely to create suspicion," but instead to "cultivate the friendship of influential people." After falling gravely ill en route and fearing he had contracted smallpox, he finally neared Lhasa. In his notes, Das recounted his approach to the holy city in the third person, his characteristic mode of writing, because he feared what would happen if he wrote in the first person and his diaries were discovered. "Drepung monastery was passed away on the left, and then the towers and glittering pinnacles of the sacred city burst upon the view. Here at length, was the object of all his dreams and all his arduous adventures, lying sedately before him on the open plain! Lhasa the mysterious, the home of occult learning, the abode of the hierarchy of all Buddhism."

Das concurred with Thomas Manning's earlier assessment of the Chinese-Tibetan relationship, deploring the "dissipated and licentious habits" of the *amban*s, whom he characterized as "the terror of Tibetans," who "abhor them from the depths of their hearts." At the same time, like so many others before him, Das found Tibetans simple and appealing. "Humanity and an unartificial gentleness of disposition are the constant inheritance of a Tibetan," he wrote.

Das described the thirteenth Dalai Lama, then an eight-year-old boy, with whom he had an audience, as having "a bright and fair complexion and rosy cheeks." His notes on how this reincarnation had been "discovered" added significantly to Western understanding of the institution of the Dalai Lama. And the Tibetan-English dictionary he compiled after he returned to India became a crucial resource for generations of future scholars.

Unfortunately, so sensitive were Tibetans to foreign incursions that, according to the Japanese monk Ekai Kawaguchi, who was studying at Drepung monastery at the time, when Tibetan officials finally learned that Das had in fact been a British agent, all those who had helped him out of sympathy suffered extreme chastisement. Sengchen Lama, a chief minister who had befriended him at Tashilhunpo monastery and helped him get to Lhasa, was stripped of his property and publicly beaten. Servants of his family had their eyes gouged out and their hands and feet cut off. Curiously, it was to the American Sinologist William Woodville Rockhill that the Royal Geographical Society in London turned to edit Das's reports about what he had found in Tibet. They were ultimately published in 1902 as *Narrative of a Journey to Lhasa and Central Tibet.* It was Das who became the inspiration for secret agent Hurree Chunder Mookerjee in Rudyard Kipling's *Kim.*

Chandra Das's adventures were not the end of pundit activity in Tibet. Among others, an illiterate Sikkimese named Kintup, alias K.P., departed in 1880 disguised as a pilgrim and accompanied by a Mongolian lama to explore the headwaters of the Brahmaputra River. Before leaving, Kintup devised an elaborate plan to determine the mighty river's source by pushing five hundred marked logs into the Tsangpo River in Central Tibet, then testing to see whether they reappeared downstream in Assam in the Brahmaputra.

Alas, Kintup's valiant efforts were in vain. His message alerting the British to the log release never made it back to India, and his trip turned into a nightmare. He was sold into slavery and then indentured to a lama as a servant. But Kintup's dedication to the Survey never wavered. Perhaps because he was unable to write, he passed into obscurity after limping back to India, serving out the rest of his life as an anonymous guide to British sportsmen and travelers.

What animated the pundits to carry out their dangerous colonial assignments so heroically between 1863 and 1893 is not entirely clear. But there is little evidence that they were possessed either of the same geopolitical fears or of the same infatuation with the mystique of Tibet as their British overlords. With the exception of Sarat Chandra Das, who seems to have absorbed some of the British fascination with Tibet, the pundits appear to have been actors loyally performing as surrogates in someone else's drama. What they accomplished, however, would soon prove of great practical significance. By the turn of the century, Graham Sandberg could write that through their efforts "large tracts in Tibet had thus become no longer geographically unknown. . . . Rivers, mountain ranges, localities of towns and villages, can now be laid down with extreme accuracy in our maps, wholly and solely by their painstaking surveys." The effort, said Sandberg, was "one of the greatest romances in geographical science."

Indeed, as late as the 1980s, when Hong Kong–born scholar Victor Chan began trekking around Tibet to write his monumental *Tibet Handbook: A Pilgrimage Guide,* pundit maps were often still the only trustworthy ones available. "It is incredible how accurate these maps were," Chan told me. "When I first started using them, I thought I'd surely get lost. But actually they turned out to be very precise and very reliable."

For the British, who now had a new sense of the lay of the land on the other side of the Himalayas, military force became an option against adversaries in a country in which stealth and guile had hitherto been their only passports. And by the end of the century, fear of Russia had begun to obsess British colonial officials. George Nathaniel Curzon, governor-general and viceroy of India from 1899 to 1905 and a politician whom the Indian historian of the period P. L. Mehra called a "prancing proconsul with a megalomania for territory," was soon complaining that Russia's ultimate ambition was "the dominion of Asia." "Whatever be Russia's designs upon India, whether they be serious and inimical or imaginary and fantastic," wrote Curzon in 1889, "I hold that the first duty of English statesmen is to render any hostile intentions futile . . . to guard what is without doubt the noblest trophy of British genius, and the most splendid appanage of the Imperial Crown." What Curzon feared about Russia was that "each morsel [of Central Asia] but whets her appetite for more and inflames the passion for pan-Asiatic domination." He was particularly worried by the likes of Przhevalsky and insistent that, at the very least, Tibet be turned into "a sort of buffer zone between the Russian and the Indian empires."

"Russia has been long at work and has already fastened two of her tentacles upon the people of the land—trade and her mystical sort of prestige," wrote Graham Sandberg. He counseled, however, that they "can yet, with an effort, be wrenched off from her prey." In his view— and he was hardly alone in espousing it—the only way to get Russia to back off was with a show of military force. As he reminded British policy makers in the best imperial style of the time, "The Tibetans are a weak and cowardly people, their very pusillanimity rendering them readily submissive to any powerful military authority who entering their country should forthwith give a sharp lesson and a wholesome dread of offending."

When British officials twice sought to make direct contact with the Dalai Lama to discuss trade and win assurances of his neutrality, their letters were returned unopened. In Lord Curzon's imperial scheme of things (he had been raised to the peerage at age thirty-nine), it would simply not do for Britain to be treated as "the pettiest of petty poten- tates" and defied by a power that "only mistakes forbearance for weak- ness." Pronounced Curzon, "Nothing can or will be done with the Tibetans until they are frightened." So he decided to force the issue. "As it is clear that they do not mean business . . . we propose to send a mis- sion up to Lhasa to negotiate a new treaty," wrote Curzon to Lord George Hamilton, the London-based secretary of state for India, in 1902. "I would inform China and Tibet that it was going, and go it should. It would be accompanied by a sufficient force to ensure its safety." Curzon placed the expedition under the command of Major Francis Edward Younghusband, a dashing young Sandhurst Military Academy graduate from the King's Dragoon Guards who had been born in the British hill station of Murree on the North-West Frontier of India (now part of present-day Pakistan) in 1863 and had developed an abiding passion for the uncharted expanse of territory that lay on the other side of the Himalayan divide. In fact, in 1887 he had traveled across much of Central Asia, all the way from Beijing to Kashmir, becoming the first European to cross the Mustagh pass over the Karakorams between India and China. It was a trip that left him "nearly burst[ing] with excitement." The book that followed in 1896, *The Heart of the Continent,* helped win him the distinction of being the youngest member ever elected to the Royal Geographical Society.

Like Curzon, Younghusband was known as a "forward thruster," meaning he believed that any Tibetan inclinations toward an alliance with Saint Petersburg must be stopped with a "forward" policy—if not by negotiations, then by other means. The British had been particularly agitated by the efforts of Przhevalsky and by the ongoing rumors that the Buriat Mongol Agvan Dorzhiev, who had accompanied him, was still serving as a vector for Russian influence in Lhasa. But while Younghusband was a military man, he was also possessed of a spiritual, even mystical, side. Indeed, many Europeans were coming to feel that, like Tibet, India, where he had spent his formative years, possessed ineffable sacred dimensions, of which the West had been defoliated. Theosophists, as we shall see, sometimes referred to India, too, as a "Holy Land" with a religion that "was molded by Divine Men." So what better place to search out this "sacredness" than in Tibet, which retained—so many British seekers believed anyway—a far purer and more concentrated form of India's own spirituality.

In describing Westerners who were smitten with the idea of Tibet as an inaccessible idyll of otherness, Peter Fleming, author of *Bayonets to Lhasa,* an account of the Younghusband expedition, writes: "The men and women of their generation regarded the East as mysterious. They saw Asia as possessing—they almost willed it to possess—some inner, hidden quality which Europe lacked. Of what this quality consisted they were not sure. Wisdom? Spirituality? Ripeness? They could not say; they knew only that there was *something* there, something of which the proudest among them was prepared to stand in awe."

Indeed, Younghusband and Colonel L. Austine Waddell—who was with the Indian Medical Service and would become the expedition's surgeon and cultural expert—had already been sufficiently drawn to Tibet that as younger men they had both made plans to secretly trek to

Lhasa. In his book *India and Tibet,* Younghusband spoke of "an abortive effort in 1889 to go to Lhasa, disguised as a Turki from Central Asia." His plans were, however, soon "nipped in the bud by the refusal of my Colonel to give me leave from the regiment."

Even before becoming viceroy of India, Curzon, as so many of his class, felt the allure of Asia. "The East is a university in which the scholar never takes his degree," he declared in a speech at an Old Etonian banquet. "It is a temple where the suppliant adores but never catches sight of the object of his devotion. It is a journey the goal of which is always in sight but is never attained. There are always learners, always worshippers, always pilgrims." Curzon was also to admit after living in India awhile that "the fascination and, if I may say so, the sacredness of India have grown upon me."

In 1903 Curzon invited Younghusband to become commissioner of a newly formed Tibetan Frontier Commission. Younghusband was promoted to colonel and, at the young age of forty, assigned to organize a negotiating team and, if necessary, to launch a whole expedition to compel the Tibetans to sign a treaty with Great Britain. "Here, indeed, I felt was the chance of my life," wrote Younghusband. "The thrill of adventure again ran through my veins."

Back in London, some in Parliament were skeptical about the confusion of motives implicit in the policies of the forward thrusters. The liberal politician Sir Henry Cotton cautioned those for whom "the romance attaching to the unknown formed the great temptation of their lives, and whose curiosity to trample out the secrets of the Grand Lama's palace was only one degree less burdensome to them than their desire to go simply for the fun of knocking the stiff-necked old exclusivist off his perch and humbling him before their 'march of civilization' merely because he just chose to be exclusive."

This certainly described an aspect of Younghusband, who was as enamored of the idea of capturing Tibet as of jousting with czarist Russia. As he journeyed by train to Darjeeling, his point of departure for initial negotiations with the Tibetans at Khampa Dzong, just inside Tibet, Younghusband waxed eloquent about the prospects of a Himalayan adventure. "As in the earliest dawn I looked out of the train window, to catch the first glimpse of those mighty mountains I had to penetrate, I saw far up in the sky a rose-tinged stretch of seeming cloud. It gave me the first thrill of my new adventure, and I forthwith drank in greedily every new impression."

Negotiations at Khampa Dzong went nowhere. The Tibetans were unalterably opposed to the idea of having their relations with Britain "put on a regular footing." To impress them with the majesty of Britain's far-flung imperial power, Younghusband ordered elements of his Thirty-second Sikh Pioneers to appear resplendent in full-dress uniform. When neither this "ceremonial effect" nor more-naked threats brought about productive talks, Younghusband received permission from London and Lord Curzon, who was becoming increasingly agitated over rumors that the Tibetans would soon give the Russians exclusive access rights, to press on toward the trading center of Gyantse. "The advance should be made for the sole purpose of obtaining satisfaction, and, as soon as reparation is obtained, a withdrawal should be effected" was how British policy was defined in a telegram. It was, as Younghusband noted, a "curious telegram," which left policy goals strangely ill-defined.

Attached to Younghusband's expedition were some 1,150 British troops—including a complement of what Lord Kitchener, India's new commander in chief called the "white faces." They were divided into eight companies of Sikh Pioneers, six companies of Gurkhas, a Royal Artillery Battery with four artillery pieces and four rapid-fire Maxim guns from the Norfolk Regiment, all under the command of Brigadier-General James R. R. L. Macdonald of the Royal Engineers, with whom Younghusband soon developed a famously fractious relationship. The expedition was also supported by a "yak cavalry" of some four thousand beasts, a train of seven thousand mules, almost two hundred ponies, six camels, and over ten thousand porters, creating a column that extended for more than four miles when strung out along the trail.

Finally, there was a contingent of four reporters from British dailies. Their job was to supply the empire with on-the-spot accounts of what Waddell would call, in the style of the times, their "little war." So began "the last great adventure of the Victorian age," as Younghusband's biographer, Patrick French, characterizes it.

"The lamas believe that . . . their religion will decay before foreign influence," wrote Edmund Candler of the *London Daily Mail* about Tibetan fears of foreign intrusion. "The Dalai Lama, they say, will die, not by violence or sickness, but by some spiritual visitation. His spirit will seek some other incarnation, when he can no longer benefit his people or secure his country, so long sacred to Buddhists, from the contamination of foreign intrusion." Uneasy about the way that the expedition was about to violate Tibet, Candler explained almost apologetically to his readers back home that "Tibetans are not the savages they are depicted. They are civilized, if medieval. . . . When they speak of their religion being injured by our intrusion, they are thinking, no doubt, of another unveiling of mysteries, the dreaded age of materialism and reason, when little by little their ignorant serfs will be brought into contact with the facts of life, and begin to question the justness of the relations that have existed between themselves and their rulers for centuries."

Expressing the ambivalence that some Westerners felt as they "brought civilization" to Lhasa, Candler added, "The Tibetans, no doubt, will benefit, and many abuses will be swept away. Yet there will always be people who will hanker after the medieval and romantic, who will say: 'We men are children. Why could we not have been content that there was one mystery not unveiled, one country of an ancient arrested civilization, and an established Church where men are still guided by sorcery and incantations, and direct their mundane affairs with one eye on a grotesque spirit world, which is the most real thing in their lives?' "

Younghusband evidently sometimes shared such feelings about the expedition himself. In fact, he reportedly withdrew frequently from others to be alone, read, and reflect on the transcendental messages of such works as Walt Whitman's *Leaves of Grass,* hardly the kind of literature associated with the commander of a military expedition. "Important as was the task upon which I was engaged," he wrote, hinting at his incipient spiritualism, "I all the time thought it of very minor consequence in comparison with the great main deeper interest of my life in which I was now absorbed."

His sensitivity to spiritual matters notwithstanding, Younghusband disregarded all Tibetan entreaties to stop the British advance. Unfortunately, the Tibetan lamas sent to negotiate were none too sophisticated as diplomats, nor did they have a very realistic sense of what they were up against. If the Tibetan soldiers were courageous, their military defenses and their armaments were laughably primitive. For example, as a form of defense the soldiers had each been issued a decree stamped with the Dalai Lama's personal seal, protection, they were assured, against the weapons of the invaders.

During the winter of 1903–04, British forces advanced into Central Tibet unopposed, stringing a telegraph line behind them to keep the expedition and its accompanying reporters in touch with India and London. As they passed through the border town of Phari, Waddell called it "possibly the dirtiest and foulest town on earth." When they reached the small mountain settlement of Tuna some 150 miles from Darjeeling, Younghusband branded it "the filthiest place I have ever seen." Reality, it seemed, had a way of tarnishing romantic projections.

Still hoping to reach some sort of agreement, a frustrated Younghusband impulsively decided one day in January 1904 to negotiate directly with his counterparts by riding boldly into the Tibetan camp unannounced. "Even if a very considerable risk was incurred in the process, . . . I thought that if we could meet and could tell them in an uncontentious and unceremonious manner what all the bother was about, we might at any rate get a start—get what the Americans call 'a move on.' " After all, he reasoned, "When I saw these people so steeped in ignorance of what opposing the might of the British Empire really meant, I felt it my duty to reason with them up to the latest moment, to save them from the results of their ignorance." His entreaties, however, failed to move the Tibetans, who, according to Waddell, viewed the British as little better than "thieves and brigands." They continued to insist that the British retreat.

On March 31, 1904, Younghusband discovered that the Tibetans had blocked the trail ahead in a mountain pass halfway to Gyantse, near a village called Guru, by building a crude stone wall across it. Again the Tibetans pleaded with the British to retreat; again Younghusband refused. "There was no possible reasoning with such people," he remembered disconsolately. "They had such overweening confidence in their Lama's powers."

When British troops set out to disarm the ragtag band of Tibetan defenders blocking the trail, "no one dreamed of the sanguinary action that was impending," wrote Candler. The massacre that followed was evidently precipitated by the sudden charge of a Tibetan general, whom Younghusband later described as having "completely lost his head." More likely, he feared the ignominy of not resisting. When he unexpectedly fired his revolver and shot the jaw off a sepoy soldier, British troops unleashed a savage fusillade. "Before a few seconds were over," wrote Younghusband, "rifles and guns were dealing the deadliest destruction on them in their huddled masses."

In the words of Waddell, "a fierce hand-to-hand melee ensued." British forces, backed by the Royal Artillery and the Maxim gun unit of the Norfolk Regiment (which included two machine guns quaintly named Bubble and Squeak), opened up on Tibetan resisters, who were armed with little more than old matchlocks and swords. As the poet Hilaire Belloc glibly noted in verse:

> Whatever happens we have got
> The Maxim Gun, and they have not.

"From three sides at once a withering volley of magazine fire crashed into the crowded mass of Tibetans," wrote Perceval Landon of the *Times*. "Under the appalling punishment of lead, they [the Tibetans] staggered, failed and ran. . . . Men dropped at every yard."

"I got so sick of the slaughter that I ceased fire, though the general's order was to make as big a bag as possible," wrote Lieutenant Arthur Hadow, commander of the Maxim gun detachment. "I hope I shall never again have to shoot down men walking away."

"It was a ghastly sight, and all the more so in such sublime surroundings . . . under the shadow of the chaste Mt. Chumolhari and her train of dazzling snow peaks," wrote Waddell. "The dead and the dying lay in heaps one over the other amidst their weapons, while a long trail of piles of bodies marked the line of the retreat for half a mile or more, and cringing under every rock lay gory, wounded men, who had dragged themselves there to hide."

It was not Britain's finest or most chivalrous hour. Even Younghusband described the battle as "a terrible and ghastly business." In less than five minutes, some seven hundred Tibetans had been killed or wounded, while the British suffered no dead and only thirteen wounded, including Candler, who had his head and one hand sliced by a Tibetan sword. For the Tibetans, "the impossible had happened," wrote Candler. "Prayers and charms and mantras, and the holiest of their holy men, had failed them. I believe they were obsessed with that one thought. They walked with bowed heads, as if they had been disillusioned with their gods."

It was not until April 1904 that British troops finally arrived in Gyantse. When a month later a forward detachment finally reached the 16,600-foot-high Karo-La, one of the last great mountain passes on the trail to Lhasa, they discovered that the stubborn Tibetans had prepared yet another line of defense behind a second stone wall. At first, the three thousand Tibetans put up stiff resistance against a detachment of flanking Gurkha troops, killing a British captain and wounding over a dozen other soldiers. But they were again no match for superior British firepower. In what Younghusband called a "plucky and daring little action," hundreds more Tibetans were killed and wounded while only four of the expedition's troops died.

Even then, the Tibetans did not seem to recognize the power of the enemy confronting them. In the midst of all this combat, the Dalai Lama wrote a high lama at Gyantse, quaintly asking him, "Will you also request the English privately not to nibble up our country?" Even though London was deeply divided about the advisability of pressing on, Younghusband phlegmatically told the Dalai Lama's emissaries, "I had the Viceroy's order to go to Lhasa, and go there I must."

As the full British force marched toward Lhasa, they met resistance at the Karo-La a second time. Again Younghusband's mountain batteries—"splendid little guns," he called them—opened up, and again the poorly armed Tibetans suffered a bloody and humiliating defeat.

Candler described this battle as "surreal": "Stretched on a grassy knoll on the left, enjoying the sunshine and the smell of the warm turf, we civilians watched the whole affair with our glasses. It might have been a picnic on the Surrey Downs if it were not for the tap-tap of the Maxim, like a distant woodpecker, in the valley, and the occasional report of the 10-pounders by our side, which made the valleys and cliffs reverberate like thunder."

By this time, the Tibetan will to resist was breaking. "This slaughter was beginning to put the fear of God into them," wrote Candler. Now virtually no impediment lay between the long British column and Lhasa. "Tomorrow we camp outside," Candler wrote excitedly in his diary as British troops finally approached the holy city that August. "Our journey has not been easy, but we have come in spite of everything." Waddell was also filled with high expectations of the fabled city. Writing of the scenery as "the most romantic we had yet seen," he described himself as in a state of "eager anticipation." Starting off that morning with the thought that "every step we took brought us nearer to our goal, and every turn of the road might reveal the sacred city," he wondered if his feelings were not "akin to the emotions felt by the Crusaders of old on arriving within sight of Jerusalem."

Younghusband, too, was gripped by the significance of the moment. After all, he had won the race to Lhasa, becoming the first Englishman since Thomas Manning to reach the "citadel of Lamaism." His description of approaching the fabled city at last would contribute to the West's mythology of Tibet long after his military feats, or savagery, had been all but forgotten.

"And then we saw, rising steeply on a rocky prominence in the midst of the valley, a fort-like dominating structure, with gilded roofs, which we knew could be none other than the Potala, the Palace of the Dalai Lama of Lhasa," wrote Younghusband. "The goal of so many travellers' ambitions was in sight! The goal, to attain which we had endured and risked so much, and for which the best efforts of so many had been concentrated, had now been won. Every obstacle which nature and man combined could heap in our way had been finally overcome, and the sacred city, hidden so far and deep behind the Himalayan ramparts, and so jealously guarded from strangers, was full before our eyes."

Despite his own excitement as he prepared to enter Lhasa on August 3, 1904, Candler felt that something ineffable was about to be lost. "Tomorrow, when we enter Lhasa, we will have unveiled the last mystery of the East," he wrote, as if he sensed that the promise of Lhasa unattained might prove more satisfying than whatever reality might offer.

So eager, however, was Waddell to see the Potala and the city itself that on the first night British troops were camped outside he could not resist riding ahead to the West Gate with several other officers. "On climbing the ridge alongside the gate, which was crowded with several hundred inquisitive monks and townspeople thronging out to see the white-faced foreigners, the vast panorama of the holy city in its beautiful mountain setting burst upon our view, and we gazed with awe upon the temples and palaces of the long-sealed Forbidden City, the shrines of the mystery which had so long haunted our dreams, and which lay revealed before our eyes at last."

Perceval Landon of the *Times* was equally elegiac. "When at last the sight of the farthest goal of all travel burst upon our eyes, it was worthy, fully worthy, of all the rumour and glamour and romance with which in the imaginings of man it has been invested for so many years."

Since members of the Younghusband expedition were the first British to reach Lhasa in almost a century, the reports and books that their exploits would spawn did much to excite the popular imagination with the idea of a "hidden kingdom" presided over by a mystical castle, even if it had at last been penetrated. But idealizations of Lhasa were quickly tempered by reality, bearing out the old saw that things are often better imagined than described. The long-denied city's unclean state and the evident oppressiveness of the theocracy proved a surprising letdown for most of Younghusband's men.

"If one approached within a league of Lhasa, saw the glittering domes of the Potala, and turned back without entering the precincts, one might still imagine it an enchanted city, shining with turquoise and gold," Candler confided. "But having entered, the illusion is lost." He found the city "squalid and filthy beyond description, undrained and unpaved. Not a single house looked clean or cared for." Even the Jokhang appeared "mean and squalid at close quarters, whence its golden roofs were invisible."

Younghusband, too, felt disappointed. "Many a traveller had pined to look on Lhasa, but now we were actually in this sacred city, it was, except for the Potala, a sorry affair. The streets were filthy dirty, and the inhabitants hardly more clean than the streets; the houses were built of solid masonry, but as dirty as the streets and inhabitants; and the temples we passed, though massive, were ungainly. Only the Potala was imposing."

Candler was especially disenchanted with Lhasa's theocracy. "I must confess, that during the protracted negotiations at Lhasa, I had little sympathy with the Lamas," he wrote. "One or two looked as if they might be humane and benevolent. . . . But most of them appeared to me to be gross and sottish. . . . No wonder that, when one looks for mystery in Lhasa, one's thoughts dwell solely on the Dalai Lama and the Potala."

On closer examination, Younghusband was hardly more taken with what had come to be known as "Lamaism": "Of the higher Lamas, my impression was not favorable as regards their intellectual capacity or spiritual attainments." Calling what he found in Lhasa "a sorry picture," Younghusband doubted "whether Lamaism has on the whole been a success." He acknowledged that, while it had "nourished peace in Tibet," he nonetheless viewed it as an institution born of "sloth and decadence." Even in Lhasa's spirituality, he found the sacred city wanting. "We could hear nothing of the wonderful Mahatmas," he reported. What he found instead was an indolent theocracy. "Practically, then, the religion of the Tibetans is but of a degraded form," he concluded.

"The Lamas ruled the country entirely in their own interests," he continued. "They were not even ecclesiastics; they never preached or educated laity, but kept the latter in ignorance and servitude, with the result that the Tibetans have become the most priest-ridden people in the world . . . sapped of their vigor and spirit." A disenchanted Perceval Landon described Lamaism as "an engine of oppression."

But Candler, at least, still yearned to hold on to some small part of the West's comforting illusions about Tibet. He professed himself relieved that the thirteenth Dalai Lama had escaped Lhasa—he had fled to Mongolia—and so was not forced to sign the accord with Younghusband in person like an ordinary mortal. "Imagine him dragged into durbar as a signatory, gazed at by profane eyes, the subject of a few days' gossip and comment, then sunk into commonplace, stripped of his mystery like this city of Lhasa, through which we now saunter familiarly, wondering when we shall start again for the wilds." For Candler, the Dalai Lama's flight to Mongolia had "deepened the mystery that envelops him, and added to his dignity and remoteness; to thousands of mystical dreamers it has preserved the effulgence of his godhead unsoiled by contact with the profane world."

Nonetheless, after asking around the city, Candler reported that "to many strangers [i.e., Nepalis] in Lhasa, and perhaps to a few Lhasans themselves, the divinity was all clay, a palpable fraud." The Dalai Lama, he concluded, was considered "a pompous and puritanical dullard masquerading as a god."

On September 7, 1904, in the Dalai Lama's own audience hall in the Potala, the British and the Tibetans signed what came to be known as the Anglo-Tibetan Convention, concluding the whole misbegotten venture. The accord forbade the Tibetans from having diplomatic dealings with any power save the Chinese without British permission, required them to open several trade routes and marts with a resident British representative, and imposed payment of a stiff indemnity. No one seemed to remember that the casus belli had been an alleged Russian presence in Tibet. Needless to say, no Russian arsenal, no troops, indeed no sign of czarist presence of any kind was ever found. Nonetheless, Lamoshar Lobsang Gyaltsen, or Tri Rinpoche, a monk from Ganden monastery whom the thirteenth Dalai Lama had designated as regent in his absence, graciously gave Younghusband a small statue of Buddha at the

final signing ceremony, saying that "when we Buddhists look on this figure we think only of peace." All he asked was that henceforth when
Younghusband looked at this statue, he "think kindly of Tibet."
Younghusband was deeply affected by this gesture and cherished the
gift for the rest of his days.

The experience of invading Tibet and taking Lhasa by force had
been disillusioning for almost everyone involved. Lhasa laid bare and
conquered was no longer the intriguing mystery it had been when still
inviolate. "Civilization has roused her from her slumbers, her closed
doors are broken down, her dark veil of mystery is lifted up," wrote
Waddell upon returning. "Thus, alas! inevitably, do our cherished
romances of the old pagan world crumble at the touch of our
modern hands!" Even Lord Curzon seemed to sense that something
ineffable had been lost. "I am almost ashamed of having destroyed the
virginity of the bride to whom you aspired, viz. Lhasa," he wrote the
explorer Sven Hedin, who described the Younghusband expedition as
the "rape of Lhasa." "War against Tibet! Why?" Hedin wondered
angrily. "The Tibetans never asked for anything better than to be
left alone." The result of the Younghusband expedition for Hedin was
to denature forever after the idea of Lhasa as an alluring, forbidden
place. "The longing I had in 1901, to penetrate the holy city in disguise,
was completely gone," he wrote. "The charm of the unknown had
passed."

As it turned out, though, Younghusband, Curzon, Candler, Landon,
Waddell, and Hedin were not completely right about Lhasa's being forever dispossessed of its mystery and allure. Perhaps for them the *mys-
terium* of Lhasa had been punctured, but what they did not take into
account was the urgency of the drive to maintain the myth for others.
In the industrializing West—indeed, in a world that would soon be
submerged in the bloodiest century that civilization was ever likely to
experience—the need to imagine a peaceful, spiritual, serene country, at
once beautiful and removed, could not be displaced for long by the
reports of a few journalists and military men and their accounts of a
bloody little "expedition" into an imagined paradise.

Candler, Landon, Younghusband, and Waddell all included a fair dose of Lhasa's mundane reality in their descriptions of their sojourn in Tibet. And yet, despite the popularity of their writings, the mystique of Lhasa continued to grow virtually unabated as the small drama of 1904 faded from memory. What would be remembered from the accounts of these newly minted Tibetan specialists was not their encounters with a filthy, corrupt, oppressive, and backward Tibet, but the exoticism of the remote world they had at last penetrated. No one would better illustrate this process than Younghusband himself.

Indeed, on Younghusband's last day in Lhasa he experienced a revelation of sorts that would play a role in the years to come in strengthening Western tendencies to view Tibet as possessing spiritually curative powers. Just before leaving the city, he tucked Tri Rinpoche's Buddha into his saddlebags and rode out alone into the mountains overlooking the Potala. "I gave myself up to all the emotions of this eventful time," he remembered in his memoir *India and Tibet.* "My task was over and every anxiety was passed. The scenery was in sympathy with my feelings; the unclouded sky a heavenly blue; the mountains softly merging into violet; and, as I now looked toward that mysterious purpley haze in which the sacred city was once more wrapped, I no longer had cause to dread the hatred it might hide. From it came only the echo of the Lama's words of peace. And with all the warmth still on me of that impressive farewell message, and bathed in the insinuating influences of the dreamy autumn evening, I was insensibly suffused with an almost intoxicating sense of elation and good will." Then, Younghusband, who had been profoundly influenced as a youth by Tolstoy's more mystical writings, such as *The Kingdom of God Is Within You,* evidently underwent an epiphany of his own. "This exhilaration of the moment grew and grew till it thrilled through me with overpowering intensity. Never again could I think of evil, or ever again be at enmity with any man. All nature and all humanity were bathed in a rosy glowing radiancy; and life for the future seemed nought but buoyancy and light."

Younghusband found himself "boiling over [with] love for the whole world" and filled with an "untellable joy" such that everything around became "ablaze with the same ineffable bliss that was burning within me." At that moment he became "convinced past all refutation that men are good at heart, that the evil in them was superficial. . . . In short, that men at heart are divine." This mystical revelation would help etch in the imagination of future generations of Westerners a sense that, whatever its shortcomings, Lhasa nonetheless held a wealth of hidden redemptive spiritual possibilities. If it could conquer the heart of its conqueror so effortlessly, then what Western heart might resist its transformative powers?

In the wake of the Younghusband expedition a British representative connected by telegraph line to the outside world was to be posted in Gyantse. Still, Lhasa itself fell more firmly than ever under Chinese control and once again closed its doors to the West. Lhasa had been invaded but Tibet did not become a European colony like much of the rest of South and Southeast Asia. Moreover, Tibet's cloistered condition would now be sanctioned not just by the Tibetans and Chinese but by the British, who had become another great power worried about the arrival of gate-crashers.

As for Younghusband, he was knighted for his controversial expedition and then retreated into mysticism. After a flirtation with Theosophy, he developed a bizarre and complex religious philosophy all his own that he hoped would promote universal love and "enrich the blood of mankind." A tireless writer, he penned a string of eccentric books that moved from such topics as "eugenic fitness" and "liberated love" to flying saucers and aliens. As Younghusband's biographer, Patrick French, notes, "By mixing philosophy with poetic descriptions of Tibet, Sikkim and the Himalayas, he aimed to draw admirers of his Eastern adventures into his mystical orbit." He even began referring to himself as Svabhava, an Indian Brahmin who was supposedly "a follower of the Gleam," an amorphous cosmic notion dreamed up by an elderly Younghusband. He also helped found a World Congress of Faiths, aimed at promoting a fuzzy ecumenical notion of international brotherhood.

At his request, when he died in 1942 his body was laid to rest under a tombstone inscribed with a bas-relief of the city of Lhasa, and the Buddha figure given to him by Tri Rinpoche was placed atop his coffin. After his death, supporters drew up plans to establish a Chair of Mysticism in his name at Oxford.

14

ILLUSION AND REALITY

Now that the real Tibet is at last open to curious Westerners, who can jet into Lhasa's Gongkar International Airport for five-day tours, not a few modern pilgrims return home feeling even more disappointed than the members of the Younghusband expedition. Due to the rapidly increasing number of Han Chinese immigrants and abundant signs of economic development, visitors from the West see the holy city turning into just another example of ugly socialist urban blight, albeit dotted by an occasional theme-park-like Tibetan Buddhist monastery or religious shrine. No longer exiled from their dreamland but disenchanted and even offended by what they find there, Westerners are caught in a strange dilemma. Where in this high-tech age besides outer space can we project our dreams and yearnings without risking disappointment? Where can we hope to find a different, a better, a deeper, more spiritual, and more meaningful world than the one we already inhabit?

Hollywood, the ne plus ultra of contemporary dream machines, has stepped in with the answer. Just as the West was being dispossessed of Lhasa as a receptor site for its projections, the film industry has chosen to lavish tens of millions of dollars creating Lhasas and Tibets that harken back to an era when Westerners were still resolutely denied access, the better to encourage our fevered imaginations to embroider what was an intriguing, but still largely unknown, reality. And to our long-standing fascination with this unusual and once unchanging place has now been added a new story line, that of Tibet's occupation, oppression, and destruction by the Chinese Communist Party. Now the imagery of Tibet as a beloved spiritual refuge and geographical escape hatch runs up against that of Tibet as a defenseless underdog, a spiritual society that was minding its own business only to get crushed under the jackboot of an aggressive, materialist overlord.

Heinrich Harrer's stay in Lhasa was the very last moment of Tibet's isolation, and the film version of *Seven Years in Tibet* grafts on to his account a hint of the coming end of our imagined paradise. One thinks of the scene of the forced execution of a monk by his acolyte or the blowing up of the peasant house that I watched being shot in Argentina. Never mind that these sequences were not in his book and that the worst atrocities perpetrated by the Chinese did not take place until the late 1950s, long after Harrer had fled, and then again during the Cultural Revolution, which began in 1966. What is undeniable is that such scenes did eventually happen, and their re-creation on movie screens in cineplexes around the world will heighten the sense that a formidable power has unfairly and savagely bullied a smaller and defenseless people into submission.

So, in the popular imagination of the West, the plight of the Tibetans as an oppressed people occupied against their will by a predatory neighbor has been added to the lure of Tibet as a mystical place of physical beauty and spiritual refinement. Particularly for Americans, who so often in their history have prided themselves on identifying with underdogs, this new twist has become a compelling part of Tibet's evolving mythology.

Jean-Jacques Annaud's film is calculated to blur the line further between the older paradisiacal Tibet and the newer human rights–oriented version to create an updated composite Western fantasy of Tibet as both the aloof Shangri-La and the invaded, oppressed victim.

It is striking that in the record of the West's Tibet—with the exception of translations of books on Buddhist philosophy and wisdom—accounts have almost all come from Westerners looking in from the outside. One does not have English-language records of Tibetan voyages in Tibet, no less in the West. Yet here on this film set, for possibly the first time, Tibetans are helping, even if in a subsidiary or purely atmospheric way, to create a Tibet aimed at Westerners and those members of the Tibetan diaspora who have had little familiarity with their homeland for four decades. For no matter how much this Argentine set may have been turned into something that even elderly Tibetans are tempted to mistake for their homeland, what will finally appear worldwide on movie screens will be another version of Tibet yearned for by Westerners. All the monks and other Tibetan exiles who have been enlisted in this project to create something that is inspired not quite by them but by a nostalgic Austrian mountain climber, a French director, an American superstar, and an Argentine landscape are just willing extras in a new Hollywood simulacrum. These perfectly real monks and other Tibetans are, in effect, playing themselves in a petrified and reorganized version of their (or their parents') stories. Indeed, the film is so bizarrely close to the mythology it both plays off and reinforces that the Dalai Lama's own sister, Jetsun Pema, plays their mother. The effect is something like having real Holocaust victims play the roles of concentration camp prisoners or having combat veterans replay their battles as, in fact, Audie Murphy, the most decorated World War II vet, did in the 1955 film version of his autobiography, *To Hell and Back.*

Casting these real Tibetans as Tibetans (Hollywood has not always excelled in casting ethnic extras) and then making almost manic efforts to keep the locations, sets, costumes, and props "authentic" is part of a strategy calculated to help actors and crew feel as if they are participating not so much in the making of a feature film as in a celluloid passion play being acted out in semidocumentary form. "It's one of those films that's much more than a movie," publicist Sue d'Arcy tells me proudly. "It's an unusual experience. Even before we started, the monks became involved in it. They even wanted to bless the set. Now, there's something that doesn't often happen in Hollywood!"

Once a vaporous dream for the West, Tibet is now becoming virtualized in more concrete and convincing ways. No longer is the creation of our Tibet largely the product of the written word working on our imaginations. Now it can be visited as if it were a multidimensional Web site. It can be seen, heard, and practically smelled in intensely vivid images on-screen and, in my case, toured in person on a location about as distant from the actual Tibet as it is humanly possible to get on this planet.

Hollywood has always been in the business of re-creating history and has always been tempted to spin the past into nouvelle historical cotton candy. Recall, for example, the massive re-creation of Babylon that D. W. Griffith constructed on a Hollywood back lot for his 1916 silent epic *Intolerance* (which as late as 1975 film historian Robert Sklar was still calling "the greatest visual experience in the history of movies"). Using its unique alchemy, Hollywood has re-created everything from Elizabethan England, revolutionary France, and Inquisition Spain to feudal Japan, warlord China, and the South Seas. It has reenacted every kind of barbarian invasion from Visigoths and Huns to Mongols and Tatars and dramatized every sort of struggle from Roman slave rebellions to nuclear war. And in between, there have been thousands of versions of Western heroes and villains—cowboys, Indians, sodbusters, cavalrymen, gold diggers, sheriffs, preachers, gunslingers, cattle herders, saloon girls, broncobusters, and bank robbers—all depicted as if they had just walked right out of the history books onto the screen. In recent decades, Hollywood has also taken to creating historical worlds of the future— *Star Wars, Stargate, Starman,* and *Star Trek*—and rendering them so vividly and concretely that it is hard for a viewer to believe that there is no basis for them anywhere in our universe.

There is a story to every aspect of Hollywood's rapacious use of the past, including the use of authentic people to play themselves as actors. In the early days of the movies, for instance, actual cowboys and range fighters like Buffalo Bill Cody and Indians like Sioux Chief Running Hawk were featured first in Wild West shows and then in films, sometimes playing themselves in reenactments of battles in which they had actually fought each other. Silent-screen historian Kevin Brownlow reports that Bill Cody made a film of the last Indian wars that included scenes of the massacre at Wounded Knee in which both he and Running Hawk played themselves. As Brownlow notes, it was shot "precisely where the massacre had occurred, over the graves of the victims."

Nonetheless, compared with *Seven Years in Tibet* these were primitive attempts at verisimilitude. In the hands of present-day Hollywood "historians," the genre has taken a quantum leap into the onrushing technofuture, where it is simple to splice a re-creation of the Potala's rooftop onto an image of the real thing or create a computer-animated character out of cyber nothingness. The Tibetans of *Seven Years in Tibet,* like those of its sibling, *Kundun,* being shot in Morocco, find themselves embedded in a virtualized reality whose import and impact not only they but few of us have yet fully begun to grasp.

The Tibetan extras for *Seven Years in Tibet* are housed at an off-season ski resort, the Hotel Ayelen in Los Penitentes ("the penitent ones"), which is situated among a collection of ski lodges perched in a mountain pass on the Argentine-Chilean border. The hotel's chalet-style ambience—large stone fireplace, cozy bar, and ads for ski boot rentals—is an odd fit with the spectacle of elderly Tibetan monks in full habit rather than après-ski wear. In the lounge area, it feels as if a misplaced Tibetan convention is in progress. Clutches of Tibetans of all ages wearing jeans, madras shorts, Birkenstocks, baseball caps, and T-shirts sit around tables chatting and eating while several small children chase a balloon through the dining room, slaloming around Argentine waiters serving steaming bowls of spaghetti. A Tchaikovsky piano concerto cascades from a PA system as if from the wrong movie soundtrack.

Since today is Sunday, there is a relaxed but festive atmosphere among the extras lodged here. Indeed, for many this film production is not only the first time they have left their homes in exile, but also their first chance to meet such a cross-section of fellow exiles, who come from the United States, India, Nepal, Bhutan, Canada, England, Switzerland, and Germany. There is no question that the production of *Seven Years in Tibet* has provided an unparalleled occasion for hundreds of Tibetans in exile to meet, work together, and get to know one another.

Most young Tibetans here at Los Penitentes regard with condescending bemusement, if not disdain, the fascination of Americans and Europeans with things Tibetan and Buddhist. "Westerners look at us with a kind of unreal awe," says a young woman who now lives in Vancouver, Canada. "They think we're all monks or at least that we always meditate. Somehow Westerners think Tibetans are so spiritual that they don't expect us to have two eyes and a nose. I mean, where did we ever get such an exotic stereotype?"

"Because so many Westerners have lost their own culture and religion, they've become fascinated with Tibet where people still believe," another young woman interjects. "But Buddhism isn't something you can get by conversion, where you can just get it. It's *nangpa,* an inner phenomenon, an interior rather than an exterior thing."

"Lama-chic Westerners don't like young Tibetans like us with long hair and jeans," a woman in a ponytail says almost derisively in accentless English. "If someone doesn't have a robe and a shaved head, they think that we're not a real Tibetan. But I've been in the West a long time and although I may look very Westernized, I'm still very Tibetan. I wouldn't even date anyone outside my race, for God's sake!"

"It's a contradiction," complains a young man sipping a Coke. "They want us to be authentic, funky Tibetans, but then they want to bring His Holiness to Hollywood, where nothing is real!"

"Yeah, I know some Westerners who call themselves Tibetan Buddhists and I must confess that I have strange feelings about them," adds a pretty woman in a "Free Tibet" T-shirt. "Western converts all seem to have their own guru or lama, a figurehead whom they expect to perform miracles. They seem so earnest and so extreme. The way they think that all monks are special really turns me off. They go to a weeklong course or to a dharma center and think that they've gone to nirvana."

As we chat, I am struck by how few of these young people from the Tibetan diaspora have ever been to Tibet, even though many of them could now go as tourists. Indeed, many of them have lost some of the most distinguishing characteristics of Tibetans in their homeland. Whereas almost every Tibetan's skin has been burned nut-brown by being out in the relentless high-altitude sun, in the West, Tibetans often become pale, even sallow. The difference in complexion is a reminder of the gap between the real Tibet and the Tibet in their minds, which yawns almost as wide as it does in the minds of many Westerners. In certain unexpected ways, especially here in Argentina with so much corroborating scenery, these exiled Tibetans seem to be drawing closer to the West's collective imagining of their homeland than to the real place in the People's Republic of China from which their parents fled.

Playing extras in this virtual Lhasa is as near as most have come, and perhaps ever will come, to their homeland. Still, after listening to them talk about the films now being made about Tibet, about their experiences of being Tibetan in foreign lands, and especially about the West's fascination with their country, I nonetheless come away with a sense that they are still distinctly the products of Tibetan culture. But it is equally evident that, here in Argentina, they feel even more disoriented than I do, and never more so than during those hours when they are costumed as and pretending to be—in fact, almost feeling they *are*—Tibetans living in Lhasa in the late 1940s.

The scene in the film that many of them talk about as if it *were* real is the reenactment of the signing of the Seventeen-Point Agreement with Beijing at a landing strip outside Lhasa. "When we rehearsed that scene, it felt so real we all cried," a young man in his thirties, his hair done up like that of a Khampa warrior, tells me somberly. "Although it never actually happened quite that way, still, for us it felt real." The actual agreement was signed on May 23, 1951, by a Tibetan delegation headed by Ngawang Jigme, not in Tibet but in Beijing. It involved no dramatic confrontations (that we know of) between Chinese and ordinary Tibetans of the sort scripted by Becky Johnston. Nonetheless, for almost everyone present the scene as shot here in Argentina was one of almost unbearable poignancy. In fact, because it was such an emotional experience, a number of these young Tibetans are now not sure whether this isn't actually the way history happened. After all, were they not there to witness it firsthand and to feel its raw power?

The point is that these real tears people are shedding tend to sanctify what is, in effect, a moment of well-meant historical fiction. "I see and feel, therefore history is" will perhaps be remembered as the maxim of this virtual era when entertainment merged with news and history to provide a more visually and dramatically pleasing, if amorphous, aggregate that is to the information revolution what genetic engineering is to biology. Of course, every filmmaker from Oliver Stone to Jean-Jacques Annaud who does historical productions is looking for added emotional punch. As the actor B. D. Wong put it one night at dinner, "Historically accurate or not, it's pay dirt for Jean-Jacques."

When I raise the question of Tibet and Hollywood with these young Tibetans at the Hotel Ayelen, everyone starts talking at once, but not about Hollywood's libertine ways with history. "The bottom line is, no Tibetan likes to see His Holiness in Hollywood," says one. "For us, he's too holy for that. I heard some Tibetans say that, while they understood it helped raise money for their country, they still weren't pleased to see His Holiness with Sharon Stone and all those Hollywood stars. It's almost commercializing him." Yet, without any evident sense of contradiction, every one of them expresses a real hope that their cause will somehow be amplified to good effect through this Hollywood film on which they are working but over which they, like all the other imported Tibetan members of the cast, have no control.

It is a measure of the West's yearning to believe in a romanticized Tibet that a book like Harrer's is being transformed into a movie. But for entertainment purposes, a key element is missing from Harrer's account of his life in Lhasa. If one is to believe Harrer, he had no contact with women, not so much as a fleeting dalliance. This was not, of course, good news for a film boasting Brad Pitt. Not only were there no mentions of torrid affairs in the book, but when I interviewed Harrer in Austria he insisted he had been completely abstinent while in Tibet.

To remedy the "love-interest" lacuna, scriptwriter Becky Johnston had to find a way to pump up the part of a young Tibetan woman named Pema Lhaki, who did, in fact, end up marrying Harrer's partner, Peter Aufschnaiter, played by British actor David Thewlis. Then, to make their love affair less peripheral to the story, Johnston called for Pema Lhaki to be not only a ravishing beauty, but someone whom Harrer was initially interested in as well. In the end, however, there was no way to change the fact that Harrer—that is, Brad Pitt—does not get the girl. Nonetheless, the two men's competition for Pema's affections does allow the comely ingenue Lhakpa Tsamchoe to be on-screen for much more of the film than Pema's relationship to Harrer would otherwise have warranted. After all, if this go-round of mythmaking about Tibet was to have real firepower, a certain quotient of on-screen pulchritude was assumed to be a necessity.

Twenty-six-year-old Lhakpa Tsamchoe is the only Tibetan with a substantial part in *Seven Years in Tibet.* I met her one night for dinner at the very Uspayatta restaurant that had curtained off a portion of its dining room for Brad Pitt in hopes that he would return again. Tsamchoe grew up in a family that fled Tibet in 1959. She was discovered by casting director Priscilla John at a party to celebrate Human Rights Day organized by the Tibetan Youth Congress in Bangalore, India, where she lives.

"I was busy dancing at a disco when I saw a foreign woman watching me," remembers Tsamchoe, an Indian lilt in her voice. "Later, Priscilla John called and asked to meet with me. Finally, she wanted to do a screen test." (In its worldwide search, said publicist Sue d'Arcy, the production was looking for "a very specific girl with simplicity and serenity, beauty and grace," all of which it found in Lhakpa Tsamchoe.) "I never thought they would choose *me!*" says Tsamchoe, smiling with embarrassment. "But here I am, out of India for the first time in my life."

Tsamchoe is a statuesque young woman with high cheekbones, flawless coffee-colored skin, limpid brown eyes, and snow-white teeth. With her long, straight, shiny black hair plaited into a cascade of Tibetan braids—seven hours of effort by Maria Teresa Corridoni—her unconventional beauty is startling and exotic.

Before fleeing his homeland in the Kyirong district of Tibet, Tsamchoe's father traded wool for sugar with Calcuttan merchants. He and his family now live in Bylakuppee, one of the many Tibetan refugee colonies that sprang up in India after the 1959 exodus. In addition to farming forty acres of ginger and maize and running a seed and fertilizer business, he serves as the local minister of parliament in the Tibetan government in exile's assembly in Dharamsala.

"I very much appreciate the education I have gotten, because my father had no education in Tibet," Tsamchoe tells me in the accented English she learned at an English-language middle school in Bangalore. "My father did not even know how to write until he got to Dharamsala."

Tsamchoe speaks of her father reverentially. "He is a very kind and helpful man with a lot of guts. That's why he was elected by the Tibetans in our community to parliament. Whatever my dad says, I listen to. Whenever I fail to listen, things turn out badly. I have always wanted to make him proud of me. If my father says nothing, then I listen to my instincts."

Indeed, Tsamchoe's instincts evidently come through to her with little distortion or background static. She appears remarkably at one with her inner thoughts, religious convictions, and emotions.

"The day we wanted to shoot a kite-flying scene, it was cloudy," remembers associate producer Alisa Tager. "So Tsamchoe offered to pray for the sun to come out. She was completely straight-faced."

"She has a true purity of spirit," says actor B. D. Wong. "There's absolutely no pretense. She has an ability to focus on what's important, which gives her enormous screen presence. Because she is so centered and spiritually focused, she has no excess, no fat to trim away. When I first met her, I was totally disarmed. In a way it's not an accident that they found her for this movie. It's like she walked right out of the pages of the script."

"You have to remember that except for Brad, David, and B. D. Wong, almost no one on this film has acted before," Tsamchoe explains to me. "But, you know, for me it's not that difficult. Jean-Jacques tells me what to do, but he very much lets me be myself." She unleashes one of her most radiant smiles.

"We Tibetans are lucky that this film is being made," she continues. "It has been a wonderful experience. Jean-Jacques has been very understanding and very determined to make the sets exactly the way Tibet was." She pauses a moment. "I used to think that only after independence would I ever see Tibet. But now, here it is before me—in Argentina!

"Maybe Westerners are interested in Tibet because Buddhism emphasizes the spiritual more than the material side of life," is her matter-of-fact response to a question about the Western mania for Tibet. "Our culture is so different. We Tibetans are very traditional, very religious, and very self-sufficient. These qualities have been a great benefit to us."

Since Tsamchoe has never been to Hollywood, I describe for her the wave of interest in Tibet and Tibetan Buddhism that has swept through it.

"Yes, the impact of Tibetan Buddhism on a lot of Westerners has been obvious to me even here," she acknowledges. "People on the crew tell me that usually they work on films just to make money, without getting very involved, but that this time they really feel something special about the subject. I am certain it has something to do with Buddhism and His Holiness."

Tsamchoe believes that China simply does not understand the spiritual side of Tibet. "If they did, they would never be so cruel and crude," she says. "We lost our country to the Chinese and now live in fear, but at least we still have our own culture." She is convinced that the Tibetans in exile will one day be able to return home.

Thinking about Lhasa with its medieval housing, refuse-strewn streets, cold, and isolation, I'm not so sure that Tsamchoe would ever be happy there, although she is utterly dedicated to the Tibetan cause and comfort is a low priority for her.

When I ask whether she is a practicing Tibetan Buddhist, Tsamchoe replies abruptly, "Yes, of course," as if the question irritated her. "What I follow is my belief that if you can help other people, that is good. If you cannot help, at least do no harm. So every day, as soon as I get up, I do my prostrations and say, 'I take refuge in the Buddha, the dharma, and the *sangha* [the spiritual Buddhist community].' Then, I pray to my personal deity, Palden Lhamo, to help me follow the right path and act well. But above all I pray for my father and my family. Now I also give thanks for all the help given to our director, Jean-Jacques, to Brad, David, and all the cast and crew."

She half closes her eyes and begins reciting a prayer right at the dinner table over her half-eaten salad. " 'Let my parents live long and suffer less in this life. Let all sentient beings attain enlightenment. I pray for the long life of His Holiness, the Dalai Lama.' " Looking at me once more, she adds, "I also pray that, when I come across people I don't like, that I will get help to be good to them." After watching me take notes for a moment, she adds, "Perhaps in my last birth I did something good to earn such karma and such a good life. How I earned it, I don't know."

The members of her family, she tells me, follow traditional forms of Buddhist practice. Each month they invite monks from the local monastery to their house for a *puja,* or prayer ceremony, which involves morning-to-night chanting. Every year her father gives ten Indian rupees to each of the local monastery's thirty-six hundred monks. As Tsamchoe says, "If you give back, it comes back."

When I ask what is most important to her, she doesn't pause. "My family," she says emphatically. "But nothing is permanent. Nothing lasts forever. Maybe that's why the older generation all have a lot of children. My mother's family had eleven kids, although only six survived. It's great to have older brothers and sisters and be part of a big family. But after me, my mother had had enough, so she called me Tsamchoe, which means 'to stop.' [*Lhakpa* means "the wind."] But then she had another anyway." Tsamchoe smiles. "We are all very close. Both my married brothers live at home. I live at home and I always turn to my thirty-six-year-old brother for advice. If I didn't have any brothers to look after my parents, I'd stay with them forever. I am so grateful to them that every day I pray for their long life. They gave us life and we should not leave them when they get old."

I comb the fissureless surface of Tsamchoe's happy but not self-satisfied existence, looking for cracks. She has no regrets, is grateful to have been born into a Tibetan family, and prays that in her next life she will be born again into a Tibetan family.

I cannot resist asking if she ever gets angry. "When I begin to argue with someone like my sister, I just walk outside for a while until she comes and says that she is sorry. I never like to hurt people, and when I do hurt them, it is always unknowingly."

She has never met the Dalai Lama but, like all other Tibetans, respects him deeply. "He is the person who leads us," she adds. "To meet him would be a great achievement for me, because he has learned Buddhist teachings so well. If we could only do our spiritual practice like him, maybe we could become Dalai Lamas too."

Tsamchoe would not agree to make more films just for the money and has no interest in becoming a fashion model or in getting married yet, especially to a Westerner.

"I don't want to marry a foreigner, because there would be lots of problems. What about the kids who get squeezed between two cultures? Maybe they would never get to know Tibetan culture, in which I believe so deeply. For instance, I believe in doing an astrological chart to see if I fit with a man."

This clear-thinking, good-hearted young woman (whose favorite pop song is Elton John's "Sacrifice") seems to have little idea what could hit her if she gets fed into the maw of the Hollywood publicity machine. When Tsamchoe reminds me that she's never been interviewed by a journalist before, I feel as if I have wandered into one of the last unexplored and unmapped tracts of land left on Planet Hollywood. It occurs to me that in a sense Tsamchoe's appeal is exactly that of her homeland.

"I suppose it would be very difficult for some people to be Tibetan Buddhists in Hollywood, but not for me," she says cheerfully. "That's just the way I am. I don't want to get attached to wealth. The Buddha teaches detachment from cravings. I have never been drunk, although since I've been here in Argentina, I started drinking wine with the other cast members. But now I've even given that up."

Of all the Tibetans who have been flown to Uspayatta, none is better known or more revered than Jetsun Pema, and nobody's presence here has done more than hers to blur the line between illusion and reality.

Cast in the film as the Great Mother, in real life she is the younger sister of the Dalai Lama. Thus, in the film she is playing her own mother. A real sister has become a virtual mother. And to blur matters further, Jetsun Pema's daughter is playing the Great Mother in Martin Scorsese's *Kundun,* meaning that she will appear on-screen as her own grandmother.

"In fact," Jetsun Pema tells me as we meet one afternoon for tea at the Hotel Valle Andino, "yesterday, I got a call from my daughter in Morocco announcing that she'd just played a scene in which, as she put it, 'I was pregnant with you.' "

Jetsun Pema is a handsome, dignified woman in her mid-fifties who, even when off the set, dresses in traditional clothing. The day we meet, her hair is up in a simple bun, and she is wearing a striped dress tied at the waist with a handwoven sash, pearl earrings, and sandals.

Having been educated from age nine, when the family went into exile, in an Indian boarding school run by Irish Catholic nuns and then in England and Switzerland, she speaks such excellent English that it is easy to forget who she is. Only when she smiles does her striking physical likeness to her elder brother become unmistakable.

In 1964, upon finishing her schooling, she took over a nursery for refugee children at the Tibetan Children's Village in Dharamsala, which had been started by her older sister Tsering Dolma. In 1980, she led the last of three government in exile fact-finding delegations to Tibet approved by the Beijing government under the liberal Party general secretary, Hu Yaobang.

"This is my first time in a Hollywood film," she says brightly as we sit on a porch and sip tea. "When I was first approached, I took some time to read the script, talked to my brothers and children. I still wasn't sure what to do. I have always been so stage-shy that I didn't know whether I wanted to act this part or not, especially to play the role of my own mother." She laughs and primly smooths her skirt. "But my whole family said I should take the part because they didn't want to see anyone else portray my mother. So I just plucked up my courage and here I am.

"I don't find it very easy to act, much less to remember all these lines. The first scene I had to do was in a golden palanquin carried by eight monks. There were all these cameras and Jean-Jacques was telling me to have this expression and that expression. The more they shot, the more confused I got. I was just a big flop. So finally Jean-Jacques said that we should stop. The next day it was a little better, and by the time we got to the third and fourth scenes I'm in, I had almost forgotten about the cameras and had learned to be less self-conscious."

I ask if she had to develop some Buddhist detachment from ego when on-camera.

She nods. "Yes, you must forget about yourself and then I think you do much better. And, of course, you must practice this every day as a Buddhist, too. But I am really hopeless as a Buddhist! Other than attending events with His Holiness and going to a few teachings, I've never really studied Buddhism. I've been so busy with my work with children. The old lamas just tell me, 'Oh, just go do your work with children, because that is really practicing Buddhism!' When I tell His Holiness of my plight, he just laughs and doesn't pay much attention. So I'm still at the kindergarten stage of Buddhism. I think I will have to wait until I am older before I can take more teachings."

Jetsun Pema maintains that her illustrious sibling "takes each individual at his or her own level." Her fondness for him is visible in her face as she speaks. "He's a wonderful listener. He doesn't impose anything on anyone, but if they want to learn, he is there. He is so open. Maybe that's why so many people are so taken with him."

As we begin talking about Argentina, she suddenly exclaims, "You know, the other day I took a walk through a meadow ringed by willows and poplars, with snow-covered mountains in the background, and I felt, Ah! This could be Lhasa! I do feel somehow very close to home here. Many of the monks are saying that the mountains and the sets make them feel that they have returned to areas they once knew at home, and this sense of familiarity has had a deep effect on everyone. But at the same time, such familiar surroundings, sets, and costumes also make me very sad. And since I am playing my mother, going up to the Potala just like we . . ." For a moment she chokes up and words fail her. "You know, when our mother went up to visit His Holiness in the Potala, she always took him food. Once or twice a month, she would bring him Amdo-style bread from where we were born. So whenever she started baking and getting really busy in the kitchen, we knew she was about to go up and, of course, we children all wanted to go with her. Then our old household master of the kitchen used to fill up his *chuba* with sweets for my brother. But as His Holiness got older, the regent forbade bringing him such things.

"When we go up the steps of the set for the Potala here and think about Tibet and remember what happened, of course it makes us sad. We begin to relive the whole thing. The scene they shot the other day where they blew up the Amdo village even made some extras have health problems afterward. One old monk had a slight heart attack. Such things have been very emotional for us. After all, this movie portrays what used to be. Then, people might have been poor and dressed in skins and rags, but they were proud and happy. But now this old Tibet is completely lost, except for here on these sets. Under the Chinese, maybe some Tibetans have electricity and cars, but they have lost their dignity and identity."

"Do you remember Harrer from Lhasa?"

"Oh yes, I remember his blond hair from riding on his shoulders. Harrer was a foreigner, but he was accepted and became a great friend of my brother and mother. He and Peter Aufschnaiter said that they would have continued to live in Tibet if the Chinese hadn't come, so there must have been something more valuable there than material comforts and progress."

Jetsun Pema's last trip to Tibet took place in 1980. "We spent over three months there and it was terrible." She strokes her cheek as if even now the pain were palpable. "Every day we cried. We shed buckets of tears over what we found. People were so poor. They didn't even have bedding and cooking utensils. Children were not being taught Tibetan in schools. Many learned monks had been imprisoned and even killed. It was a terrible situation. And everything was so controlled, it made me feel oppressed.

"There seemed to be no balance. The Chinese go either to one extreme or the other. First they were Marxists, and now they've gone to the other extreme and become capitalists. There's no middle path." She smiles wanly. "Actually, what they could really use is a little Tibetan Buddhist philosophy. They are so rigid and blind.

"When we Tibetans encounter an obstacle or adversity, we don't get angry and aggressive or go on strike. That's putting your needs first. An individual must think what is in the interest of the majority, not just oneself. We are made to be aware that not only *we* have rights but others have rights, too, and other people's needs and rights are more important than our own. So Tibetans often just let others have their way. Because of this, many of us say that maybe Buddhism has made us too flexible and weak. But I suppose it's also given us inner strength. Losing one's temper is easier, but it really shows inner weakness. It takes strength to control one's temper and promote harmony. Maybe this is why Tibetan immigrants to the States find Western behavior so different. In the West, you must become aggressive to survive and that's against Tibetan nature. For us it's a kind of mental torture."

If it were up to Tibetans, Jetsun Pema believes, the film would never have been made. "Tibetans would say, 'You're crazy to drive yourself this hard!' All the monks are really shocked by how hard Jean-Jacques and the crew work. His nose is burned red by the sun and he keeps staying out there with such perseverance." The film makes her sad, but it also makes her feel hopeful. "Most Westerners really don't know what Tibet is and what has happened to it. When His Holiness got the Nobel Peace Prize, then, at least, people started to know that Tibet meant the Dalai Lama. Millions will watch this film and perhaps it will create knowledge and awareness. If people can just understand that Tibet was once a peaceful country minding its own business before the Chinese came and occupied it, that will be the point."

— 15 —

THE LAND OF THE SPIRIT

It has been many years since Jetsun Pema was growing up in Lhasa, and then, of course, she saw the city with the eyes of a child. So it is hardly surprising if, after all this time, she remembers life there through a haze of juvenile wonderment and nostalgia. What is far more puzzling is that so many Westerners, most of whom have never been there at all or at best have visited only briefly (and certainly never as children), imagine Tibet with a similar kind of unalloyed wonderment, as a sacred oasis for humanity. But as we know, much of their perception was gained from the romanticized memoirs of explorers and from tales of adventure first read when many of them were young. It is these accounts, mostly written by those who ventured into Tibet during the latter half of the nineteenth century, that have irrigated an ever more fertile ground of fascination and fantasy.

The degree of romanticism in these works often seems to correlate with the extent of hardship suffered in Tibet and the amount of time spent futilely trying to get to Lhasa. Those who traveled briefly in the border regions are more inclined to write airily of crossing "the limits of the unknown" and to suggest that entrance to Tibet was something akin to ascending into an exalted universe or an enchanted land, even into an extraplanetary realm.

In 1899, L. Austine Waddell proclaimed the Himalayan foothills "a stupendous staircase hewn out of the Western border of the Tibetan Plateau." In 1902, William Carey described his passage through the Himalayas and up onto the Tibetan Plateau as mounting "the grandest stairway in the world," leading through "mysterious portals" into a "vast silence of mountains muffled in snow." Here indeed, implied such florid, overblown language, was the entryway to a remote spiritual utopia with a cure for every ailment of advanced civilization.

From the middle of the nineteenth century on, an increasing amount of purple prose was written by Westerners trying to describe Tibet as somehow ineffable, a place where, in the ripe language of the poet John Gillespie Magee, one could imagine having "slipped the surly bonds of Earth." Even supreme realists like Lord Curzon confessed that the "sacredness" of India haunted him "like a passion." In Tibet, to believe many of these turn-of-the-century pilgrims, one might enter a space where history came to a stop, where matters of the soul transcended matters of matter, where the paranormal was normal, and where even the yeti, or "abominable snowman," a creature that defied ordinary ideas about evolution, was suddenly believable.

At the time, expeditions to the last unprobed places on earth were viewed by Westerners as a form of transcendent adventure, promising spiritual epiphanies in otherwise mundane lives. "We had pierced the veneer of outside things," wrote Sir Ernest Shackleton after he and his men almost perished in 1914 when their ship was crushed in an Antarctic ice floe while trying to reach the South Pole. "We had 'suffered, starved and triumphed, grovelled down yet grasped at glory, grown bigger in the bigness of the whole.' We had seen God in His splendours, heard the text that Nature renders. We had reached the naked soul of man."

But Tibet was seen as more than simply a stern test of man against and over nature. It was the land of unexplored lands, the place, as the explorer and popular novelist H. Rider Haggard wrote in his classic adventure novel *She,* where "wisdom" reigned. And no person did more to convince an important group of wisdom-hungry Westerners that such a land existed than Helena Petrovna von Hahn, better known as the inimitable Madame Blavatsky.

Born in 1831 of a mother who was a well-known Russian novelist and an aristocratic German father who had settled in the Ukraine, the young Helena was enamored of mysticism and the occult from an early age. On visits to her maternal grandmother, who worked with Tibetan Buddhist Kalmyks from Dzungaria in the Caspian city of Astrakhan, she met up with some distant cousins who were practicing Buddhists. "For Helena, all nature seemed animated with a mysterious life," her sister Vera remembered. "She heard the voice of every object and form, whether organic or inorganic; and claimed consciousness and being, not only for some mysterious powers visible and audible to herself alone in what was to everyone else empty space, but for visible but inanimate things such as pebbles, moulds, and pieces of decaying phosphorous timber."

At age seventeen, Helena Petrovna von Hahn became Madame Blavatsky, thanks to a short-lived marriage of convenience with an elderly Russian of little note, Nikifor Blavatsky. Shortly after her betrothal, she fled alone to Constantinople, setting off on the first of her many legendary travels, which would in the years to come take her to points around the world, especially to Ceylon and India, where she even met, among others, the pundit Sarat Chandra Das. On the subcontinent she claimed to have sought out the teachings of well-known mystics and guardians of a so-called Secret Doctrine, who, despite living "beyond the Himalayas," were "in communication with Adepts in Egypt and Syria, and even Europe." Of course HPB, as she came to be known, was such an "adept" herself and thus was able to converse through various psychic means with this secret "brotherhood," who arrayed themselves against the "dark force."

Having absorbed the writings of George Bogle and Samuel Turner, she became especially fascinated with Tibet. She even came to claim that during her various peregrinations she served a seven-year "apprenticeship" in that land studying occult phenomena as an initiate in a mystical group she called the Great White Brotherhood. Whether she actually spent any significant time anywhere in Tibet, much less a sojourn of seven years, remains unclear but is considered dubious by many who have studied her life.

Even Marco Polo had alluded to the occult aspect of Tibetan culture in the account he professed to have kept as he journeyed across Central Asia to China during the thirteenth century. He told of passing through a Tibetan border region inhabited by "skillful enchanters" who, "among other wonders," were able "to bring on tempests and thunderstorms when they wish, and stop them at any time." Although he never actually reached Lhasa—some scholars now doubt whether he ever even reached China—Polo was the first Westerner to titillate Europe with the idea that in Tibet there were powerful magicians who could "perform the most potent enchantments and the greatest marvels to hear and to behold by diabolic arts, which are better not to relate in our book, or men might marvel overmuch."

Whatever her real travels were, Madame Blavatsky claimed that she regularly received paranormal missives on rice paper from Great Souls, or "Mahatmas" (the title later conferred on Mohandas Gandhi, a friend of hers), who existed in out-of-body states somewhere in Tibet. These revelations were, she insisted, channeled through her in a "secret sacerdotal language" called Senzar and then "translated" by her into English.

Madame Blavatsky ended up in New York City, where she evangelized in literary salons and in 1875 founded the Theosophical Society with an attorney, Colonel Henry Steel Olcott. The society claimed to be dedicated to the scientific investigation of religion and the advancement of universal and ecumenical brotherhood. Theosophy, meaning "divine wisdom" in Greek, proved a bizarre mishmash of beliefs and occult practices. In Blavatsky's séances, the living communed with the dead, flowers mysteriously fell out of thin air, and silverware passed magically through walls. Much of her occultism was "explained" in a treatise entitled *Isis Unveiled*. This two-volume, twelve-hundred-page tract ("revealed" to her in Senzar) is a gaseous tome larded with words and phrases in Greek, Latin, Egyptian, and Sanskrit, all languages that she had not evidently mastered. And then there was her five-volume *Secret Doctrine,* an even weightier and more undecipherable opus.

"Many Victorians, stranded high and dry by an increasingly rational Protestantism, thirsted for miracles and hungered for the wondrous," writes Jeffery Paine in his book *Father India.* "To them Madame Blavatsky served a satisfying manna, apparently baked in Tibet and India."

Whereas Christian missionaries, who abounded in India, tended to see Tibetans as heathen primitives, Madame Blavatsky and other Theosophists saw them as highly evolved, enlightened beings. Although she had some concerns that "Lamaism," because it was not "original Buddhism," had been corrupted, she felt that it was "yet far above Catholicism." In fact, she and her followers came to see Tibet as a fountainhead of true spirituality that would be "maintained in its purity only so long as Tibet is kept free from the incursions of Western nations, whose crude ideas of fundamental truth would inevitably confuse and obscure the followers of the 'Good Law.' "

"For centuries we have had in Tibet a moral, pure hearted, simple people, un-blest with civilization, hence untainted by vices," wrote Mahatma Koot Hoomi, allegedly the master of Blavatsky's Great White Brotherhood. "For ages has been Thibet the last corner of the globe not so entirely corrupted as to preclude the mingling together of the two atmospheres—the physical and spiritual." Blavatsky and her followers hoped that "when the Western world is more ripe in the direction of philosophy," the "splendor of [Tibet's] truth will then illuminate the whole world."

Whatever one thought of her occult belief system, by 1885 she had helped establish well over one hundred Theosophical Society "lodges" around the world and her mysticism had become a global phenomenon.

Although she had no way of knowing it, Blavatsky would leave an occult trail that would be picked up many years later by the Nazis. It was her belief that Aryans (from the Sanskrit word meaning "noble"), a group she associated with Tibetans, were the descendants of the lost race from the submerged continent of Atlantis. And since she believed that the secrets of this lineage were somewhere archived in Tibetan Buddhist monasteries, it was she who first adopted the Buddhist swastika symbol in the West, making it the emblem of the Theosophical Society.

In her later years, Madame Blavatsky not only became obscenely obese—she described herself as "a hippopotamus of a woman" and at one point had to be boarded onto a steamer by means of a special chair attached to a deck winch—but faced much ridicule and public accusations of fraud. Richard Hodgson, writing in 1885 as an investigator for the London-based Society for Physical Research, which sought to debunk claims of occult powers, described her as having "achieved a title to permanent remembrance as one of the most accomplished, ingenious, and interesting impostors of history." In our time, as noted by Donald Lopez, the anthropologist Agehananda Bharati has characterized Blavatsky's Theosophical doctrines as "such a melee of horrendous hogwash . . . that any Buddhist and Tibetan scholar is justified to avoid mentioning it in any context." Those who mention it do so wryly. "Perhaps she was a charlatan," American Buddhist aficionado Alan Watts ventures, "but she did a beautiful job of it."

Crackpot though she may have been, Madame Blavatsky was hardly an irrelevant force. Indeed, she played a seminal role in galvanizing a Western fascination with the occult and with Tibet as the epicenter not only of an ancient spiritualism but of a future spirituality that would someday transform the world. The ensuing Western infatuation with Tibet and its form of Buddhism was somewhat reminiscent of the idealization of China by the Physiocrats and philosophes during the French Enlightenment. Only then, Europeans admired China's practicality and rationality, whereas now they admired Tibet's propensity for the irrational and supernatural.

Although scholars dismiss Theosophy as a pseudoscience and Madame Blavatsky's work as hokum, she did help usher in a period when many members of the intelligentsia fell under the sway of Eastern mysticism and spiritualism. As Sir Arthur Conan Doyle wrote in his two-volume *History of Spiritualism,* this urge moved through certain circles of European intellectuals "like some psychic cloud on high showering itself on those persons who were susceptible . . . with many eccentricities and phases of fanaticism." Madame Blavatsky herself rapturously proclaimed in her short-lived magazine, *Lucifer,* "The tree of Occultism is now preparing for 'fruiting,' and the Spirit of the Occult is awakening in the blood of new generations." Indeed, everywhere in Europe, America, and Russia, manifestations of the "awakening" were evident. In Russia, where the "holy man" Gregor Rasputin's influence ruled over Czar Nicholas II, Count Sergei Witte, Nicholas's finance minister and his policy adviser on the Far East, spoke of how the "soft haze of mysticism refracts everything he beholds."

In Western Europe, the young William Butler Yeats was calling Madame Blavatsky "the most living person alive" and studying with one of her Indian "holy men," Mohini Chatterjee. As part of his "revolt of the soul against the intellect," Yeats even went on to translate the mystical Hindu scriptures, the Upanishads, with another Indian guru.

This "revolt" spawned a whole host of Western lovers of Tibet, who, although they could read neither Tibetan nor Sanskrit, nonetheless managed to become Occidental Buddhist gurus. There was, for instance, the New Jersey–born and San Diego–based Walter Wentz, (read by Richard Gere) who, after a sojourn at Oxford, appropriated the more distinguished-sounding hyphenated name Walter Y. Evans-Wentz. It was his 1927 introduction and preface that transformed *The Tibetan Book of the Dead* from an obscure Tibetan theological text into a basic building block of Western spiritualism. What seeker could resist Evans-Wentz's descriptions of "learned lamas" who "since very early times" were privy to "a secret international symbol-code in common use among initiates, which affords a key to the meaning of such occult doctrines as are all still jealously guarded by religious fraternities in India, as in Tibet, and in China, Mongolia and Japan"? Such proto–New Ageism touched not only Yeats but the philosopher of religion William James and scientists like Thomas Edison and Albert Einstein, who reportedly kept the volumes of Madame Blavatsky's *Secret Doctrine* on his desk.

While some settled for traveling to Tibet in their minds and exploring and interpreting its spiritual and cultural aura by proxy, William Montgomery McGovern was living proof that the mystique of Tibet and the lure of its "forbidden city" as a geographical goal had not died with Younghusband's "unveiling." A precocious American student of Buddhism at Oxford turned lecturer in Chinese and Japanese at the School of Oriental Studies at the University of London, McGovern became the first European to reach Lhasa solo since the inimitable Thomas Manning a century before. Setting forth in 1922 from Darjeeling, India, dressed as a caravan porter in the service of a Sikkimese noble, his skin darkened with walnut juice and iodine and the color of his blue eyes blurred with lemon juice, the tenacious McGovern helped perpetuate a model of Tibetan travel in disguise that would be much imitated—especially after his adventures were published in the *Daily Telegraph*—during the decades to follow.

After a trip to Tashilhunpo monastery with a Buddhist delegation, he returned to Darjeeling and began to plot a solo reprise trip, this time to Lhasa, posing as the servant of a traveling Sikkimese aptly named Satan. Crossing the Tibetan border in January 1923 during the dead of winter, when Tibetans guarding the trails to Lhasa were less vigilant, McGovern endured a series of unspeakable hardships before reaching his goal. He nearly froze to death, became infested with lice, was reduced to eating raw meat, almost died from dysentery and pneumonia, and was, of course, always in danger of being discovered. Indeed, before McGovern ever had a chance to run into hostile village headmen, his quest almost foundered due to inclement weather. "We had exhausted all our energies in our battle with the snow and starvation in the passes, and now that we had come through, it was as if we were not at the end but at the very beginning of our difficulties," McGovern wrote of this discouraging moment. "Every step that took us nearer the Sacred City brought with it greater danger of detection; for the watch against foreign intrusion, which is sometimes slack on the outer and more sparsely inhabited parts, becomes the stricter the nearer the capital is approached. Knowing all the difficulties which lay in our way, it seemed to us impossible ever to reach our goal."

But reach Lhasa he did, and Tibetan officials allowed McGovern to stay while he recovered from an illness. Only when crowds of angry monks discovered his presence and began shouting "Death to the foreigner!" out in front of his lodgings did he leave.

After returning home in 1924, he published *To Lhasa in Disguise,* a popular account of his exotic adventures in book form. McGovern had certainly been impressed by the strangeness of a city without electricity, wheeled vehicles, or anything in the way of what might have been considered worldliness. "They asked me several questions about life in England," he wrote, "but . . . they were appallingly ignorant of everything which took place outside of their own country. To them, Tibet was the center of the world, the heart of civilization."

Once McGovern was in Tibet—"a paradise of filth," he called it— not even the landscape seemed to captivate him. "There's no country which appears so bleak and dreary as the lifeless plains of Tibet," he later wrote, elsewhere adding, "In Tibet, the lice—and there are plenty of them—lead a happier existence than human beings." Of the people, he was hardly more admiring. "Certainly in Tibet salvation from sin seems extraordinarily easy, and it is, I think, a facility which is greatly needed by its inhabitants." With a certain disparagingly imperial arrogance, McGovern noted that "Tibetan dogs are like Tibetan men, fierce and threatening creatures, whose main idea is to terrorize all around them, but like most bullies, arrant cowards at heart."

To Lhasa in Disguise raised the tantalizing question: What provokes a man to risk so much on such an arduous, dangerous, and unnecessary journey to a place that is so manifestly unappealing when he at last gets there? To the Tibetans, at least, such a useless trek seemed nonsensical. McGovern wrote of his efforts to explain his motives to an incredulous Tibetan official in Lhasa: "It was impossible to get him to understand the pleasures of undertaking an adventure and dangerous journey. Had I talked about anthropological research he would have thought me mad."

What drew McGovern to Tibet was now well established—the challenge of breaching its still-closed door. Being able to break through the formidable barrier of mountains *and* to sneak past vigilant Tibetan officials guarding all trailheads to Lhasa was for Western adventurers the very source of their sought-after satisfaction. And naturally enough, to prevail over such seemingly insurmountable obstacles was pointless unless triumphs could later be displayed before real audiences, who were, of course, neither Tibetans nor Chinese but readers back home.

"I had always had it in the back of my mind to reveal myself when I got to Lhasa," McGovern admitted of his own trip. "This was partly out of a silly, boyish feeling of braggadocio—to show the Lhasa Government that I had been able to get there in spite of their efforts to keep me out. I was also afraid, if I came back to India and told anyone that I had gone to Lhasa and come back from it in disguise, that my tale would not be believed, so that by revealing myself I should have definite proof that I had been successful in my undertaking." Tibetan Buddhism may call on followers to diminish their egos, but getting to Lhasa was by now an ego trip of uniquely Western proportions.

Nonetheless, if only out of deference to the popular demand for a Tibetan journey that possessed some measure of romance, even McGovern could not help but wax poetic about his odyssey. In a style already so familiar in 1923 as to be clichéd, he wrote, "The Tibetan adventure was, at last, at an end. But I had still with me vivid memories of the Sacred City, the far-off and forbidden abode of the gods, to which in the end I had penetrated in spite of every obstacle; and these memories were worth all the terrible hardships which the journey had cost."

However dour his overall assessment, *To Lhasa in Disguise* helped define this exciting genre of Tibetan travel writing. Although McGovern's quest was not overtly spiritual, his dependence on disguise and subterfuge and his willingness to submit to any danger or privation to reach what was for him, after all, a kind of sacred destination, certainly suggested a pilgrimage. In this sense, he was very much part of the zeitgeist.

During the first half of the twentieth century, no one more successfully combined the spiritualism of Madame Blavatsky with the adventurousness of William McGovern to penetrate the geographically forbidden than Alexandra David-Neel. Born in Paris in 1868, she was the daughter of a Belgian mother and a stern, neglectful French father who was an idealistic journalist and a friend of Victor Hugo's. In the loneliness of her childhood, she turned to books and to her own fantasies for solace, devouring the novels of James Fenimore Cooper and Jules Verne and any accounts of exotic travels she could get her hands on.

"Ever since I was five years old, a tiny precocious child of Paris, I wished to move out of the narrow limits in which, like all children my age, I was then kept," she recalled toward the end of her century-long life. "I craved to go beyond the garden gate, to follow the road that passed it by, and to set out for the unknown. But, strangely enough, this 'unknown' fancied by my baby mind always turned out to be a solitary spot where I could sit alone, with no one near. . . . My imagination did not evoke towns, buildings, gay crowds, or stately pageants; I dreamed of wild hills, immense deserted steppes and impassable landscapes of glaciers!"

Even as a young girl, she was constantly escaping from her parents' custody and later from convent schools. Rejecting the Catholicism in which she had been raised, she began studying Buddhism at the Paris Theosophical Society. And in the quiet solitude of the Musée Guimet in Paris, renowned for its collection of Eastern art, she was able to read about the Orient and Buddhism. It provided a refuge that she called her "holy of holies." It was at the museum, in the shadow of a magnificent statue of Buddha dominating the grand stairway, that she had her first spiritual revelation.

After spending a year in London studying under the aegis of the Society of the Supreme Gnosis and hobnobbing with the English occult community, she came into a modest inheritance from a godmother. This enabled her, like Madame Blavatsky before her, to travel to Ceylon and then India, where she stayed at Theosophical Society hostels as she quested for a more contemplative life. It was on this trip that she became permanently fascinated with the East.

Returning to France due to a shortage of funds, she spent most of the Belle Epoque of the 1890s singing with the Opéra Comique, which took her to Indochina. In 1904 she married Philippe-François Neel, a railway engineer in Tunisia who (inexplicably for his time) allowed his new bride long periods of conjugal separation so that she could travel alone. Yearning both for her freedom and for Asia, David-Neel left for India in 1911 to study Sanskrit, "the great passion of my youth," as she called it. But she also wanted "to live philosophy on the spot" and to "undergo physical and spiritual training, not just read about them." So in 1912 she headed for Darjeeling, in the foothills of the Indian Himalayas, on assignment for the magazine *Mercure de France* to interview the thirteenth Dalai Lama, who had fled Lhasa after a Chinese invasion in 1910. His Holiness was so impressed with David-Neel's knowledge of Sanskrit and Buddhism that he urged her to take up Tibetan. Taking his advice, she began studying at a monastery in Gangtok in the tiny Himalayan kingdom of Sikkim. It was here that she acquired her lifelong friend and sidekick, a then-fifteen-year-old Sikkimese monk named Aphur Yongden, whom she adopted as her son. It was here also that she fell in love with the mountains and with the idea of Tibet.

"The track now entered the fantastic region near the frontier passes," she wrote of a 1914 trek to the Tibetan border and what she called "the intense silence of these wild majestic solitudes." She described her progress rhapsodically: "Up and up we went, skirting glaciers, catching occasional glimpses of crossing valleys filled by huge clouds. And then, without any transition, as we issued from the mists, the Tibetan table-land appeared before us, immense, void and resplendent under the luminous sky of Central Asia."

"Nothing," she later said, "has ever dimmed in my mind the memory of my first sight of Tibet," which she said put her "at last in the calm solitudes of which I had dreamed since infancy."

David-Neel did not return to Europe for fourteen years. Instead, she became an apprentice of sorts to a Tibetan *gomchen,* or hermit, under whose tutelage she lived for two years in a cave on the Tibetan border. "I feel the hermit's life, free of what we call 'the goods and pleasure of the world,' is the most wonderful life of all," she effused of her ascetic regimen—living in a tent, studying with her *gomchen,* and meditating. In her long conversations with her new guru, David-Neel became "closely acquainted with Tibet, its inhabitants, their customs and their thoughts: a precious science which was to later stand me in good stead."

In her letters to her husband, she began describing herself as a *solitaire,* "a recluse," and expressed a revulsion at the idea of returning to "civilization." Despite the fact that both the British and the Tibetans were forbidding all travel to Tibet, in 1916 David-Neel and Yongden set off without permission for Shigatse and Tashilhunpo monastery. Here they were received as warmly by the Panchen Lama as George Bogle had been a century and a half earlier and Sven Hedin just eleven years before. The elaborate monastery and the "special psychic atmosphere" that radiated from it made David-Neel pine all the more to see Lhasa.

Upon returning to Sikkim, she learned that news of her unauthorized travels to Tibet had not been well received by British authorities in India. In fact, they ordered her prompt deportation from Sikkim and levied a fine against her. Naturally, such treatment just hardened her determination to reach the holy city. "What decided me to go to Lhasa was, above all, the absurd prohibition which closes Tibet."

Realizing that her chances of reaching Lhasa from British India were now very poor, she left in 1917 for Japan and then China. In Beijing, she met the abbot of the great Kumbum monastery in Amdo, who invited her to accompany him back home on the sixteen-hundred-mile trip to the northwest of China to help him write a book on astrology. It was at Kumbum, in "the lulling calm of the monastic citadel," where "the mind experiences, to the point of intoxication, the subtle voluptuousness of solitude and silence," she wrote, that "the idea of visiting Lhasa really became implanted in my mind." She swore that she would reach it and "show what the will of a woman could achieve!"

David-Neel spent three years in residence at Kumbum and another two and a half years traveling with Yongden some eight thousand miles through nearby Tibetan border regions, readying herself for her grand journey. In a paean of praise to her new life, she wrote, "I delightedly forgot Western lands, that I belonged to them, and that they would probably take me again in the clutches of their sorrowful civilization."

Finally in 1923, at age fifty-four, she and Yongden set off from Yunnan province as penniless pilgrims. Like William McGovern, she devised an artful disguise for her trip. Camouflaged in a Tibetan robe and cap, she donned a yak-hair wig and powdered her face with a mixture of charcoal and cocoa powder. All that she brought with her was a small cache of gold and silver, a single cooking pot, some maps, a compass, a flimsy tent, a rosary, a prayer wheel, and a small revolver tucked into her robe.

Nothing that she had yet experienced compared with the hardships she and Yongden encountered. Throughout her ordeal, however, David-Neel's spirit remained unbent. "I felt exhausted and walked mechanically, half asleep," she wrote of the earliest stages of their daunting trip, undertaken mostly at night to avoid detection. "At last utter exhaustion compelled us to rest . . . perched on the edge of a precipice whose depth was unfathomable at night. In such wise we spent the second happy night of our wonderful adventure!" That over the next few months she survived the punishing winter cold, the harsh alpine terrain, and the lack of food with such stoicism has amazed all who have read the account of her adventure, *My Journey to Lhasa.*

She and Yongden finally neared Lhasa in 1924. "As we advanced, the Potala grew larger and larger. Now we could discern the elegant outlines of its many golden roofs. They glittered in the blue sky, sparks seeming to spring from their sharp upturned corners, as if the whole castle, the glory of Tibet, had been crowned with flames. . . . Now that I stood on the forbidden ground at the cost of so much hardship and danger, I meant to enjoy myself in all possible ways. . . . It was my well-won reward after all the trials on the road and the vexations by which for several years various officials had endeavored to prevent my wanderings in Tibet. This time I intended that nobody should deprive me of it."

Her book appeared in 1927 and ended with these lines: "The gods have won! The first white woman had entered Forbidden Lhasa and shown the way. May others follow and open with loving hearts the gates of the wonderland, 'for the good, for the welfare of many' as the Buddhist scriptures say."

It is not difficult to see why Alexandra David-Neel would be rediscovered by so many feminists of a later time as an example of bold independence. But besides her courageous journeys and her learned studies on Tibetan Buddhism, what she became best remembered for was her fascination with the occult. In an era when Europeans were infatuated with reports of paranormal phenomena and esoteric spiritual practices, David-Neel's twenty-eight books—such as *With Mystics and Magicians in Tibet, The Secret Oral Teachings of Tibetan Buddhist Sects, The Magic of Love and Black Magic, Immortality and Reincarnation,* and *Initiations and Initiates in Tibet*—formed a corpus of work that slowly gained cult status in many languages. It seemed that Westerners could not get enough stories about astral projection or lamas who had mastered *lung-gom,* the ability to "fly" while in trances; oracles who could predict the future; lamas who could perform disappearing acts; charms that could ward off evil spirits; and monks who practiced *tumo rekïang,* the arcane art of controlling one's body temperature while virtually naked in sub-zero weather.

In fact, David-Neel claimed that she herself mastered *tumo rekiang.* She wrote how on one freezing night, "I began to doze. Yet my mind continued to be concentrated on the object of the *tumo* rite. Soon I saw flames arising around me; they grew higher and higher; they enveloped me, curling their tongues above my head. I felt deliciously comfortable." And in *With Mystics and Magicians in Tibet,* one of her most popular translations into English, she offered an account of seeing a flying monk while trekking somewhere in Northern Tibet. According to her description, she first saw a small black speck approaching her on the horizon at a rapid speed. When she looked at it through binoculars, she discovered that a man was advancing "at an unusual gait" and "with extraordinary swiftness" through a series of high-altitude vaults that seemed to defy gravity. "The man did not run. He seemed to lift himself from the ground, proceeding by leaps. It looked as if he had been endowed with the elasticity of a ball and rebounded each time his feet touched the ground." In such descriptions, David-Neel's scholarly knowledge of philosophical Buddhism did not prevent her from being deeply fascinated by the paranormal aspects of Tibetan religious life or from presenting lamas in ways that suggested they might comprise a "higher" plane of spiritual practice than what passed for religion in the West. She liked to recount tantalizing anecdotes from her own experience, telling, for instance, of a Tibetan master who told her that certain "teachings considered secret . . . will remain 'secret' for the individuals with dull minds." Said master also stressed that only those "endowed with an intelligence better equipped for acute perceptions, who are fit to penetrate below the surface of the world of physical phenomena and grasp the causes which are at work there" are able to understand such truths.

Alexandra David-Neel died in Digne, France, on September 8, 1969, just before her 101st birthday. By that time her reputation as avatar of Eastern occult practices was firmly established. "I did not altogether disbelieve in that mysterious world that is so near to those who have lived long in the wilds," she acknowledged. While her myriad books on Tibet and Buddhism discussed supposedly paranormal phenomena in her adopted land, they were nonetheless a far cry from the mumbo jumbo of Madame Blavatsky. While publishers and readers alike often emphasized their mystical aspects, she was also a serious empirical observer with extraordinary linguistic abilities and unsurpassed first-hand experience living among Tibetans. At the same time that she could be fascinated by the occult, she could also describe herself as "a rational Buddhist." Her watchword was: "Everything that relates, whether closely or more distantly, to psychic phenomena and to the action of psychic forces in general, should be studied just like any other science."

What eluded her was a recognition of just how uninspired spiritual life could sometimes be in the Tibetan theocracy. While the great Italian Tibetologist and art historian Giuseppe Tucci could speak of a "withered theology" that all too often replaced "the yearning for spiritual rebirth" in Tibet's great monasteries, David-Neel's deep admiration for Tibet and Buddhism made such an acknowledgment impossible. So without perhaps quite meaning to, she would become the guru of choice for those Westerners with a yearning to believe in an idealized Eastern never-never land.

The yearning to believe that Tibet held secrets of profound spiritual wisdom also dovetailed with a number of other popular fascinations to create an incipient Tibet mania early in the first part of the twentieth century. In fact, while in Lhasa, William McGovern noted that Western interest in Tibet was running so high that the Dalai Lama had been receiving ever-greater quantities of mail from abroad. Since a post office had been set up and connected to the British postal service to India via Gyantse, hundreds of letters had begun arriving in Lhasa from Westerners eager to "assure His Holiness of their rigid adherence to his creed, their acceptance of his divinity." McGovern reported that many beseechers insisted that they were "different from the average materialistic Westerner" and "would be pleased if the Dalai Lama would permit [them] to come to Lhasa and study the ultimate mysteries in the home of the secret doctrine."

Around this time a new factor contributing to the growing interest in Tibet grew out of the attention that began to be focused on efforts to climb Mount Everest. In the 1920s, the British mounted three expeditions to conquer the world's tallest mountain, which straddles the Tibet-Nepal border. When Andrew Irvine and George Leigh Mallory died trying to reach the peak's summit in 1924, the event attracted a tidal wave of new attention to the Himalayas and Tibet. Interestingly enough, Mallory and Irvine's expedition was organized by none other than Francis Younghusband, who had become the president of the Royal Geographical Society and then chairman of the Alpine Club's Mount Everest Committee.

For Mallory (as for Younghusband before him), the Himalayas had a special, almost divine attraction. (Upon first seeing K2, the highest peak in the Karakorams, as a young man, Younghusband rhapsodically wrote, "My whole being seemed to come to a standstill, and then go rushing out in a kind of joyous wonder. The sight of that tremendous mountain, so massive, firm, and strong, so lofty and so dazzlingly pure, left an impression that has lasted through life.") There was, of course, already a tradition in Hindu and Buddhist culture on the Indian subcontinent of thinking of the Himalayas as the abode of the gods. Indeed, the heroes and heroines of both the *Ramayana* and *Mahabharata* were believed to have come from these mountain peaks.

"Presently the miracle happened, . . . like the wildest creation of a dream," Mallory wrote on seeing Everest for the first time. "As the clouds rolled asunder before the heights, gradually, very gradually, we saw the great mountainside and glaciers and ridges, now one fragment, now another, through the floating rifts, until far higher in the sky than imagination dared suggest, a prodigious white fang—an excrescence from the jaw of the world—the summit of Everest, appeared." Seeing Everest emerge from the mist at night was for Mallory akin to an ecstatic experience. He described it as "immanent, vast, incalculable—no fleeting apparition of elusive dream; steadfast like Keats's star, in lone splendour hung aloft in the night, diffusing, it seemed universally, an exalted radiance." And in a letter he wrote just before his death in 1924, he claimed explicitly that for him "the Everest Expedition has become a sort of religious pilgrimage." Indeed, when a memorial service was held for him at Saint Paul's Cathedral, with the King, Queen, and Prince of Wales all in attendance, the main eulogy, given by the bishop of Chester (in whose diocese Mallory's father was a rector), touched on just this idea of mountain climbing as a holy experience. The bishop described the ill-fated expedition as if it had been as much a quest for spiritual enlightenment as an effort to physically conquer a peak. "Was it only love of high mountains that was set in hearts like these?" he asked rhetorically. "No, but rather that with the love of mountains was the ascent of spiritual altitude ... the ascent by which men of clean hands and pure hearts ascend into the hill of the Lord and rise up in His Holy Place."

Suffice it to say, with the beginnings of an Everest mania—which continues today (as the recent success of books like Jon Krakauer's *Into Thin Air* and the IMAX film *Everest,* shot by climber David Breashears, reminds us)—yet another layer of the West's expectations and dreams was laminated onto Tibet. In the wake of Mallory's and Irvine's mysterious deaths—Mallory's body was finally discovered in May 1999 by an expedition that was launched specifically to search for it—fascination with Tibet scaled new heights of its own. Typical of those who answered the call to explore this new Bethlehem of mountains, adventure, and spiritualism was the Scandinavian adventurer Theodore Illion, whose 1934 trip to Tibet led, of course, to a book. *In Secret Tibet: In Disguise Amongst Lamas, Robbers, and Wise Men—A Key to the Mysteries of Tibet* borrowed from almost every stereotype, fantasy, yearning, or projection any Westerner ever had about this much-imagined land. Part

Blavatsky, part Younghusband, part Hedin, with an ample dose of David-Neel thrown into the hopper, *In Secret Tibet* promised to enlighten those "who want first-hand information about the strange mentality and unexplained phenomena in one of the most mysterious countries in the world."

Since Illion never bothered to explain exactly where he went and when he went there, however, his book has an almost chimerical quality to it. What is more, the text is so larded with clichéd allusions to "Tibetan mysteries and psychical phenomena" and "strange things, seemingly contrary to all known laws of nature," that it is hard to take it seriously.

In a chapter entitled "Tibetan Miracles," Illion spoke, of course, of the ability of "Tibetan saints" to be clairvoyant, perform magical cures, endure subzero temperatures, and fly. But "people who imagine that the flying lamas are numerous in Tibet are mistaken," he wrote in language of pseudoauthority that sounds rather comical today. "On an average, one must keep one's eyes wide open for many weeks before one meets even one flying lama. . . . I saw flying lamas only on two occasions." He quickly added that his camera had been destroyed by robbers and that, "even had I still been able to use it, the light would not have been good enough to have taken a photograph." To be sure!

The Illion package was digestible by the Western mind because the template for its acceptance was already in place. Tibet had been firmly enshrined as the new Mecca of suspended reason and mysterious adventure. In an age of growing tourism, no other land called on Westerners to engage in such elaborate and risky subterfuges simply to gain entrance. No other land seemed so able to transform ordinary travel into adventure or simple yearning into instant spirituality. Just to get there—even to try and fail to get there—was to gold-plate oneself with the exotic. The actual or purported fantastic journeys of Tibetan adventurers helped transform the land into a strange earthly nirvana where the imperatives of the outside world seemed to exist in a state of semidivine suspension. They drew to Tibet's embrace the likes of Theos Bernard, a blond-haired lawyer from Arizona who went back to

Columbia University to get a Ph.D. in Buddhist studies and managed in the 1930s to gain entrance into Tibet to study at a monastery. Ultimately he was initiated as a lama by none other than Tri Rinpoche, who had signed the Anglo-Tibetan Convention in 1904 and given Younghusband his Buddha statue before the colonel departed. In *Penthouse of the Gods: A Pilgrimage into the Heart of Tibet and the Sacred City of Lhasa,* published in 1939, Bernard wrote about being plunged "into the innermost depths of human consciousness" in Tibet, where he suddenly "understood the wonder which held the faithful to this ancient cult." Of his initiation ceremony he professed, "It will never be possible for me to express in words what actually took place. It was something beyond the realm of the mind, therefore, beyond the expression of name and form."

So impressed was Bernard with the beauty of Tibet that he declared, "It is little wonder that the Tibetan never leaves his country, but that he aches inwardly for return, and is not happy until he does." In his view, the words "joy of living" are "no idle phrase" when applied to Tibetans, because in the "matter of living the average Tibetan exhibits great gifts." In fact, Bernard came to believe that if he himself could only "have been left alone with the Tibetans, all would have been perfect." Such statements by Occidental converts were powerfully suggestive incentives, indeed, for other Westerners to become entranced with the tonic powers of Tibet.

James Hilton's *Lost Horizon* was not only the world's first paperback book but a monumental best-seller that is still popular today, though when first published in October 1933 during the depths of the Depression, it attracted virtually no notice. Only after critic Alexander Woollcott raved about it on the radio some time later did this mother of all escapist novels finally begin to attract notice.

"Welcome to Shangri-La," trumpeted a blurb on the original book cover that showed a plane crash-landing in a valley near a golden monastery surrounded by a range of magnificent snowy peaks. Written at a time when the world's international economic system seemed to be teetering on the edge of total collapse, Nazism was growing, and fears of world war were already in the air, *Lost Horizon* conjured up a paradise hidden safely away behind the Himalayas, where nothing was wanting, everyone was cultured, and no one grew old. It proved the perfect antidote to a gathering global fear of the collapse of the civilized world. As one of Hilton's characters despairingly observes, "The whole world seems to have gone completely mad all round me."

Director Frank Capra's 1937 film version of the book was even more influential and helped crystallize in the popular imagination the notion of Tibet as a place in which a separate peace might prevail. Although Tibet was not explicitly mentioned in either book or movie, the creation of an idyll called "Shangri-La"—which quickly achieved a mythic, if kitschy, perfection as a universal concept—borrowed heavily from previous imagery that depicted Tibet as having managed to remain apart from the compromised outside world.

As the novel begins, a plane takes off from a city somewhere in China during a time of upheaval. Meant to fly three Brits and an American to Peshawar, Pakistan, it is mysteriously forced to land somewhere in Northern Tibet in the desolate Kunlun Mountains. One passenger, the urbane Robert "Glory" Conway, who in Capra's movie is played by the debonair British actor Ronald Colman, is an Oxford man ("Rowing Blue and leading light at the Union"), a former member of Parliament, and an officer in the British Consular Service; conveniently enough, he is also a student of Oriental languages (he even knows a little Tibetan). "Our civilization doesn't often breed people like that nowadays," notes the author admiringly.

The tall, handsome, intelligent Conway is the perfect candidate for a Tibetan utopia. Having been disillusioned by the horrors of World War I, Conway is a man possessed of "a love of quietness, contemplation and being alone," someone "searching for truth, for peace and ever aware of their sadly diminishing quantity in the world." Even before the plane crashes, the reader has intimations that Conway is being spirited away to a mysterious but exalted fate.

As Conway realizes he and the others aboard are about to crash in a remote mountainous area, Hilton uses language redolent of half a century of overheated Western musing about Tibet. "The whole situation, no doubt, was appalling. . . . [Nonetheless,] there came over him . . . a glow of satisfaction that there were such places still left on earth, distant, inaccessible, as yet unhumanized." Conway feels intoxicated by the air, which, "clean as from another planet, was more precious with every intake," inducing "an almost ecstatic tranquility of mind."

On the ground, Conway and the others are met by a mysterious Oriental elder named Chang, who not only speaks English but guides them up a mountain pass through a raging blizzard to a curious arch that is not unreminiscent of the West Gate into Lhasa. As they pass through it, the storm magically abates and calm descends. They have arrived in Shangri-La, the Valley of the Blue Moon; they are inside the most powerful utopian myth of a largely dystopian century.

This "strange culture pocket" is presided over, of course, by a venerable and wise High Lama, played by Sam Jaffe, an actor who got his start in New York's Yiddish theater. He rules his "loose and elastic autocracy" with "a benevolence that was almost casual." As it turns out, Conway has been chosen from afar as the High Lama's heir apparent because of his intelligence and humanity.

Even though, as it turns out, he has been abducted, Conway is intrigued by his place of exile. Indeed, he finds it "nothing less than an enclosed paradise" where time (and aging) are suspended and where peaceful feelings merge "in the deeper sensation, half mystical, half visual, of having reached at last some place that was an end, a finality." Conway cannot help but be drawn to the "austere serenity" of this lost valley in which "forsaken courts and pale pavilions shimmered in repose from which all the fret of existence had ebbed away, leaving a hush as if moments hardly dared to pass."

"Do you fail to recognize one of your own dreams when you see it?" Chang slyly asks Conway in the movie during one of their many long talks. Indeed, Conway comes to recognize Shangri-La as a promised dream. While "a reek of dissolution" hovers over the world outside, Shangri-La remains "in deep calm." Such a vision of outer turmoil and insular peace carried an irresistible allure in the 1930s. "The Dark Ages that are to come will cover the whole world in a single pall," wrote Hilton, anticipating World War II. "There will be neither escape nor sanctuary save such as are too secret to be found or too humble to be noticed. And Shangri-La may hope to be both of these."

As the High Lama tells Conway when they finally meet, "To be gentle and patient, to care for the riches of the mind, to preside in wisdom and secrecy while the storm rages without—it will all be very pleasantly simple for you, and you will doubtless find great happiness."

But if Shangri-La is suggestively "Tibetan," it is not too much so. Hilton's Valley of the Blue Moon is a carefully constructed model Tibet without all those aspects, such as filth, that had repelled so many earlier sojourners, a reassuring but unlikely hybrid perfectly designed for Westerners looking for cultural refinement and spiritual depth in the Orient. It is a Tibet in which, after all these centuries, a white man could feel comfortable, even become the Dalai Lama; a Tibet in which *they* finally want the best of *us* enough that, instead of turning Westerners back, they forcibly bring our most noble representatives into the heart of their mystery to help preside over *our* dream. It is, in short, the resolution of the dreams of hundreds of frustrated explorers and adventurers and millions of curious and emotionally needy ordinary people back at home in Europe and America.

In this Tibet, thanks to Father Perrault, a Capuchin friar from Luxemburg (obviously modeled on the real Father Orazio della Penna di Billi) who stumbled into Shangri-La in the eighteenth century and never left, "*Te Deum Laudamus* and *Om Mani Padme Hum* are now heard equally in the temples of the valley." *Lost Horizon,* then, offers Occidentals the perfect fantasy blend of East and West: the spiritual ecumenicism of Madame Blavatsky and Alexandra David-Neel raised to the nth power, a potpourri of Buddhism merged with Christianity, the crepitations of traditional Tibetan horns leavened with harpsichord music by Rameau, a mélange of Buddhist sutras in Tibetan and "the world's best literature" in every European language—in short, a Buddhist Shambhala with a Western humanistic sensibility set in a magic valley ruled over by a benevolent Catholic missionary gone native who now wishes to pass his benign monastic mantle on to an erudite ex-Oxford sage.

Shambhala is the mythical earthly paradise depicted in the Kalachakra tantra—texts that the Buddha is believed to have entrusted to the king of Shambhala—where a succession of benevolent rulers is guarding the highest Buddhist teachings until such time as the outside world ceases its warmongering and turns to peace. Described as a figurative lotus-shaped kingdom protected by towering mountain peaks entrusted to King Kalkin by the Buddha, Shambhala is a beautiful valley where everyone follows the dharma, all needs are provided, and no one ever becomes sick or grows old. It is believed that at this magical kingdom's center is the mandala of the Buddha Kalachakra itself.

Shambhala is part of a larger fund of Buddhist legend suggesting that hidden within Tibet's mountains are other mystical sanctuaries, called *beyul*, in which the enlightened may find refuge from the pain and suffering of the world. It is just a few more steps to Shangri-La.

It is no surprise, then, that Hilton portrays Conway as experiencing Shangri-La as if it were Shambhala, "a living essence, distilled from the magic of the ages and miraculously preserved against time and death," where civilization will be protected until the savage world outside is finally ready to receive it. In one of the novel's most famous lines, Conway philosophizes, "There are moments in every man's life when he glimpses the eternal."

Shangri-La is a distillation of a borrowed piece of Tibetan mythology overlaid with a Western dream of dreams that was two centuries in the making. It is the mythic embodiment of the idea of sanctuary—a place where all civilized yearnings are satisfied. There could, in truth, have been no other place on earth in which such a fantastic reverie might have been grounded than the seemingly unknowable otherness of Tibet. Generations of wanderers, adventurers, marauders, spiritualists, and mountain climbers had prepared the way for the coronation of the idea of a Shangri-La in the popular imagination. Indeed, so compelling was the notion of a Tibetan Shambhala that the name

Shangri-La would become far better known than the title of the book that spawned it. Coterminous in millions of minds around the world with the notion of refuge, it came to grace a bizarre range of things, from a World War II U.S. aircraft carrier to a chain of five-star luxury Asian hotels.

Nothing did more to popularize the notion of Shangri-La than Hollywood's version of the novel. In many ways director Frank Capra, already a specialist in Depression-era cultural mythmaking about an idealized America, was the perfect choice for the project. After all, many of his previous films had celebrated small-town America, with its hard-working families, friendly neighborhoods, and community-minded Christian values ("plain, ordinary, everyday kindness, a little looking out for the other fella, loving thy neighbor," as Jimmy Stewart would put it in Capra's later film *Mr. Smith Goes to Washington*).

Cooked up on the back-lot Columbia Pictures "ranch" in Burbank and shot in a large cold-storage warehouse and the Ojai Valley near Los Angeles, Capra's $2-million *Lost Horizon* features a lamasery that looks like something Frank Lloyd Wright might have designed on a bad day for a Mormon golf club. Massive and white, Deco-modern with fountains squirting everywhere, Hollywood's Shangri-La was a curious and implausible pastiche of modernism, Orientalia, and generic fantasy that had precious little to do with the Potala—or anything else Tibetan, for that matter. Indeed, just as in the making of *Seven Years in Tibet,* Indians were used to play Tibetans, in this case Indians from the Pala tribe in the mountains around San Diego.

Shangri-La was for Frank Capra "a place to go where you can get away from things, a place in your mind as well as in actuality" during a historical time when "the human spirit was at a low ebb" and "the fog of anxiety blanketed the globe." Indeed, for readers and viewers of *Lost Horizon,* Shangri-La became a place that was located almost completely in their minds. With Capra's film, the Tibet of filth, ferocity, arcane religious practices, grinding poverty, barren wastes, inhospitable weather, serfdom, disease, and theocratic absolutism vanished totally from public consciousness. In their place appeared the earliest fully realized Western version of a virtual Tibet. It was visually crude on the screen—

actors and actresses wearing funny fur hats in the southern California sunshine—because Capra lacked the special-effects technology that the end of the century would bring, but *Lost Horizon* still had a stunning impact on the popular imagination. No one from Albert d'Orville to William McGovern had been able to do what Capra and Hollywood accomplished—to so fully expropriate Tibet for their own fantasy and commercial use. (This did not stop the People's Republic from announcing in the late 1990s that it had "found" Shangri-La in the Diqing Tibetan Autonomous Prefecture of Yunnan province, just north of Burma, or from turning it into a tacky tourist destination complete with a Shangri-La Airport in the local prefectural town, Zhongdian, and a proliferation of Shangri-La restaurants, karaoke bars, hotels, and mock Shangri-La villages.) Tibet had been penetrated, engorged, and digested, and those parts that had proven indigestible in terms of Western dreams had been expelled as so much waste. The distilled residues were now almost completely in the West's possession, harbored safely outside the boundaries of the otherwise unpredictable and perilous land of their origin. The road to Tibet's mysteries no longer lay exclusively through mountain passes to Gyantse or across the northern grasslands patrolled by hostile Golok tribesmen. Now it was possible to reach Tibet via southern California.

As the chaos of war engulfed Asia, Europe, and Russia, a conflict that would level much of the globe and destroy tens of millions of lives, two places on earth that seemed utterly safe were the actual (and largely ignored) Tibet—into which Heinrich Harrer stumbled in 1944 looking for a neutral country where he could ride out the war—and that fountainhead of other imagined utopias in the sunny American playland of California. With Frank Capra, the two utopias merged. In a manner of speaking, *our* Tibet came home, and home was Hollywood. It was hardly surprising, then, that when Sir Francis Younghusband died in 1942, his *New York Times* obituary framed his life thus: "If as James Hilton strongly suggests in *Lost Horizon,* Shangri-La is somewhere in Tibet rather than merely somewhere—anywhere . . . then Sir Francis Younghusband probably came closer than anyone else to being Robert Conway."

Perhaps. But in the middle of the twentieth century, the mantle had clearly passed to Heinrich Harrer. Because he had actually been able to act out Robert Conway's fictional odyssey and because his best-selling account of his sojourn in Lhasa was so alluring, his story became the nonfiction equivalent of *Lost Horizon.*

16

THE ANNUNCIATION

Ffter returning from Los Penitentes, I realize that although I have been in Argentina on-set for several days I have yet to glimpse Heinrich Harrer's reincarnation, Brad Pitt. Everywhere, however, I run into evidence of both his immanence and his eminence. I have seen his abode (through the fence of a military base, to be sure), scanned sheaves of his publicity shots in publicist Sue d'Arcy's office, heard endless, often flattering comments about working with him as a colleague from cast and crew members, run into his full-time makeup woman, Jean Black, and then, this evening, found myself having dinner with his two bodyguards, along with several other members of the cast.

By all accounts, Pitt has been touched by the experience of working with the Tibetans here in Uspayatta. He is reported to have decorated his trailer with Tibetan cushions and butter lamps and even to have tried some Tibetan tea. But he has remained as aloof and elusive as the young Dalai Lama, who, in Lhasa during bygone days, showed himself to commoners only on rare occasions, such as his seasonal processionals by sedan chair between the Potala and the Norbulinka, his summer residence.

Finally, I am visited with an annunciation of sorts. As I walk through the lobby of the Hotel Uspayatta, Sue d'Arcy appears to proclaim that today Brad will, at last, be revealed to me. The revelation is to take place, she announces with a mixture of solemnity and triumph, on the set of the Barkhor, the main bazaar in front of the Jokhang, where the scene in which Harrer and Aufschnaiter first enter Lhasa in rags is being shot.

Like the Dalai Lama's mother, who cautioned Harrer never to stand higher than her sainted son, never to look him directly in the eye, and never to turn his back on him while in his presence, d'Arcy archly reminds me of the ground rules for being allowed within sighting distance of the star. No unauthorized approaches of any kind are to be countenanced. It is acceptable to gaze upon him from afar but out of the question to address him. The taking of photographs is unthinkable. All private cameras (except his own) are verboten on-set. In short, I am put on notice to abandon any lingering hopes I may still harbor of encountering this modern-day God-king face-to-face. As d'Arcy puts it, "He is such a nice guy that, if he meets you, he might then feel obligated to talk with you."

At this penultimate moment, I am admonished to consider myself fortunate just to have been granted access to the peripheries of this hallucination of Tibet. It is not so much a question of whether I might commit lèse-majesté that makes her so wary, I am told, but simply that Brad does not want to be disturbed, something that happens each time his staff lets down their guard and he is forced to enter the world of mortals.

I find to my befuddlement that, despite my skepticism about stardom, I am nonetheless filled with a thrill of expectation at the thought of actually seeing Pitt. In anticipation, I head out to the set particularly early the next morning. As this long-awaited moment approaches, I want to be certain not to miss anything. At work everywhere on the set, among piles of construction materials, heaps of equipment, and rows of vehicles of every sort all connected by an elaborate grid of electrical cables, are men in shorts, T-shirts, and baseball caps girthed by bulging tool belts. A cacophony of hammers, nail guns, gas-powered generators, and Skil saws fill the desert silence. A crew member with a grizzled beard trims two-by-fours; a young man antiques a giant prayer wheel; a middle-aged woman in the back of a truck inventories stacks of snow leopard and fox skins.

Over by the white catering tents, I find a complement of Tibetan monks, nobles, and nomads eating breakfast. Heading back to the fortress of steel scaffolding that supports the set for the Jokhang, I round a corner and suddenly find myself transported into one of the alleys near the Barkhor. The sets appear authentic down to the last detail. The stone walls of the blocky Tibetan houses—although made out of mesh and plaster backed with plywood—are completely convincing in their stolid, crumbling disrepair. Prayer flags flutter authentically against an azure blue sky. Running down the middle of the alley there is even a carefully contrived rivulet of dirty water covered with a thin skim of fake ice, all garnished with more of the production's definitive collection of ceramic yak turds.

Emerging from the winding alley, I find myself facing the Jokhang. There, gleaming in the sunlight over the shrine's sacred double-doored entranceway, are two fabled golden deer holding a wheel and flanked by two huge gold bell-like objects. On either side of this hallowed portal are the huge butter sculptures that I observed the monks making at GAM 8. And just in front is a weeping willow tree, the *jowo utra,* or the "hair of the Buddha," so named by Tibetans who believed it to have been planted by Princess Wencheng, wife of King Songtsen Gampo, over a millennium ago.

The person most responsible for creating this extraordinary feeling of "realness" is production designer Hoang Thanh At, who has also done sets for other historical films, including *The Lover* (1992) and

Germinal (1993). He is a soft-spoken Vietnamese resident of France who has a reputation for unfailing faithfulness to original locations. Having grown up in Vietnam, a land with its own Buddhist tradition, and having traveled to Tibet, At has a unique fix on the West's Buddhist and Tibetan fascination.

"Perhaps it's because Westerners have had so many crises in their own religiosity that they feel the need to look for a new religion and spirit," he tells me in French, as we sit at the edge of the Barkhor to talk. "At the same time that Westerners are drawn to competition, they also seem to want to escape the aggressiveness of their own lives and to find an opening into something more tranquil."

Smiling shyly, he says, "This film will be like a bomb blast when it comes out because it is one of the first feature films about Tibet and it has such a human theme. And the fact that Jean-Jacques is focusing less on religion and more on the Chinese invasion of Tibet will make it very incendiary."

When he actually went to Tibet himself, he remembers feeling strongly that he was in an occupied country. "I think many Westerners feel this way and it makes them sympathetic toward Tibetans," says At. "It has made me not even want to go to China anymore. In many ways, what's happened to Tibet is not too dissimilar to the Vietnam War. The Tibetan refugees in India are like the Vietnamese and the Laotian refugees at the end of the war in Indochina. So, in a way, I am working on this job more for the Tibetans than for the film."

As At gazes out across the Barkhor and the frenzy of activity that always precedes a shot, his face softens. "People have told me that they feel as if they were in a dream on this set. Many older Tibetans have come up to me with tears in their eyes and said that they had forgotten what Tibet was like until they came here. When sets bring back such memories to people who have actually lived the experience, that is the best reward for me. After all, I, too, am a refugee, so I feel very close to these people."

A piece of lore known to almost everyone in the production is how a group of the Buddhist monks on first arriving at Uspayatta and seeing the Jokhang set became so emotional that they wept. Then they organized a ceremony to bless it before shooting began.

As I watch, the public square in front of At's masterfully designed set
slowly fills with meticulously costumed and coiffed street peddlers selling food, incense, and religious trinkets; monks chanting sutras; pilgrims spinning prayer wheels; nomads in ratty sheepskin *chuba*s making
reverential circumambulations; mendicants with begging bowls; nobles
sporting absurdly marvelous hats and furred finery; and ragamuffin children skipping through the crowds. Everywhere there are set dressers,
cameramen, equipment handlers, workmen, hydraulic cranes, snarls
of electrical cables, and piles of carrying cases. But to look within the
frame, as if one's eyes were a camera lens, is to be transported to another
world. Only when a crew member in a Chicago Bulls cap wearing a
backpack sprayer walks into the shot to spritz the wax-butter sculptures
with water to prevent them from melting in the hot desert sun is the illusion momentarily shattered.

For several hours I watch the day's shoot move sluggishly toward the
first take. Hundreds of extras have to be blocked in place in front of the
Jokhang, animals have to be positioned, and smoking incense has to be
readied before Pitt and Thewlis can arrive in Lhasa. As camera angles
are checked, the assemblage of extras waits patiently under the baking
sun. An elderly Tibetan woman in a fur cap and robe sits in the shade of
the hair-of-the-Buddha willow tree interminably working her prayer
beads as if she were indeed in Lhasa.

In the midst of this dense Tibetan crowd scene, a little whirlwind of
activity suddenly develops. Two robed monks have broken spontaneously into a Spanish song. As laughter ripples across the set, nearby
extras turn to see what is happening. Moments later two other monks—
evidently from Argentina—suddenly hike up their robes and, like a pair
of nightclub performers egged on by an enthusiastic audience, start to
dance the macarena.

As this little entr'acte is ending, I leave the set and head for a huge
flatbed trailer on which rows of chemical toilets have been positioned. I
approach one of the bright yellow plastic boxes just as a door swings

open and out comes a Tibetan nobleman in full regalia topped by one of Michael Jones's sublimely tasseled chapeaux. As he hoists his pantaloons up under a dazzling fur-trimmed brocade robe, he gives me a wink.

On my way back to the set, I run into Dennis Murray, the man in charge of plaster, which is what the whole set's faux masonry veneer is made of. To protect himself from the relentless sun, Murray wears a white cloth napkin tucked under a baseball cap so that he looks like a French foreign legionnaire. He stands behind a small cement mixer that grinds away next to stacks of unopened paper bags of powdered plaster. Like a baker, he is coated from head to foot with white dust.

"We've got about forty or fifty plasterers at work on the set and I guess we'll use . . . oh, I don't know, maybe a hundred tons of plaster before we're done," he tells me jauntily. "The art department shows us a picture of something and then what we do is to make a model out of fibrous canvas and plaster, reproduce the surface, and paint it."

Back at the set, there is still no sign of Pitt and very little evidence of progress toward the first shot of the day. Another hour passes before the first assistant director gets all the extras positioned so that a walk-through can begin. There is a countdown, and suddenly a commotion from one of the alleys makes everyone turn. Standing on tiptoe to see over the heads of the crowd, I glimpse a young man with blond hair, followed by another Westerner, trudging down an alley in a T-shirt and sunglasses. It's him, appearing to rehearse his entrance! At last! I crane to get a better look.

But no, wait! He's not quite tall enough and there is no suggestion of the renowned Pitt musculature. A false alarm—it's only the stand-ins for Pitt and Thewlis, who must walk through each scene many times before the actual take so that the director of photography can get the proper camera angles. However, I am assured a moment later by d'Arcy, who is ever on patrol and evidently catches me looking somewhat let down, that I will not be disappointed for long. Brad's advent, she pledges, will still be today.

Ennui descends on the set once more as hundreds of extras are rearranged and a horse carrying a noblewoman is marched repeatedly through its paces. Annaud strides around checking details.

The sun continues to blaze down.

The butter sculptures are spritzed again. And then again, and again.

The ceramic yak dung is rearranged.

Meanwhile all the extras stand patiently in place gulping bottled water.

I'm beginning to feel a little light-headed myself from all the beeswax smoke wafting around in imitation of burning juniper incense.

"Give me five more nomads and two monks," someone calls over the walkie-talkie system that ties the whole production together.

"I want those dogs down here now," another voice barks over the airwaves, probably to Paul Ball. "And let's get those chickens ready to go, too."

More time elapses. It is late morning when things finally begin to galvanize.

"Ready on the set!" the first assistant director finally calls out, an order immediately translated into Tibetan and Spanish. The cameramen hunch over their equipment like gunnery crews over their weapons.

"Cameras! Action!"

And as if some elaborate mechanical window scene in an elegant Fifth Avenue department store were suddenly coming to life, the whole stationary scene in front of the Jokhang clicks into motion. Moments later, out of the alleyway, with chickens and dogs scattering underfoot, comes Brad Pitt. Before us, however, is no American golden boy but a bearded, exhausted, half-starved, sun-scorched Heinrich Harrer in a ragged, filthy Tibetan *chuba*. He and David Thewlis hobble into the Barkhor amid a medieval tableau of Tibetans.

Although seeing Pitt at last before me is, of course, somehow immeasurably less exciting than imagined, the scene itself takes my breath away nonetheless. Despite the fact that I am surrounded by cameras, piles of equipment, and numerous Caucasians in contemporary dress, the scene is still powerfully convincing. Indeed, I find myself unexpectedly swept away in a wave of nostalgia.

But nostalgia for what? I'm not sure. All I know is that I feel over-whelmed by a yearning for a place like the one I see being set in motion before me—a fantastic island of escape from the prosaic, the rapacious, the speed and falseness of modern life. The irony does not escape me that I am actually looking at one of the most false of all modern con-juries. But then, as I drink in the wonder of the scene unfolding all around, it occurs to me that at last I really have reached the true goal of my quest: the ultimate Hollywood illusion of Tibet . . . with me inside it.

The next day an even more complex scene is to be shot at the Jokhang, but, alas, another one that never actually happened in Lhasa. It involves the dramatic if mythical arrival of a delegation of People's Liberation Army generals sent to negotiate Tibet's acquiescence to the Chinese occupation in 1951. Again, hundreds of extras wait as the set is laboriously prepared. I strike up a conversation with one of them, Ngawang Jinpa, an elderly professor of Tibetan Buddhism at the Manjusri Institute in Darjeeling. Ironically, it was at the real Jokhang that Jinpa took his *geshe,* or divinity degree, in 1958 while he was a monk at Drepung monastery. He has been cast in the film as a Tibetan minister and wears red, white, and blue traditional felt boots, a gold brocade robe with a crimson sash, a single turquoise and silver earring, and a piece of millinery from the Ministry of Funny Hats that consists of a saucer-shaped brim embroidered with flowers, a spike at the top, and a fringe of red tassels.

"Oh, it's very nice to be in these lovely hats again just like the old days," he exclaims with delight, noticing me inspecting his head-gear. "Most of the younger Tibetans have no idea what each of these hats signifies. But for us old people, they bring back such wonderful memories."

When Professor Jinpa first saw the Jokhang replica, he felt, "Oh, my goodness, I am home. How amazing to be back in front of the sacred Jokhang." He looks up at this replicated sanctum sanctorum of Tibetan Buddhism with the wonderment of a pilgrim who has arrived, at last, in the promised land. "Aiyaaa!" he exclaims. "The climate, the scenery, the dust, the bright sunshine, the blue sky make me feel so much at home. In Lhasa we used to say that perfect food came from China, perfect robes and hats from Mongolia, and perfect religion from India and Tibet."

As we continue to wait, Professor Jinpa takes me on an ecclesiastical tour of the shrine before us, pointing out the iconographic significance of all the details that have been incorporated into the Jokhang's replica exterior. He tells me that the two golden deer holding up the wheel above the entranceway represent the Buddha embracing the dharma during his first sermon in a place called Deer Park. The bells under the eaves engraved with mantras stand for peace and prosperity. He offers a learned exegesis on the elephant-trunked divinity riding a rat, the four-face Indra mounted on a duck, the ferocious Makhala borne aloft on the mythological Garuda. Then he points out the fluted columns of the *khyamra gochor* and the *dhochal* where the devout have worn the flagstones smooth by prostrating themselves over the centuries. Flanking this sacred portal are murals of the four guardian kings and the *thunpa punzhi,* the four friendly brothers (an elephant, a rabbit, a parrot, and a monkey). To the left is the window from which the Dalai Lama once viewed the ceremonies below. And just above, hidden behind a large yak-hair curtain, is a balcony where the *kashag,* Tibet's cabinet, used to sit on ceremonial occasions. Suspended over the whole amazing structure are *gyaphip,* the individual gilded pagoda roofs of the various interior chapels.

Professor Jinpa lectures on as clouds of smoke wreathe the set and several grinning Bolivian Indians dressed as monks practice turning their hand-held prayer wheels like a group of teenagers learning how to spin hula hoops. One is chewing bubble gum.

"Inside the Jokhang is the Jowo Shakyamuni, a statue of the young Buddha that was made during Buddha's time and actually blessed by him," Professor Jinpa continues rhapsodically. "The statue has a jewel that is said to move around inside its body. You can place your forehead against its knee, say a prayer, and make a wish. Then, if the jewel comes into the knee, your wish will come true." He grins. "When I last was in the Jokhang, I prayed that I would not have to stay under Chinese rule. Of course, I had no idea then that I would be going to India."

When Professor Jinpa must take his place again in the scene, I walk to the sidelines to watch. Turning to one side I am stunned to find that Brad Pitt and Gwyneth Paltrow have silently materialized only a few feet away from me. They stand near a street stall that sells prop incense, prayer flags, and charms. Looking at Pitt, who is now out of costume, I think of Dustin Hoffman's comment that "next to Brad Pitt, everyone else looks like an onion." With his dazzling white teeth and his handsome face topped off by a Heinrich Harreresque head of dyed blond teutonic hair, Pitt seems almost too perfectly beautiful. Today, wearing a collarless tunic and khaki trousers, he is busy taking snapshots of the rehearsal.

In shorts and sandals, Paltrow is an exaggerated version of the tall, thin, leggy, fey look so popular in Hollywood and fashion circles. Without makeup and with her straight blond hair in a simple French twist, she looks far more mortal than I ever imagined possible. In fact, next to Pitt's, her beauty seems almost commonplace.

They stand together next to a pair of folding canvas chairs inscribed with their names—the Hollywood version of thrones—which are kept ready at all times. Here on the set, they are a royal couple, carefully shrouded from the profanity of public view. For a moment, I feel as Heinrich Harrer must have felt the first time he gazed upon the Dalai Lama. I realize that my heart has even started beating faster.

As I glance around, however, I can see that no one else is paying much attention. Of course, they are with Pitt every day, whereas I, an *auslander,* am seeing him out of character for the first time.

Still, the thrill of the moment cools quickly. Only when Brad suddenly flashes one of his million-dollar smiles—rendering him slightly craggier than I remember from his films—does a flicker of his star power seem to kindle.

When he lights up a cigarette, I consider accosting him, even though I know it would win me eternal damnation from Sue d'Arcy. For a moment it feels necessary to seize my opportunity. After all, have I come all this way merely to acquiesce, when decisive action might allow me to meet my quarry? But that moment, too, quickly passes. More than the displeasure of Sue d'Arcy, it is the fear of capping my quest with a disappointingly flat instant of direct contact that finally holds me back.

"Stand by for rehearsal," calls out the first assistant director in a voice of strained calmness that undoubtedly masks a reservoir of anxieties.

"Let's get a shot through the monks' hats," suggests Annaud, who wanders by beaming at all that he has wrought. "Are we short of hats?" he inquires, spotting a group of bare-headed monks. "More hats, please. More hats!" he orders, waving his hands like a traffic cop. A factotum instantly appears with a pile of fringed monks' bonnets of the type that gave the Gelugpa sect the name "Yellow Hats."

As gongs start ringing and robed monks commence to chant, dancers in skeleton masks begin a slow-motion danse macabre. Two long, curved copper horns, stretching to the ground like giant elephants' trunks, bleat out a welcome to the delegation of generals in Mao suits. Unctuously squiring them toward the Jokhang is B. D. Wong, or rather the collaborationist Tibetan nobleman Ngawang Jigme. He is costumed in full sartorial splendor with a minimalist yellow hat that sits on top of his strange coiffure like a popover, making him look like a cross between the Philip Morris boy and Mickey Mouse.

In the scene, the script calls for the Chinese generals to march into the sacred Jokhang and trample contemptuously through a sand mandala that the monks have been laboriously preparing on the floor in welcome. Throughout this indignity, the script indicates that the young Dalai Lama continues to sit on his throne in utter equanimity. Even when the scowling generals refuse to sit lower than him as custom requires, he keeps his composure. It is a quintessential good-guys-meet-bad-guys Hollywood moment, meant, no doubt, to help enshrine in popular culture a view of China as ruthless in its dealings with Tibet. But, of course, of all the horrendous things that China did to Tibetans, this particular insult by PLA generals is not among them. If Chinese Communist Party leaders, perturbed by the film, complain of this unfair and cynically unfriendly depiction, they will be technically justified.

As the shot ends, I spot David Thewlis, Pitt's costar, with whom d'Arcy has offered me an interview as a substitute for the Pitt interview that can't be. Thewlis is a slender, laconic actor. Mustachioed and far scruffier looking than Pitt, he has the air of someone whose life has not always worked out smoothly and who is capable of self-neglect and self-doubt. From Blackpool, England, he came to the notice of critics through the raunchy realism of such films as Mike Leigh's *Life Is Sweet* (1990), in which his character licks chocolate off the anorexic body of his girlfriend, and Leigh's *Naked* (1993), in which he plays a strung-out dope addict, a role that won him the award for best actor at the 1993 Cannes Film Festival.

Since Thewlis is not yet overwhelmed with media attention or relentlessly hounded by screaming fans, he is still willing, perhaps even a little gratified, to reveal himself in interviews. However, what makes his relation to *Seven Years in Tibet* unusual is the fact that he began to cultivate an interest in Buddhism about five years earlier.

"One time I was in an Oxford hotel room that had no TV or books except for a copy of *The Teachings of Buddha* and I read it until the end of the night," he tells me as we sit in his air-conditioned trailer. "Since then, I've continued to read these teachings and they actually helped me give up smoking." He gives a wry little laugh as, with a certain defiance, he lights a cigarette. "I've always had an interest in philosophy and religion, but until reading that book, I had never really taken notice of Buddhism in a spiritual way, nor did I know much about Tibet. It seemed very far away and mystical. Not until I started to read some history and politics did I gain any familiarity with the place and begin to really admire the Dalai Lama for his rejection of violence."

As for the likely effect of the upcoming Tibet films on popular culture, Thewlis says, "Under the generic title of 'New Age religion,' they will probably make Tibetan Buddhism come out top of the pops. It's a real phenomenon right now, maybe part of some kind of millennium fever. We're so out of nature and so surrounded by technology that it's easy to get spiritually lost."

Thewlis was raised as a Christian. "If I was in trouble," he says, "I'd often turn to the Bible, but it never did anything for me." He stubs out his cigarette, immediately lights up another, and lets a plume of smoke curl up past his mustache as he sucks it back in through his nostrils.

When he sees me glancing at a dog-eared copy of *The Tibetan Book of the Dead* that sits next to his ashtray on the trailer's kitchen table, he says matter-of-factly, "I've always been fascinated with death. But Tibetans have a far more positive view of dying than Christians. I used to joke that I could just give it all up and go to Tibet. In fact, at one point I did just go and live on an island in the Philippines. It was a kind of paradise and all the stress *did* melt away in a manner that made me seriously consider dropping out permanently. But then along came this big Hollywood film." He shakes his head. "My first reaction was, 'Oh no! No!' But then they said, 'Hey, it's big-budget! It's got Brad Pitt, but you get the girl!' " He laughs. "Frankly speaking, one of the reasons I'm doing this film is because of Buddhism. It's been the most fascinating thing I've done since 1993 and *Naked*. The Tibetans are really beautiful. Brad and I went to meet some monks and I'm not sure who was more amazed. They have such presence, such a generous, compassionate aura, such a glowing, benevolent sense of well-being. They seem so easily pleased and not to demand much. On the other hand, we are all about demands and owning our things. I live simply, but even so I have far too many things. The Tibetans seem almost entertained by what makes us so stressed out. I feel they know something that I don't. When I meet them, I just feel humble."

Unlike Heinrich Harrer who, by the time he departed from Lhasa in 1950, had become close friends with the young Dalai Lama, I left the set of *Seven Years in Tibet* several days later to return home to California without ever even speaking to Brad Pitt. And I departed from Uspayatta feeling somewhat disconcerted by the whole experience of being let into this manufactured Lhasa. Harrer had been able to end his book elegiacally by writing about a real place and a real experience that enabled him to say, "Wherever I live, I shall feel homesick for Tibet." When he was finally able to return to Lhasa in 1982 with a tour group, he was deeply disappointed by what he saw, forced to console himself with the idea that he had lived "a dream that mankind wanted to dream." As I boarded a United Airlines jet in Santiago de Chile for Miami, all I felt was an inchoate sense of homesickness for a chimera of a place that had been created in my mind not so much by my visits to Tibet as by the books now lying inertly in my duffle bag and by those flimsy plywood-and-plaster sets—soon to be dismantled—on the Uspayatta desert.

17

THE LAST OF THE QUESTERS

Tibet remained largely undisturbed as World War II swept through both Europe and Asia. One French expedition, under André Guibaut and Louis Liotard, did manage in 1940 to head out the same route taken by Huc and Gabet and Bonvalot and Henri d'Orléans. In the border town of Kangding, where they met Alexandra David-Neel and Aphur Yongden, Guibaut wrote with great excitement and anticipation about what lay ahead. "We are at the end of the world—of our world—and on the fringe of a new one . . . a starting point for those whom faith or the spirit of adventure have driven out into the unknown like caravels across the ocean."

Although Liotard was killed en route by Golok bandits and Guibaut failed to reach Lhasa, Guibaut's book, *Tibetan Venture*—which described Tibetan lands as "being so near the clouds that they seem to belong rather to the sky than the earth"—served to help keep the still-evolving myth of Tibet as a rare and transcendent place alive in the West.

When the war finally ended, a few Western stragglers once again took up the challenge to act out dreams that had been put on hold. Guibaut was a beacon for another pilgrim, a French physician and expert on Buddhism named André Migot. Proclaiming that Tibet had been a "magic name" that had kept him "going through the tragic days of collapse and the dark years of the occupation" of France by the Third Reich, he set off in 1946 through Tibet's eastern border regions from China.

Although, like so many others before him, he was finally thwarted in his "spirit quest," he departed Asia no less enamored of the idea of Tibet than when he arrived. He spoke fondly of the land's "irresistible attraction," declaring that he would not soon forget "the grandeur of the bitter nights under a great vault of stars; the misery while I waited for the sun to come out and warm my numbed limbs; the thrill of pressing on, step by step, into forbidden territory; the nerve-racking suspense when we involuntarily met strangers; and the perpetual fear of being unmasked." What was important to Migot was not so much that he had failed to reach Lhasa but that he had lived out a part, at least, of his Tibetan fantasy.

When CBS broadcaster Lowell Thomas received the news in May 1949 that his request to visit Lhasa with his son had been approved by the Tibetan government, he was both incredulous and ecstatic. "It may be hackneyed to say so, but this trip seemed to be one of those dreams that come true," wrote his son Lowell Thomas Jr. in their best-selling book about their journey, evocatively entitled *Out of this World*. "Perhaps Dad even had visions of Tibet when he was a boy in the old Colorado gold camp of Cripple Creek," wrote the younger Thomas. "At any rate, . . . the desire to travel eventually nourished a craving to reach Tibet and make that most impossible journey to Lhasa, because for centuries it has been the classic of the difficult."

The radio broadcasts that Lowell Thomas Sr. tape-recorded for CBS were done on a prototype battery-run recorder, one of the earliest of its kind to be used in broadcast news. Because they represented the first voices ever to be heard from Tibet, they had an enormous impact on listeners when they aired back in the United States. For the first time in history—and the last for over three decades—the English-speaking world was in direct contact with Tibet via the electronic media. And the tone of these reports made it sound almost as if both Thomases imagined themselves to be in a waking reverie. "It often seemed as though we were dreaming—acting the parts of characters in James Hilton's novel, on our way to Shangri-La," the son reported. "Once we crossed the Himalayas into Tibet, we were indeed travelers in the land of the Lost Horizon."

Nor were the Thomases disappointed with the reality of Lhasa. Like Harrer, they glimpsed the city at that last moment when the outside world still remained at bay. "With the gold-roofed Potala, the monasteries and temples glistening in the sun, the crowds of people in their gay, picturesque costumes, Lhasa seemed to me like a rich illustration from a medieval manuscript, magically brought to life," wrote Lowell Thomas Jr. "As an enthusiastic traveler to far-off places, I felt that I had come about as close as ever I would to finding that pot of gold at the end of the rainbow."

He was even able to speak admiringly of Lhasa's backwardness. "Two world wars have brought startling change to most of the globe, but so far, not to Tibet. It remains a feudal theocracy, ruled with an iron hand by two hundred thousand all-powerful Buddhist monks who have fiercely resisted nearly every attempt by unwelcome intruders to invade their solitude," he wrote with obvious approval.

As the Thomases made their way back to India, they described their progress thus: "We felt that we were coming out of the Seventh Century into the Twentieth." And while they were emerging from the interior of an actual geographic place, the imagery they employed was that of awakening from a dream of an "incredible, fabulous, story-book country."

But even as Thomas and son were absorbing their paradisiacal experiences, Tibetans were concerning themselves with far less dreamy thoughts as the Chinese Communists began speaking about "reuniting the motherland." Suddenly Lhasa officials found themselves in a desperate search for outside allies.

It is an astonishing fact that, until 1979, only 1,250 Westerners were estimated to have ever visited Lhasa, and many of them had been part of the 1904 Younghusband expedition. Following China's occupation, which began in 1950, Tibet's doors once again swung shut to the West. This time the gatekeepers were not wary lamas or Manchu *amban*s but high Communist Party cadres and People's Liberation Army generals.

Once more off-limits, Tibet continued to burn on vividly in the Western imagination. While the real Tibet was undergoing tectonic and destructive changes at the hands of Maoist revolutionaries, in the Western mind it remained a place of changeless tradition frozen in time. "Tibet seemed not to belong to our earth, a society left on the shelf, set in amber, preserved in deep freeze, a land so close to the sky that the natural occupation of her people was to pray," Huston Smith, a professor of religion, commented in a 1968 PBS film, *Requiem for a Faith.*

In reality, there was not much chanting or public meditating going on just then. The Cultural Revolution had begun and thousands of monasteries were being razed, tens of thousands of monks were being persecuted, imprisoned, and tortured, and some were being murdered. As ever, though, self-styled spiritualists were on hand in the West, succored by Buddhism and animated by a rich legacy of past accounts, to keep the idea—or perhaps it would be more accurate to say the hope—of a changeless Tibet alive.

One such spiritualist, whom Tibet scholar Donald Lopez profiles in *Prisoners of Shangri-La,* was Ernst Lothar Hoffman, aka Lama Anagarika Govinda. The son of a Bolivian mother and a German father, he had been interested in the esoteric since his youth. His books, including *Foundations of Tibetan Mysticism According to the Esoteric Teachings of the Great Mantra Om Mani Padme Om* (1956) and his popular *The*

Way of the White Clouds (1966), did much to both explain Tibetan Buddhism and keep the old mythology of Tibet and the Himalayas as being sacred alive in Western consciousness.

By Lama Govinda's account, his conversion to Tibetan Buddhism came after he took refuge in a Tibetan monastery while trekking in the Himalayas near Darjeeling in 1931. It was here that he had "opened to him the gates to the mysteries of Tibet." In the late forties, he claimed, he not only was "initiated" into the Kagyu order after meeting a certain *rinpoche* at Tsecholing monastery in Western Tibet but had a spiritual revelation that caused "a strange transformation" to take place in his soul. "It is as if a weight were lifted from the mind, or as if certain hindrances were removed," he wrote, so that "consciousness seems to be raised to a higher level, where the obstacles and disturbances of our ordinary life do not exist."

Although he had traveled widely in India, Burma, and Ceylon, where he had become a Theravadin monk in the 1920s, there is no evidence that Lama Govinda could speak or read Sanskrit, Tibetan, or Chinese. He did, however, have a talent for playing the part of the Westerner turned Eastern guru who had been imbued through special sensitivity and training with an ability to understand "the wisdom of the Ancients." He called himself a "Buddhist adept" (a word borrowed from the Blavatsky era), wore "Tibetan" clothes of his own design; sported a long, Fu Manchu–style beard, and in familiar fashion claimed that Tibet was "the last living link that connects us with the civilizations of a distant past" and to "the mystery-cults of Egypt, Mesopotamia and Greece, of Incas and Mayas . . . [which] are forever lost to our knowledge."

Like so many other Western seekers, Lama Govinda, too, cherished Tibet and its mountains as places that had escaped the spiritual decline and physical desecration of the modern world outside. As he wrote reverentially in the introduction to *Foundations of Tibetan Mysticism,* "Tibet, due to its natural isolation and its inaccessibility (which was reinforced by the political conditions of the last centuries), has succeeded not only in preserving but in *keeping alive* the traditions of the most distant past, the knowledge of the hidden forces of the human soul and the highest achievements and esoteric teachings of Indian saints and sages." Of the Himalayas, he observed, "The power of such mountains is so great and yet so subtle that, without compulsion, people are drawn to it from near and far, as if by the force of some invisible magnet; and they will undergo untold hardships and privations in their inexplicable urge to approach and worship at the center of this sacred power."

Interestingly, however, although Lama Govinda's works were touched by the ardent fervor of the true (even if non-native) believer, they nonetheless offered clear and informative explanations of Tibetan Buddhism to Westerners. As fascination with Tibetan spiritualism converged in the 1960s with the imperatives of the psychedelic revolution, Lama Govinda became an ever more popular translator of Tibetan Buddhism. This was, of course, the era when psychedelic experimenters Timothy Leary and Richard Alpert burst onto the scene. After reconstituting himself as the guru Baba Ram Dass, Alpert began proselytizing for the idea that enhanced spiritual consciousness could be born not only from yogic exercises and meditation but from LSD, mescaline, and other hallucinogenic drugs. Leary and Alpert's 1964 book, *The Psychedelic Experience: A Manual Based on the Tibetan Book of the Dead,* threw Tibet and psychedelics into the same blender, creating a novel mix of chemistry and spirit that would have surely bewildered Tibetan lamas back home. For sixties flower children in search of holy lands abroad, however, India and Nepal had to stand in as default destinations in a still-Tibetless world.

The Western mythology of Tibet, like all other deeply rooted living myths, has managed to endure by evolving with the times, not just resisting but even transforming and absorbing the most extreme challenges reality has had to offer. When, after three decades, the Chinese government began opening Tibet to trekkers, mountain climbers, and tourists and a new generation of Western adventurers, spiritual seekers, teachers, and political activists were able to travel there, what this next wave of pilgrims found soon fused with what they wanted to find. As the collective unconscious that had been accumulating for two centuries merged with the reality of China's occupation, yet another chapter in Western mythology about Tibet began to take shape.

Beginning in the early 1980s, thousands of starry-eyed Caucasian pilgrims began to make reverential journeys to Lhasa, their rucksacks filled with the writings of Heinrich Harrer, Alexandra David-Neel, and Lama Govinda, their minds filled with visions of medieval monasteries, thousands of chanting monks, and legions of ascetic hermits meditating in mountaintop grottoes where, as Donald Lopez writes, it was assumed that "ancient wisdom was held in safekeeping for the modern age." By the early 1990s, however, roads criss-crossed much of Tibet, Lhasa had traffic lights, the entire city had been electrified, an international airport had opened, telecommunications reached virtually anywhere in the world, and a Holiday Inn (complete with CNN and yak burgers) was offering reservations through an 800 number in the United States.

With a certain well-intentioned innocence, the new devotees tried to make some sense out of what had happened to the promised land during its three decades off-line. Nostalgically receptive to the Tibet of old, they naturally felt immediate sympathy for any defrocked monks they encountered and for Tibet's "lost culture." New, however, was a fierce sympathy for the Dalai Lama, his government in exile and the Tibetan people, which grew in intensity in direct proportion to the indignation these sojourners came to feel over China's undeniably savage occupation. While historically speaking there had often been an incipiently anti-Chinese aspect to the West's infatuation with Lhasa—one has only to think of the litany of unflattering remarks from Manning to McGovern about arrogant and meddlesome *amban*s—as Westerners began to realize the magnitude of destruction the Cultural Revolutionaries had wreaked on Tibetan culture and society, anti-Chinese sentiment became stronger and more explicit.

It was hardly surprising, then, that much as China appreciated the hard currency visitors brought with them, Communist Party leaders came to look on these arriviste pilgrims with increasing distrust and even ended up blacklisting some of them for helping the Tibetan freedom movement. After all, the Chinese had their own myths about Tibet—especially that Mao's revolution had "peacefully liberated" an oppressed and thankful people—and Party leaders in Beijing did not appreciate being forced to watch their myths compete unsuccessfully with those of the West. Behind China's determination to hold on to Tibet and the myth of liberation is a long historical legacy that has been absorbed by most Han Chinese, who enthusiastically support the way the old empire, after a century and a half of being preyed on and partially dismembered by the West and Japan, was stitched back together by Mao in the 1950s.

Joan Chen is a Chinese actress who left Shanghai for the United States in the early 1980s and has starred in films ranging from Bernardo Bertolucci's *The Last Emperor* (1987) to Oliver Stone's *Heaven and Earth* (1993) and Steven Seagal's *On Deadly Ground* (1994). Her directorial debut was the Chinese-language independent feature *Xixiu: The Sent Down Girl,* set in a Tibetan ethnic border region of China during the 1970s. Because Chen had shot her film in China without Party permission, before it was released in May 1999 she was roundly criticized by officials from the Film Bureau in Beijing and banned from working in China. Also in 1999, Chen was working on a new film with Richard Gere and Winona Ryder in New York City.

When I asked her about the West's tendency to romanticize Tibet, Chen offered a reminder of how dependent perceptions of the world are on cultural context. "When I came here to America, I found it quite strange to see how Westerners idealized Tibet," she told me. "For us growing up in Mao's China, the Dalai Lama was a slave owner, Tibetan Buddhism was a tool for oppressing and exploiting the serfs, and Tibet was considered a backward, feudal place that we didn't want to go to. That's what we were taught, so that's the way we saw it.

"On the other hand, I can also remember how totally exotic America seemed to me when I was in China. I think that's the way Tibet must seem to many Americans. They think they like Tibetan Buddhism, but actually when you ask them to tell you about it, many of them can't make much sense out of it. People in Hollywood like the idea of Tibetan mysticism because they don't really understand it and so can interpret it any way they want. It's a lazy way of achieving enlightenment.

"Maybe their fascination has something to do with Tibet's visual landscape, how cinematically exotic it is and how it seems to promise Westerners a remote hope of something other than what they have. But Westerners do to Tibet exactly what Third World Asians do to the United States. In terms of fantasies, Westerners crave a place in the East where everything is pure and spiritual, while those who grew up in China crave the West because they see it as the land of materialism. Each group tends to idealize the other by projecting their yearnings onto it."

While most Tibetans have deeply negative feelings about China's occupation of their homeland, in recent years some have taken a clear-eyed look at the historical record and acknowledged the gross inequities in traditional Tibet's social and political system. For example, Tsering Shakya, a research fellow at the School of Oriental and African Studies in London, writes in *Dragon in the Land of Snows: A History of Modern Tibet Since 1947* that before 1950 Tibet was not a "land of happy contented people" but a kind of "hell on earth ravaged by feudal exploitation." Although he does not excuse the Chinese for their savage occupation and cultural cleansing, Shakya observes that what China's Party leaders and many leaders of the Tibetan exile movement share is their unwillingness to let "complexities . . . intrude on their firmly held beliefs."

This also tended to be true of the new generation of Western pilgrims who began flocking to Tibet in the 1980s. For many of them, the exploratory and questing aspects of their experience of Tibet were subsumed by the imperatives of a political or moral crusade that grew out of an understandable outrage over Tibet's fate as a Chinese occupied area. It did not take long before thousands of touring, trekking, climbing, motoring, biking, meditating, kayaking, hang-gliding, yak-riding, and sometimes even English-teaching foreigners who were drifting around Tibet began forming their own unregimented views. Like those who preceded them, many wrote about their experiences upon returning home—even after only weeklong packaged tours controlled by the new Chinese *amban*s of Lhasa. *New York Times* correspondent Harrison Salisbury, a man of an earlier generation, highlighted this mind-set when, as one of the first Westerners to visit Lhasa in the early 1980s, he lamented, "Once identified with Shangri-La, a mythical place of peace and contentment, [Tibet] is now a dark and sorrowing land."

The repressive authoritarianism that the new generation of travelers observed seemed shockingly at odds with the tenets of Tibetan Buddhism as they understood them. Catriona Bass, a young British woman who attended Oxford, was the rare foreigner able to arrange an eighteen-month visa to teach English in Lhasa. It was not long after arriving in 1986 that her "childhood image" of Tibet as "a snow kingdom huddled in the peaks around Everest" was rudely challenged. In her book, *Inside the Treasure House,* she compares the West's view of Tibet (as "swathed in the romance of Western nostalgia") with the East's view (as steeped "in centuries of contempt"). But the image of Tibet that was left burning in her mind's eye was not of a secluded spiritual oasis but of a land that had aspired to mind its own business being overrun and oppressed by "barbarian inhabitants."

In 1987, American physician Blake Kerr and civil rights lawyer John Ackerly, former classmates at Dartmouth College, headed for Lhasa. Kerr remembers "longing for some sort of adventure," and appealing to Ackerly's "sense of adventure" by presenting him with copies of Heinrich Harrer's *Seven Years in Tibet* and Alexandra David-Neel's *My Journey to Lhasa.* They, too, however, found their original idea of Tibet quickly assaulted by other realities. After a trip to Central Tibet via Chinese bus from Gansu Province, Kerr was thrilled at the sight of the Potala as they entered the city. ("My heart beat faster as I imagined exploring the palace," he wrote.)

But they soon found themselves in the middle of one of the largest proindependence demonstrations in the capital since China's occupation began and ended up being detained by Public Security Bureau police. The fact that the demonstrations led to a bloody crackdown, with Kerr ministering to wounded monks, and that martial law was ultimately imposed in 1989 had a profound influence on how these two Americans would henceforth see Tibet. As Kerr later told Bernard Shaw in a CNN interview, "Tibetans have been living under Chinese military occupation for thirty-seven years. China is committing genocide in Tibet."

Such outrage over China's role in Tibet, not uncommon among visitors in the 1980s and 1990s, also helped forge a Western cadre of activist sympathizers. John Ackerly went to work at the International Campaign for Tibet, while Blake Kerr ended up spending much of the next six years documenting human rights abuses in Tibet and writing a book about his 1987 experiences. In the last lines of *Sky Burial,* he suggests just how much he continues to idealize the old Tibetan society—one that he missed seeing—as a model of innate peacefulness and humanism. When mixed with the injustices of Chinese rule, it created a potent hybrid cocktail. "If China's colonization of Tibet and enforced family planning policies continue, the world will lose one of its most peaceful cultures. China and the West have much to learn from Tibet; but there is little time left."

Indeed, as of 2000, the streets of Lhasa and Shigatse were still being patrolled by fleets of new white and green Japanese jeeps filled with vigilant policemen in dark glasses, many of whom were Han Chinese and unable to speak or read Tibetan. Like other imported officials, they could never be sure what conspiracies were being hatched under their noses, all too often, they suspected, with the complicity of sympathetic foreigners like Bass, Kerr, and Ackerly.

Ironically, as in the earliest days of contact, Tibetans now tend to be extremely friendly to Western visitors because they know that only through outsiders can they make their plight known to the rest of the world. Like a river that has reversed its course, Tibetans now desperately turn outward rather than inward. And the most significant manifestation of this outward turning, of course, is the steady flow of refugees into Nepal and into a Tibetan diaspora that has rooted exiles in foreign lands around the world.

Given the relative ease with which tours and expeditions to Tibet can be arranged—sometimes even with overseas Tibetans along—a growing number of journalists, human rights activists, politicians, and filmmakers concerned with the "Tibet question" have managed to enter Tibet surreptitiously as "tourists," thus continuing, in slightly modified form, the tradition of Westerners stealing into Lhasa in disguise. Only instead of donning yak-hair wigs, darkening their skin with walnut juice, or wearing the rags of Buddhist pilgrims, they now arrive clad in Patagonia outdoor wear, their rucksacks filled with trail mix and sunblock and their shoulders draped with digital cameras. These modern-day pilgrims seek the possibility of both spiritual enlightenment and a chance to somehow aid the cause of the Dalai Lama.

One such convert was Mathieu Ricard, a French molecular biologist and the son of the philosopher Jean-François Revel. In 1972 Ricard renounced not only his father's rationalism but science as well, to become a Tibetan Buddhist monk at the Shechen monastery in Nepal and a personal interpreter for the Dalai Lama. In a best-selling 1998 book coauthored with his father, *The Monk and the Philosopher,* Ricard remembers thinking that despite all his accomplishments as a scientist "something was still missing." Feeling "like a bird in a cage," he writes, he "had only one idea—to be free." Having met many great and admirable people in his life, he "couldn't help noticing that the mastery such people possessed in their particular field was often not matched by even the simplest human perfection—like altruism, goodness and sincerity."

After seeing films of some of the earliest Tibetan lamas to be exiled from Tibet, however, he was impressed by how they seem to have "matched the ideal of sainthood, the perfect being, the sage—a kind of person hardly to be found in the West." To Ricard, they were "living examples of wisdom" and "deeply inspired perfection," and he remembers saying to himself, "If it's possible to reach perfection as a human being, that must be it. . . . Their way of being seemed to reflect what they taught. So I set out to find them." Almost thirty years later, he is still pursuing the dharma. "When I see my teacher, his physical appearance, the way he speaks, what he does, what he is—it all makes me feel utterly convinced that there's something essential here that I want to go deeper into."

A similar book, coauthored in 1999 by activist Tibetologist Robert Thurman, *Circling the Sacred Mountain: A Spiritual Adventure through the Himalayas,* recounts Thurman's trip with a group of Westerners on a dharma quest around Mount Kailash, which is described on the dust jacket as "the most magical place on earth," where "one's prayers are answered instantly." Indeed, "one trip around the sacred mountain at 18,600 feet can wipe away the sins of a lifetime." Thurman, who was soon dubbed "Buddha Bob" by fellow pilgrims, sees Mount Kailash "as the core of the global structure of life, the sacred heart of the joy that makes life worthwhile." At the mountain he hoped "to find access to forces capable of transforming the world out there, not just myself."

In August 1997, Congressman Frank R. Wolf acted out an updated variation on the time-honored scenario of Lhasa-by-disguise. A Republican representative from Virginia whose concern for international human rights violations had previously taken him into the Soviet gulag, Ceauşescu's Romania, and war-ravaged Chechnya, Wolf wanted to document religious persecution and other abuses. Disguised in what he referred to as "traditional tourist garb," Wolf arrived with a faithful native retainer, an unnamed Tibetan carrying an American passport who, like Alexandra David-Neel's Sikkimese monk, served as interpreter and factotum. To avoid detection while in Lhasa, the two interlopers stayed not at the Lhasa Holiday Inn (with which Holiday Inn Worldwide was to sever ties due in part to the unfavorable publicity of being associated with the oppressive Chinese government), where they might have been recognized by officials, but at a small backpackers' hangout, the Hotel Kyichu.

"At no time was I asked nor did I make known that I was a Member of Congress," Wolf later admitted. "Had I done so, I am sure that my visit would not have been approved just as other Members of Congress requesting permission to visit Tibet have been turned down." Describing Tibetans as suffering "boot heel subjugation" at the hands of their Han overlords, Wolf declared that in Tibet, "humane progress is not even inching along, and repressed people live under unspeakably brutal conditions in the dim shadows of international awareness."

Upon discovering Wolf's subterfuge, China reacted swiftly. The New China News Agency accused him of trying to foment trouble. It quoted Raidi, the Chinese-appointed chairman of the People's Congress of Tibet, as saying, "All people with a sense of justice, including the Tibetan people, are enraged by his actions." Calling Wolf a "slanderer," the news agency insisted that his allegations of human rights abuses in

Tibet were "malicious attacks," "sensational lies," and "claptrap." Henceforth, it announced, all individual visitors would be banned from Tibet until further notice and group tours would have to be vetted by officials in Lhasa. Finally, the small hotel where Wolf had stayed was closed to foreign guests. The news agency also stepped up its denunciations of the Dalai Lama as "a tool of imperialist forces trying to undermine China" and as a "splittist."

Like many members of the Younghusband expedition, Wolf viewed himself as trying to bring a modicum of civilization to a land controlled by China and ruled by an oligarchy. In this case, however, it was not Tibetan Buddhism and its attendant theocracy that Wolf found fault with, but Marxism-Leninism and the authoritarian bureaucracy of Party cadres from Beijing who now ruled the land. Wolf's reaction to what he found bespoke the new force that was drawing Westerners to Tibet: indignation over the way they perceived China as having oppressed Tibetans and strangled Tibet's traditional religion and culture. In the view of most of these activist political pilgrims, Tibet could now only be "saved" by outside intercession, exactly what China feared most and was most sensitive to.

While Wolf's pilgrimage highlighted Chinese control and the erosion of Tibetan religion and culture for the outside world, in the end it also helped reinforce the idea of Tibet as a guarded citadel that continues to tenaciously protect its inner secrets and can thus be plumbed only by the stealth and guile of those willing to go undercover.

Approaching Lhasa today, one tries to imagine what it must have been like to arrive on foot in disguise a century ago. However, as one's jeep or bus labors up over the mountain pass on the road from Nepal above Lamdrok Tso, the sacred Turquoise Lake that lies just beyond the last mountain pass above the Tsangpo River valley, one gets a prefiguration of the changes that the Tibetan landscape around Lhasa has undergone. A large Chinese hydroelectric project has blasted a tunnel through the mountain ridge over which the road passes for a power station capable of generating electricity for the expanding city below by slowly draining the waters of the magnificent lake above.

In the river valley, one travels along a wide, paved highway, a far cry from the narrow, winding yak caravan trails of yore. Then, just as one's sense of arrival is building, one reaches the suburbs (even the word grates in the context of Lhasa), where new People's Liberation Army bases have been constructed, their concrete barracks standing in rows like tombstones. A cement factory belches smoke into the clear mountain air. A tannery issues forth a contemporary brew of chemical effluent. Acres of modern greenhouses sheathed in plastic grow vegetables once unknown in these high-altitude climes. All vestiges of enchantment seem to have vanished, when suddenly, there it finally is! The Potala! As in the accounts of old, it towers above the distant city, its golden roofs gleaming in the late-afternoon sunshine as if illumined from within. For a moment, it's possible to imagine the wonder, reverence, and relief that this same scene must have evoked in those few weary Western pilgrims who beheld it at last, after so many months of arduous, dangerous travel.

But the sense of elation does not last long. Just as Thomas Manning and Edmund Candler found little enchantment once they allowed their eyes to wander from the Potala to the streets below, so now the new city that has grown up around Red Hill holds little romance or luster for the expectant traveler. Over the past two decades much of Lhasa has been transfigured by graceless, cell-block-like Chinese buildings that make one feel more in a drab, provincial Chinese city than in a Shangri-La.

Were Heinrich Harrer to return today, he would hardly recognize his former home. He would certainly be confused by the new roundabout at Fuxing Road outside the old city, with its massive kitsch sculpture of two golden yaks, presented to the Tibetan people by the government in Beijing to help them celebrate the fortieth anniversary of their "peaceful liberation." Harrer would undoubtedly note with some confusion that the old West Gate and its *chorten*s—through which he passed on January 15, 1946, and which were so meticulously reproduced in Argentina—are now gone. And once beyond the spot where the West

Gate once stood, he would undoubtedly feel thoroughly disoriented by the city's grand new plaza, which has recently replaced the old *shol,* an area just below the Potala where government and army offices once stood and past which caravans used to make their progress as yaks grazed peacefully in the surrounding pasture. Suffice it to say, the city's new "miracle mile," with its traffic jams and its welter of shops, eateries, video-game parlors, photo studios, karaoke bars, and massage parlors (owned and run almost exclusively by Han Chinese), would also be a bewildering sight.

The Jokhang still lies at the center of the old city; the revered seated figure of the young Buddha, the Jowo Shakyamuni (on which Professor Jinpa had waxed so knowledgeably in Argentina) is still inside; and the Barkhor, the bazaar that surrounds the Jokhang, continues to exert a powerful spiritual magnetism that draws not only worshipers but also protesters to its embrace.

Looking down from the Jokhang's gold-leafed roofs onto the *dhochal,* the area in front of the main doorway into the Jokhang—where at almost every hour of the day flocks of ragged pilgrims still reverently prostrate themselves on flagstones worn as smooth as skin by centuries of devotions—one does get a whiff of the past. Crowds of true believers spinning prayer wheels and fingering rosaries still circumambulate the Barkhor past a tableau of street merchants hawking goods and black-market money changers badgering tourists for hard currency as mendicant monks chant *Om mani padme hum.*

But beneath this hurly-burly of devotion and commerce, there exists a discernible undercurrent of tension. Because this is Lhasa's Tiananmen Square, the Jokhang, the Barkhor, and the graceless modern-day square built in front all remain under constant surveillance from police and from rooftop video cameras. Moreover, the crowds that gather every day are always infiltrated with plainclothed operatives ready to spring into action should there be any unacceptable expression of public dissent. That the police station now standing on the south side of the Barkhor was burned during demonstrations that shook the city in 1987 serves as a reminder of what a tinderbox this epicenter of Tibetan life and Western dream culture can be.

Although most Chinese strenuously object to accusations of Han colonialism in Tibet, many nonetheless evince a kind of colonial superiority in their attitudes toward Tibetans. Their hauteur is not so far from what earlier visitors observed in the imperial *ambans*. Most Han Chinese see themselves accepting responsibility for providing tutelage to a lesser, more primitive people just as American missionaries once saw China as a place where "manifest destiny" could be acted out (even if the impulse was rouged up as a selfless saving of souls and a bringing of civilization to an uncivilized world). There can be no doubt that many Chinese find a certain pleasure in assuming this imperial burden and bringing the gospel of progress to a benighted land of dark-skinned natives.

The fact that most Tibetans never wished to be "liberated" by anyone except the Lord Buddha is, for the Chinese, beside the point. The rationalizations of a superior power for occupying and governing another land autocratically invariably have their own logic, one that seldom has much to do with the occupied land. To say that China and Tibet are, in the words of the well-known Chinese saying, "sleeping in the same bed but dreaming different dreams" would be an understatement.

For Tibet, there is now probably no turning back from some sort of union with China. Tibet has become so dependent on its rapidly developing Chinese infrastructure that surviving on its own, even if Beijing did unexpectedly grant it self-determination, would be a daunting task. Without Tibetans wishing for it or consenting to it, their fate and future have become irrevocably intertwined with China's in ways that make some sort of long-term accommodation with Beijing almost inevitable.

The West, too, is deeply involved, even though no nation disputes China's sovereign right to Tibet. Because Westerners themselves are so enmeshed in complicated emotional ways with the idea of Tibet, if not with Tibet itself, they have become an ineluctable part of the equation.

When Heinrich Harrer finally revisited Lhasa in 1982, it seemed unimaginable to him that he could fly there in a jet passenger plane and look down upon "the greatest infinity on earth" that only several decades earlier had for him and Peter Aufschnaiter been a "terra incognita, unknown to any man." It is indeed strange to depart from Lhasa for Kathmandu and the outside world on a sleek commercial aircraft and, while sipping a cup of hot coffee, to look down on the amazingly rugged terrain that took Harrer almost two years to navigate on foot. And as one passes over a snow-wreathed Mount Everest looming above the vast ridge of peaks that stretches as far as the eye can see, it is difficult even to imagine what possessed those who once had to endure so much privation to make their uncertain ways to the heart of this fabled land. Their journeys share so little with ours that they seem to have happened not years ago but in another universe.

Yet as remote as their experiences now seem—as remote in a way as Lhasa must once have seemed to them—there is still an enduring connection. The body of lore that grew up around their journeys (even their imagined journeys) has been passed on to us, encoded as a kind of DNA that over and over again has expressed itself in our dreams and fed our fantasies, until they seem more real than the place itself.

"Why is [it that] the fate of Tibet has found such a deep echo in the world?" asked Lama Govinda in the 1930s. "There can be only one answer: Tibet has become the symbol of all that present day humanity is longing for, either because it has been lost or not yet realized, or because it is in danger of disappearing from human sight: the stability of a tradition that has its roots not only in a historical or cultural past but within the innermost being of man, in whose depth this past is enshrined as an ever present source of inspiration."

PART III

18

WHERE THE VIRTUAL HEINRICH HARRER AND THE REAL BRAD PITT DIVERGE

Call it unfinished business or simply a cosmic sense of life's perpetual incompleteness, but despite my return to the San Francisco Bay Area and my normal, distinctly nonvirtual life of friends, family, and meetings at the journalism school where I work, I found myself unable to abandon the idea of meeting Brad Pitt. For reasons I did not bother to analyze, I continued to call Pitt's personal public relations agent, Cindy Guagenti, of the Beverly Hills firm of Baker Winokur Ryder. Perhaps like that of Tibet itself, the lure of Pitt lay in his elusiveness. But when none of my many calls produced much more than friendly but vague promises that Guagenti would "try" to arrange something, I finally began to lose hope.

Then one July afternoon in 1997 a call unexpectedly came from

Guagenti inviting me to a preview screening of *Seven Years in Tibet* in New York. Would I also be able to interview Pitt? I hastened to inquire. He would, I knew, be in the city because he was enacting the role of an angel-messenger from the great beyond come to harvest the well-heeled soul of a character played by Anthony Hopkins in the film *Meet Joe Black,* just then in production. Yes, Guagenti said with a simplicity that made the endless months of rebuffs seem absurd.

And so, several days later, I found myself sitting expectantly in a trailer inside the vast turn-of-the-century Park Slope Armory in Brooklyn making small talk with Pitt's makeup artist and a Cockney bodyguard, both of whom I had met in Uspayatta. It must be said that when at last Pitt came through the trailer door dressed in jeans and a T-shirt and sat himself down at the dinette table, my breath did catch for a moment. After all, it was as if a movie character had magically stepped off the screen and taken a seat beside me in the theater. But it might also be said that my own odyssey—to the real Tibet and Hollywood's Tibet—ended as well. It was there, in yet another mobile home, amid yet another flotilla of filmland trailers, trucks, forklifts, and catering vans, that my circuitous journey, begun at age thirteen in New York City with Harrer's book and involving ships, planes, yaks, trekking expeditions, and limos as well as trips to China, Tibet, Austria, Argentina, Hollywood, and now Brooklyn—a journey that had taken me not only through history but also through endless layers of fantasy and fiction— seemed to reach a conclusion.

It wasn't Brad Pitt per se who put the last piece of punctuation on this long personal tale. He was a perfectly likeable man who seemed to have learned the painful way that, faced with the relentless, often frivolous probing of the media, it was best to say nothing. His attitude toward Tibet was, if anything, admirably matter-of-fact and modest for a Hollywood star. He had, for instance, responded to a question by a *Time* magazine reporter on China-Tibet policy by saying, "Who cares what I think China should do? I'm a fucking actor! They hand me a script. I act. I'm here for entertainment. Basically, when you whittle everything away, I'm a grown man who puts on makeup."

When I asked Pitt how he had been affected by the many Tibetan exiles on the set, he replied with unpretentious directness: "I'm not a politician and I'm not a historian. I just have no place jumping into a political ring talking about the future of Tibet. I haven't lost a family member or had my home taken away. I haven't had my rights taken away."

Well, then, perhaps he could describe how he imagined Tibet before he made this film? "I don't know," he began diffidently, "I had this idea of this peaceful, tranquil, utopian Shangri-La where everyone loves each other and people are good to each other. You know, it's a bit naive once you get into it. But that's basically it. I didn't know that much."

And so it went, from familiar question to familiar question and from cautious answer to cautious answer, none of which contained much more than truncated fragments of thoughts. When I left an hour and a half later, I knew that there was nothing on my tape recorder that was really relevant to what I was writing.

Only later, as I pondered the strange letdown the meeting proved to be, was I able to make any sense of the prosaic way my quest had come to an end. For if Brad Pitt the actor could be dazzling on-screen and if his offscreen life—at least from afar—also radiated a certain presence, Brad Pitt the person was, by all appearances, rather ordinary, whatever his intellectual resources or acting skills. Before me in that trailer, so far removed from Tibet, no less from Argentina, was neither Heinrich Harrer nor an angel; nor even a larger-than-life superstar, but a well-defended young man with a certain sadness around the eyes who was expending a great deal of wary energy on divulging nothing of his true self, a self that may or may not have been interesting without makeup. In truth, there was no way for me to tell. And besides, it didn't really matter. I had unavoidably run up against his strategy for survival—a kind of reaching out for sanity in a world where what everyone yearned to know was why his engagement to actress Gwyneth Paltrow had broken off. In any event, meeting this Hollywood God-king was anything but exotic. Walking out of that gloomy armory into a muggy Brooklyn afternoon, I found it quite preposterous that this nice yet ordinary embodiment of a megastar was part of anyone's fantasy of either Hollywood the glamorous or Tibet the mysterious. But then, from another perspective, it was hardly less preposterous that I and many other Westerners like me had managed to make such a powerful fantasy out of Tibet.

19

COPING WITH THE REAL
HEINRICH HARRER

If Heinrich Harrer had just been an adventurous mountain climber from Austria who found humanity in the magic kingdom of Tibet, Brad Pitt might have been an appropriate choice to play him on-screen. But, as it turned out, of the two of them, Harrer proved to be the better actor. He had, in fact, for decades lived his own vivid, artfully airbrushed life offscreen and in real time, as became clear only months before the film version of his book was due to open. Then, an unexpected revelation, an unseemly intrusion of actual history, lanced the bubble within which the virtual version of Harrer's life as a hero in Tibet had been evolving and radically altered the circumstances in which Pitt's portrayal of him would be viewed. It was as if, just before Harrer became canonized as an adventurer saint and the newest version of Tibet as a dreamland was projected onto thousands of screens worldwide, the fantasy context was suddenly, if momentarily, switched off.

A crucial part of Harrer's fantastic story had always lain outside ethereal Tibet. Now it seemed that there was a very practical reason why in his book and his interviews Harrer had always skipped so lightly over his POW camp experience with other prisoners from Germany, Austria, and Italy and why he never offered his public a real glimpse of his inner life. Just as postproduction work on *Seven Years in Tibet* was ending, Gerald Lehner, a young reporter with the Austrian National Broadcasting Corporation—who, like me, had read Harrer's book as a teenager and who had been doing research at the U.S. National Archives in College Park, Maryland, where many Nazi records seized at the end of World War II are still warehoused—stumbled on some long-forgotten microfilmed files. They revealed a new Heinrich Harrer, one who had been a longtime Nazi Party member, not just a courageous mountain climber who had innocently appeared with Hitler in that 1938 photograph hanging in his Huttenberg museum. The records showed that as far back as the Nazis' ascension to power in Germany—and well before Hitler's troops marched into a welcoming Austria in 1938 to incorporate it as part of the German Reich—Harrer had voluntarily joined the SA, the Sturmabteilung, or "storm troopers." In fact, when he joined in 1933, the SA was still an illegal organization in Austria. (It was the SA that before the 1936 Berlin Olympics—at which Hedin delivered the opening address and shared Hitler's box—popularized the slogan *"Wenn die Olympischen Spiele vorbei, schlagen wir die Juden zu Brei"* ["Once the Olympic Games are over, we will beat the Jews to a pulp"].)

The files also revealed that on April 1, 1938, Harrer upgraded his Nazi bona fides by joining the SS, the Schutzstaffel, or "protective echelon"—Hitler's elite corps of secret police, headed by Heinrich Himmler—where he ultimately gained a rank equivalent to sergeant. This was the same year Harrer bore the Nazi swastika to the top of the north face of the Eiger, proclaiming, "We have scaled the summit all the way for our Führer."

At a sports festival organized in Breslau by the Third Reich to honor Harrer and his three climbing mates, Hitler was effusive. "My children, what a feat you have accomplished!" he exclaimed. "After the north face of the Eiger, we are all the more the masters of our resolve." As Lehner revealed in a June 1997 article he wrote for the German magazine *Stern*, Harrer also voluntarily provided Himmler with a pedigree for himself and his fiancée to prove that they were "true Aryans" entitled to have the SS Reichsführer give their marriage his official blessing.

There was more to the Nazi-Tibet axis than the surfaces of Harrer's story suggested. How much of it Harrer was aware of is impossible to know, but just as Hollywood is presently fascinated by Tibet, so in the 1930s the Nazis had also fallen under its thrall. Third Reich mythmakers had already borrowed the somewhat reconfigured swastika, a symbol of good fortune in Hindu and Buddhist cultures, as the official Nazi insignia. And in 1935 Himmler set up a Nazi Party organ under the SS called the Ahnenerbe, or Office of Ancestral Heritage, which was, among other things, charged with investigating reports of paranormal Tibetan phenomena and formulating rationalizations for bizarre Nazi racial theories.

In Nazi lore, Central Asia was supposedly the place of refuge for what remained of an Aryan race from Scandinavia after the sinking of the lost continent of Atlantis. Conveniently overlooking the fact that Tibetans were not blond Vikings or Teutons, the Nazis nonetheless came to the view of Madame Blavatsky—that the Tibetan Plateau was an enclave of racial purity long protected by the Himalayas from the miscegenating influences of the outside world. The idea that Sanskrit was somehow linguistically connected to Latin, Greek, and even German and that Teutonic people were somehow descendants of Aryans from Central Asia was first lofted by the German scholar Friedrich Schlegel in the early nineteenth century.

Indeed, as early as 1926, long before they were a force to be reckoned with, future Nazi supporters managed to send the first of several "anthropological" expeditions to the area under the leadership of zoologist Ernst Schafer, whom one scholar of the period has dubbed "a Nazi Indiana Jones." In 1938, Himmler dispatched Schafer and a well-funded, well-equipped team of Ahnenerbe filmmakers, all of them, like Schafer, SS members, to shoot a documentary entitled *Geheimnis*

Tibet, or *Mysterious Tibet.* Released in 1943, it is still sometimes screened today, albeit with its swastika images and propaganda about race edited out.)

In 1939, concerned about the British position in India, Himmler once more turned to Schafer, this time to organize a military reconnaissance expedition to Tibet. Although it never actually departed, its mandate was to gather geographic and ethnographic information with the ultimate intention of fomenting a guerrilla war against the British in the area. At the same time, a coterie of Tibetan monks was reportedly assembled in Germany under the direct tutelage of Himmler, who, like Hitler, was fascinated with their supposed oracular and clairvoyant abilities.

Even the renowned Swedish explorer Sven Hedin, who had studied in Berlin as a youth and whom Harrer so greatly admired, ended up supporting the Nazis. Although his great-grandfather had been a rabbi, Hedin not only allowed the Nazis to name the Reich Institute for Central Asian Research in Munich, where Ernst Schafer worked, after him in 1943 but he came to the opening, with Heinrich Himmler in attendance, and then accepted an honorary degree from the University of Munich. Indeed, a document from the institute's files cited in Karl E. Meyer and Shareen Blair Brysac's encyclopedic *Tournament of Shadows,* quotes Hedin as telling Schafer in 1942 that "I myself had not a single doubt: the future of the Nordic lands is closely connected to Germany's."

Thus, Harrer's expedition to Nanga Parbat must be seen as part of a broader mosaic of Tibet-related Nazi activity that went far beyond simple mountain climbing. Indeed, the French journalist Alain Giraudo has claimed in *Le Monde* that it was Himmler himself who invited Harrer to join the Nanga Parbat expedition.

Whatever the case, Lehner's revelations about Harrer swept around the world in short order. Soon accounts of Harrer's secret Nazi past were being trumpeted from the pages of *Le Monde,* the British *Spectator,* the *New York Times,* and various Hollywood trade journals. ("Austrian Tutor, Played by Brad Pitt, Was a Nazi" the *Times* headlined.) Although neither Annaud nor Harrer—each horrified in his own way by the disclosures—would have agreed, there was something reassuring in knowing that it was still possible for a bit of historical reality to derail a powerful and convincing virtual creation.

Harrer and his supporters did not wait long before launching a defense. "As much as Mr. Clinton likes to shake the hand of Michael—what's his name, Jordan?—or Michael Tyson before he raped women and bit people's ears off, Hitler liked to surround himself with the athletes of his time," protested Harrer's lawyer Johannes Burger, to *Vanity Fair* reporter H. G. Bissinger. In his own statement, Harrer pointed out that he had only once publicly worn a Nazi uniform—at his wedding. He found the revelations "extremely unpleasant," he said, and emphasized that he had joined the Nazis simply to further his mountaineering career. (There are not that many moments in life when to claim to be a craven careerist of the most calculating sort is a step up from ignominy.) As far as anyone could tell, it was at least true that Harrer had no history of Nazi ideological activism or of ever having participated in other Nazi activities.

"My personal philosophy grew out of my life in Tibet," he somewhat lamely explained, as if mere association with that enchanted Buddhist land might help cleanse the stain of his Nazi past. "It is a belief that reflects many tenets of Buddhism and places great emphasis on human life and human dignity. . . . It is a philosophy that leads me to condemn as strongly as possible the horrible crimes of the Nazi period." Of course, as Harrer had not been hesitant to tell me when I visited him in Austria, he had never had much truck with the Buddhist or spiritual side of Tibetan culture even while in Tibet.

Harrer went on to protest that "everybody has something they are not proud to show off" and that he now regarded "the events that involved the SS as one of the aberrations in my life, maybe the biggest." He regretted deeply that "these events may give rise to false impressions" but steadfastly maintained that his conscience was "clear on my record during the Hitler regime." There was nothing, he said, to be done but "grin and bear it."

Meanwhile, the film executives who had been busily preparing for the opening of *Seven Years in Tibet* found themselves suddenly in need of a strategy to spin Pitt's portrayal of Harrer so that it would not seem to glorify an unreconstructed Nazi. Jean-Jacques Annaud issued a statement of his own, saying, "I had suspected for a long time that one of the hidden scars Heinrich Harrer had to heal was left by a possible connection with the Nazis when he left Austria in 1939. . . . When he returned after the Second World War and seven years in Tibet, he devoted his life to nonviolence, human rights, and racial equality." Lest potential viewers or reviewers not get his drift, he added, "The film *Seven Years in Tibet* revolves around guilt, remorse, and redemption."

Personal transformation was hardly a new theme in the West's relationship with its imagined Tibet. After all, there had often been a presumption that enlightenment, even redemption, might be the reward for those who managed to reach the holy city. But the transformation of a Nazi who hadn't bothered to admit to the particulars of his errant past in the nearly half century since his book appeared might be a tougher sell to movie audiences. Admittedly, Steven Spielberg had managed to turn Oscar Schindler, a careerist Nazi who transformed himself by saving "his" Jews from Auschwitz, into an on-screen global phenomenon. And years earlier, George Lucas had tamed the storm troopers of recent European history by transforming them into the carapaced imperial soldiers of *Star Wars*. But what of an unconfessed, previously unrepentant Nazi who had escaped a British prisoner-of-war camp to become the tutor of the most peaceful, compassionate, and spiritual man on earth? That was a somewhat less palatable dose of reality to swallow, especially so late in the production process, when there was little Annaud could do to reedit the story his film told.

The best that he could accomplish was to add a few new lines of voiceover. For instance, as that phalanx of belligerent PLA generals arrives in Lhasa to force concessions from the Tibetans, Brad Pitt was made to say, "I shudder to recall how once, long ago, I embraced the same beliefs, how at one time I was no different from these intolerant Chinese."

"It's about redemption, OK?" John Jacobs, head of marketing for Peter Guber's Mandalay Entertainment production company, explained to a reporter from the *Spectator*. "The fact that he was a Nazi only explains that the character had to change. This is a movie about guilt and remorse. The bulk of his life, when you measure eighty-five years, is pretty exemplary."

Gerald Lehner's further research did nothing to reassure anyone hoping that the real story of Harrer's life was one of unpublicized redemption. In the Austrian magazine *Profil* Lehner wrote a follow-up article no less devastating than the first, claiming that since the end of World War II, Harrer had even kept up with several old Nazi friends. One was Bruno Beger, an anthropological colleague of Ernst Schafer's and a former member of the Ahnenerbe who had gone to Tibet on the 1938 SS trip to search for some connection between the Tibetan people and the Nordic races. He had also played a later role in selecting subjects at Auschwitz to be turned into living skeletons in research projects dedicated to proving some of Himmler's more outré racial theories. In fact, one Sven Hedin Institute research paper speaks of a trip Beger made to Auschwitz in 1943 to measure body size and study the physiognomies of Central Asian inmates in an effort to help corroborate Himmler.

In 1971, Bruno Beger was convicted in Frankfurt of complicity in the murder of eighty-six Russian Jews at Auschwitz and sentenced to three years in prison, although the sentence was ultimately suspended. His freedom allowed him, as Meyer and Brysac point out, to appear at a reunion in Austria between Heinrich Harrer and the Dalai Lama, who had no notion of the company he was keeping.

Gerald Lehner's revelations were a reminder of how uncooperative history can sometimes be to those interested in fabricating virtual worlds of entertainment from fragments of real people, places, and events. Not unlike trying to fit the ugly sister's oversized foot into Cinderella's delicate glass slipper, wedging an unreconstructed Nazi Party member into roseate Western fantasies of Tibet was to prove difficult, even with some last-minute spin-doctoring. Perhaps a different, more complex script and an actor capable of playing a more subtle Tibetan version of Oscar Schindler might have been possible. But whether bottom-line-conscious Hollywood could have countenanced such an effort and whether a mass audience would have paid to see a closet Nazi who got along by going along recycle himself through the purifying medium of Tibet and Buddhism is another matter. One can imagine an interesting small-budget film wrestling with the ironic question of an unreflective hero without much of a conscience ending up as the Dalai Lama's tutor and friend. That version would probably have been unrecognizable, however, to those who keep the West's Tibetan fantasy world alive.

---- **20** ----

THE CHINESE REACT

There was yet another shock awaiting the Tibet that was about to come into focus on the screens of American theaters. As Beijing's leaders began to realize that they were confronting what appeared to be a massive Hollywood-inspired propaganda campaign against them, the Party-controlled media seized on the revelations about Harrer's Nazi past as if it were one of those ferocious biting Tibetan mastiffs described by Marco Polo as being "as big as donkeys." China's official press proceeded to sink its teeth into the new Heinrich Harrer and refused to let go. After all, what blacker mark could one imagine on the West's benign version of Tibet and on the Dalai Lama's status as a living saint than for unliberated Tibet to have been the ultimate haven for an unconfessed Nazi?

Wasting no time, the *People's Daily* ran an article headlined "Harrer,

Dalai Lama's Former 'Teacher,' Was a Nazi." "The Tibet craze set off by
Hollywood is being used by a Nazi to advertise himself," crowed the
paper. "Should Hollywood sing songs in praise of Nazis?" a commen-
tary in the *Beijing Review* wondered triumphantly.

Indeed, even before Harrer's public fall from grace, the Party
had launched an offensive against what it saw as a Hollywood con-
spiracy to prejudice the world on Tibet. Its strategy was two-pronged.
The first prong was, of all things, the production of a movie, a $1.8-
million Tibetan epic—an extravaganza by Chinese standards—released
by Shanghai Film Studios in April 1997. Set at the time of the
Younghusband expedition, and shot in Tibet, *Red River Valley* was a far
more shameless piece of fictionalized history than anyone involved with
Seven Years in Tibet could ever have imagined creating. But it hardly
mattered. There was no way a Chinese-made film could compete against
Hollywood's big-budget onslaught. The film, acclaimed in the Party
press, and only there, for showing "both the Hans and Tibetans united
to defend their homeland against British colonists hoping to claim
the exotic area as their own," mainly showed that, when it came to
re-creating virtual history on-screen, the Chinese were hopelessly backward, mired in cinematic techniques and a propagandistic mind-set that
could almost be called "feudal."

But the second prong of China's offensive against Holllywood's Tibet
was to prove more formidable. It was to be launched between sovereign
realms on something more like a level playing field as the Chinese
took on not screen images, elusive virtual worlds, global celebrities, or
Hollywood's peerless publicity machinery but the corporate side of the
entertainment industry. And here, as it happened, the Chinese could
bring to bear a mythology that, since the mid–nineteenth century, had
had as strong a grip on the imagination of the West's traders and busi-
nessmen as the lure of Tibet had had on its explorers and spiritual seekers. This was the promise of the boundless, fabled China market.

In the nineteenth century, as Western traders looked to China to buy
their goods, it was said that if every "Chinaman" would only lengthen
his shirttail one inch, it would "save the mills of Manchester." By the
turn of the century, even the U.S. Bureau of Foreign Commerce was

extolling China as "one of the most promising targets" for an "American invasion of the markets of the world." Hollywood's late-twentieth-century version of this promise went: put *The Lion King,* Adam Sandler, *Titanic,* and Mickey Mouse before Chinese consumers, and if each Chinese—or even one in ten—would see just one American film a year or visit one theme park, the pockets of the entertainment industry's multinational corporations would soon be bulging with cash. After all, didn't China now have 1.3 billion people and wasn't it the world's fastest-growing economy? As the chairman of the New York Life Insurance Company enthusiastically observed after a deal to let China into the World Trade Organization was worked out with the United States in November 1999, 1 percent of China's market share would double the volume of his company's business.

In recent years, China had made just enough deals with film studios and media conglomerates to tantalize entertainment CEOs, too, with visions of profits inconceivable in the wildest dreams of nineteenth-century textile manufacturers. Although, as of 1999, China still allowed only ten foreign films to be shown each year—with promises to raise the number to twenty with admission to the World Trade Organization—most were extremely well received by audiences weary of technologically backward and politically didactic homegrown films. When *The Lion King* was shown in 1996 and *Titanic* in 1998, attendance records were shattered. Despite the restrictions, Hollywood releases were already accounting for approximately half of all local box office yields, unofficially estimated at $300 million.

Among those hard on the trail of even more Chinese dollars was the Walt Disney Company, the parent corporation soon to release Martin Scorsese's *Kundun.* Under chairman Michael Eisner, the company had hired Creative Artists Agency superagent Michael Ovitz as president, and one of his assignments was to serve as point man for opening the China market to Disney products. After signing on, Ovitz had started courting Martin Scorsese to come to Disney, even though *Kundun* was his next project. Ovitz had evidently overlooked the politically controversial nature of the film and the fact that Universal Studios had earlier refused to make a distribution deal with Scorsese out of fear that China might react hostilely. From a corporate point of view, Ovitz's oversight was a grave error because, after great success in China with *Toy Story* and *The Lion King,* Disney executives were hoping to sell limitless amounts of merchandise and toys to Chinese children through more than 130 "Mickey's Corner" stores, to further penetrate China's cable-television market with China Disney Club programming, and to open a large new Disneyland-like theme park in Shanghai. Soon to be released, as well, was *Mulan,* a full-length animated film based on a Chinese legend about a heroic young woman who disguises herself as a man to take her ailing father's place in battle.

With such fevered dreams, Disney executives were loath to do anything that might jeopardize a future in which, as every studio executive was painfully aware, foreign sales would be an ever more important component of a film's success. Indeed, in the new global economy, four out of five of the top summer blockbusters of the past five years— *Saving Private Ryan* (1998), *Men in Black* (1997), *Independence Day* (1996), *Batman Forever* (1994), and *Forrest Gump* (1994)—have grossed more overseas than at home (only *Batman* in 1995 grossed more at home). Disney was hardly alone in its fears of being shut out of the People's Republic of China, and China's leaders, well aware of the extravagance of Western dreams of global profit, were about to throw a deft counterpunch at Hollywood.

In December 1996, before either *Seven Years in Tibet* or *Kundun* was completed, a transpacific cinematic cold war erupted. The Chinese Ministry of Radio, Film, and Television declared through its spokesman in Beijing, Kong Min, that because *Kundun* "intended to glorify the Dalai Lama," it constituted a form of "interference in China's internal affairs." The vice-director of the ministry, Yang Buting, came right to the point. Because, he said, Disney had "indicated a lack of respect for Chinese sovereignty," China was "thinking over our business with Disney." It was quickly rumored that Disney might actually be excluded from future deals.

While Chinese officials had often pressured other kinds of foreign businesses into doing their bidding by threatening to shut them out of their markets, this was a somewhat new tack for the Party to take in dealing with foreign entertainment conglomerates. They had, of course, long censored films made domestically but had never previously thought to pressure the parent companies of foreign entertainment corporations into doing their political bidding. Disney executives were suitably alarmed by China's sudden and aggressive reaction, but they were caught in a strange public relations bind. The fact that Tibet had become Hollywood's inamorata and that Martin Scorsese and scriptwriter Melissa Mathison (the wife of Harrison Ford, no less) were involved made it almost impossible for them to quietly bury the film. It did not help that the news division of Capital Cities/ABC, also owned by Disney, had to continue covering China for the ABC network.

After much vacillation in what *Variety* referred to as "the lama drama," Disney finally issued a statement supporting *Kundun.* Many in the media applauded, maintaining that because the company had not yielded to Chinese pressure, Disney had shown its mettle and won a genuine victory over the forces of cultural censorship. Disney's statement, editorialized the *New York Times,* was "a welcome stand at a moment when the American government and American companies seem increasingly prepared to put aside important democratic principles in hopes of expanding commerce with China." The *San Francisco Examiner* referred to the rhubarb as "the mouse that roared." And *Newsweek* ran a cartoon showing Mickey Mouse heroically blocking the path of an oncoming tank, playing off video footage still indelibly engraved in the public's consciousness from the days of the 1989 Beijing massacre.

The truth was, however, that even though *Kundun* was not unceremoniously done away with as a low-budget bother to larger corporate interests, Disney did try to distance itself from the film. Michael Ovitz even explained to Mayor Xu Guangdi of Shanghai, where Disney was angling for its first China-based theme park, that since *Kundun* was being coproduced by Touchstone, a mere subsidiary, Disney itself could not really be considered directly involved with the film.

But Beijing was not willing to relent. In the weeks that followed, Party media organs kept up a steady drumbeat of anti-Disney and anti-Hollywood propaganda. The New China News Agency joined the fray, quoting someone identified as a Tibetan scholar from the China Tibetology Center as saying that *Seven Years in Tibet* "distorts history" and is "really cheap stuff . . . that prettifies Nazis while vilifying Tibetans." An editorial in *China's Tibet,* a Party-sponsored magazine, asked, "Should we regard this follower of those who committed towering crimes against humanity as a hero of human rights? Should Hollywood sing songs in praise of Nazis?" And the *China Daily* warned Hollywood that it would "never be forgiven" for all the movies it was making on Tibet that "hurt our nation's feelings."

Because Chinese efforts to pressure Disney were greeted with almost universal disapproval outside China, it initially seemed as if Beijing's campaign was an unmitigated public relations disaster. It was one thing to try to blackmail a corporation like Boeing, whose executives were used to complying when major aircraft contracts hung in the balance, but quite another to threaten Hollywood, whose figurative lords and ladies were used to speaking out independently. Over the following weeks, however, it became less clear who exactly had won what. After all, China's leaders were interested in far more than consigning a single film about Tibet to oblivion. What they hoped to accomplish was to let the whole world know that projects on Tibet—indeed, any project on any subject deemed politically sensitive by the Communist Party— might henceforth create problems for parent companies aspiring to gain a share of the growing China market. CEOs at entertainment corporations as well as at news companies around the world had undoubtedly gotten the desired double message: that jumping naively onto the Tibet bandwagon was an instant way to lose friends in Beijing and that it is far easier to reject such projects early on than to halt them later in a hailstorm of embarrassing and damaging publicity.

In the spring of 1998, another kind of American company learned the hard way. Only after the Apple Computer company had launched a new ad campaign featuring large black-and-white photos of celebrities like Pablo Picasso, Rosa Parks, Amelia Earhart, Albert Einstein, and the Dalai Lama under the caption "Think Different," did its executives realize that they had walked into a similar minefield. It had evidently escaped Apple's attention—as it had Michael Ovitz's—that Beijing had called His Holiness a "splittist" and a "political insect" and had even compared him to leader David Koresh, the leader of the Branch Davidian cult. In this case, China did not even need to growl. Apple's campaign had hardly begun when its executives had a sudden change of heart and removed the Dalai Lama's visage from its billboards.

"Because movies are so visible, and many of the companies that make them are now so big and so dependent on the foreign marketplace for their product—whether it's merchandising, theme parks, liquor or electronics—this will have a chilling effect on anything that could interrupt the businesses that are really profitable," explained former MCA vice-chairman Thomas P. Pollock. "The movie divisions of these conglomerates are the most visible, but often the least profitable, arms of these companies. . . . The question that's going to be asked is: 'Are we going to get ourselves in political hot water because of some movie?' "

"As movie studios look to China as one of the last unconquered realms of the global marketplace, executives at both Disney and Sony may wonder what their good intentions will cost," *Entertainment Weekly* bluntly noted. Then it quoted a source as saying that Sony "doesn't want any association with the Dalai Lama. . . . Sony's afraid of China."

When asked by an interviewer on PBS's *Frontline* whether he was accustomed to having his films run headlong into such "foreign policy" questions, Martin Scorsese shook his head dolefully. "This is new territory," he said. "It's incomprehensible to me that things could get a certain way in our country where books can't be written and films can't be made because it might affect the economics of . . . a corporation. That's a very dangerous situation."

After the treatment Harrer had gotten in the Chinese press, Sony-TriStar executives were understandably worried that their studio, too, might find itself paying a high price for Jean-Jacques Annaud's politically provocative film. But what was Sony-TriStar or Disney to do? Even as China launched its offensive, their PR machines were revving up multimillion-dollar campaigns that would involve cast members, directors, scriptwriters, and producers in a global media blitz to promote movies at whose heart lay images of a rapacious China occupying

Shangri-La. Anxious corporate executives urged those who would be representing the films to the media to gloss over sensitive political questions in interviews, as if the films had nothing to do with one of the great political tragedies of this century.

Disney even hired China über-fixer Henry Kissinger to calm down Party leaders in Beijing. Suddenly, it seemed, Hollywood needed a foreign policy of its own to manage the international affairs of the illusory worlds that its studios were spinning forth, lest they antagonize the keepers of rival illusions and create havoc in the real world. And who better to mediate between these two fantasy projections than an ex–secretary of state who could masquerade as his former self, a virtual diplomat, as one magic kingdom negotiated with the other in the world of surrealpolitik?

21

TIBETAN QUESTIONS

In the swirl of globalized bottom-line anxiety, conflicting imagery, bad publicity, political threats, wanton boosterism, and furtive negotiations, the Tibetans themselves—not those of the 1940s but those still oppressed within Tibet or scattered around the world in their diaspora—stood oddly in danger of being forgotten. It wasn't that Tibet was being forgotten. Certainly not. As *Seven Years in Tibet* and *Kundun* neared their October and December 1997 release dates, the buzz in the media about China's occupation of Tibet, Buddhism, Tibetan adventures, the Dalai Lama, and Hollywood stars smitten with any of the aforementioned subjects hit near manic proportions. One could, to quote from book titles then massing on store shelves, try *Surfing the Himalayas* or *Snowboarding to Nirvana* (thanks to blond Los Angeleno yuppie guru Dr. Frederick P. Lenz III, who, before his suicide in 1998, went by the name of Zen Master Rama) or be *A Jewish Mother in Shangri-La* (following the experiences of Rosie Rosenzweig, who "lost" her "nice Jewish boy son" to Buddhism). If shorter takes were one's thing, one could explore Heinrich Harrer's relationship to Nazism in *Vanity Fair*, read about "Why Tibet Matters" in *Entertainment Weekly,* or enjoy the ins and outs of "Tibet Gets Chic" in *Newsweek.* Amid this surge of Tibetiana and Buddhist spiritualism one could even check one's everyday elation quotient in *The Art of Happiness: A Handbook for Living,* a best-seller by no less an eminence than His Holiness the Dalai Lama (with a helping hand from Arizona psychiatrist Howard C. Cutler). With Tibet running rampant in pop culture, it was difficult for those who took their Tibetan politics or Buddhism seriously to know quite how to deport themselves so as to avoid the imputation that they, too, were trendmongers or spiritual parvenus.

And yet, as the struggle between the titans of Hollywood entertainment and the leaders of China's mutant People's Republic played itself out, the tiny overseas communities of Tibetans who had looked to the two upcoming films as catalysts for their potential deliverance from exile seemed ever more irrelevant. With the premieres of the two films approaching, it seemed less and less appropriate to wonder whether a virtual world could help bring about the liberation of a real land and an actual people.

Back in Uspayatta, as designer Hoang Thanh At and I gazed at the wondrous Jokhang he had just wrought, he had expressed his hopes that *Seven Years in Tibet* would be "like a bomb blast." Indeed, in that lifelike setting under an azure blue sky reminiscent of the Himalayas, with real Buddhist monks chanting and a brisk wind whipping strings of genuine Tibetan prayer flags overhead and wafting clouds of incense smoke heavenward, it did not seem so far-fetched to imagine that the magic of this lovingly rendered re-creation might somehow rouse the world to Tibet's indisputable tragedy. One could almost believe that the release of these films might prove to be like Mao Zedong's proverbial "spark that lights the prairie fire," igniting some kind of mass revelation, if not revolution.

Of course, nobody was quite sure where exactly that figurative "prairie fire" should be lit or who exactly might be swept up in it. The Chinese Communist leaders? The Chinese people? The American government? The United Nations? Members of the European Economic Community? Ordinary people? Heads of state? Governments and political leaders had so consistently failed Tibet that among Tibetans there was a desperate, if inchoate, hope that maybe Hollywood's treatment of their land and situation might finally make someone somewhere pay attention.

Especially among supporters of the Dalai Lama, Hollywood's arrival on the scene sparked a renewed sense of hope, perhaps the only prairie fire to be lit during the whole prolonged, painful affair. With the help of Hollywood, might not Tibet be redeemed? With its global economic reach and its ability to animate popular sentiment around the world, was not Hollywood more omnipresent and mighty than even the American military? Compelling big-screen scenes of the halcyon days of Tibet, it was hoped, might somehow force the issue of what was lost onto the American foreign policy agenda for the first time in decades. Political arguments had been an insufficient means to accomplish this end, but might not mesmerizing images of the Dalai Lama's life and the religious culture in which he had grown up do the trick? Among many exiled Tibetans there arose an almost millenarian hope that the release of these films and the identification with Tibet of such pop icons as Martin Scorsese, Steven Seagal, Brad Pitt, Richard Gere, and the Beastie Boys might precipitate the long-awaited moment when China would feel compelled by the power of world opinion to address the question of Tibet in a more humane and conciliatory way.

The International Campaign for Tibet even began to organize a national effort to coincide with the opening of Annaud's film. Labeled "Seven Days for Tibet" and optimistically described as a "grass-roots uprising," it was to involve the distribution of some 300,000 "action kits," many to be given away outside theaters showing the film. It was also to include a week of educational activities and protests in thirty-four states, all calculated to capitalize on the anticipated attention and publicity the film would generate.

It was tempting to imagine that this morality play would have a happy ending, that Tibetans scattered to the far corners of the globe might at last find deliverance and be led out of their exile by an on-screen Dalai Lama. If truth be told, there were moments in following this drama when I, too, allowed myself to become swept up in such dreams. It was too bitter a reality to accept that there would be no salvation for Tibetans, that no Hollywood cavalry would at the last moment ride to the rescue.

In retrospect, such dreams were, if anything, less realistic than the exotic ones Westerners had so long held about the redemptive, transformative powers of Tibet. In a world of gigantism—whether of IMAX movie screens, megastars, superpowers, billion-dollar global box office grosses, worldwide publicity blitzes, ever more elaborate special effects, or, for that matter, ever more draconian forms of repression—the hopes of Tibetans were so modest yet so utterly unrealizable. In every sense, these were people incapable of operating on the same scale as the vast, impersonal worlds now colliding around them. There was, sadly, no wisdom the Dalai Lama possessed, nothing he could pass on to an American psychiatrist/author for Hollywood's nouvelle royalty or his own frustrated people that seemed truly capable of altering this equation.

22

VIRTUAL TIBET MEETS
THE REAL PUBLIC

It is probably best to leave places that we have idealized from afar or remember nostalgically from long ago unvisited and thus unperturbed in our imaginations. After all, what we cherish about them is seldom the places themselves as they currently exist, but what they have come to mean to us in a complex set of remembrances and associations. Unlike dreams, which have a will of their own and sometimes betray us as nightmares, certain fantasy places, even if rooted in undeniable reality, are ours to reimagine as we struggle to answer our very human need to believe that our earth and our lives still offer the possibility of escape to something better, deeper, more beautiful, more truly transcendent.

This is not to impugn the singular beauty of real Tibet, the integrity of the Dalai Lama as he moves among us, or the great tragedy that has befallen the Tibetan people. But from time to time it is worth reminding ourselves that, in the process of our making their acquaintance, they have become freighted with layers of Western projection born of our search for some imagined place of ultimate escape. Large as certain painful realities are to many Tibetans, they are too easily distorted, especially by sympathetic Westerners who live, as most of us do, bound by the gravity of so many years of dreaming about Tibet.

Long before the special-effects re-creation of Lhasa in *Seven Years in Tibet,* in fact long before Hollywood and Silicon Valley heaved up their versions of a cyber-revolution, we Westerners were already experts in conjuring up virtual worlds and in possessing perfectly real places in the name of our fantasies. Tibet was such a world and our urge to escape into it, to capture and use its wildly imagined essence to improve the quality of our lives, even at its expense, has been with us now for over two centuries. Whether it will be with us even half a century from now is another question.

Harsh as the thought might at first seem, perhaps we should hope not. After all this time, all those expeditions, pilgrimages, spirit quests, adventures, wanderings, and forced penetrations, perhaps it is finally time to try and separate our fantasies of escape—including what is most valuable about them—from the realities of Tibet.

Indeed, it is ironic, if not misguided, that we citizens of the wealthiest and strongest nation in world history—one that also has a culture of awesome (and voracious) dynamism—should choose to invest a land that is occupied and a leader who has been exiled and dispossessed of almost everything with the presumption of such mythic wisdom, power, and hope. Perhaps it just demonstrates that even the most powerful sometimes find it necessary to project unattained ideals somewhere else in order to maintain faith in the future. Like children, who as they grow up seek independence of mind, we cannot bear to completely abandon some belief in the infallibility of elders. Such transference is all well and good, except that probably only we rather than the Dalai Lama can do something about Tibet's lamentable situation, because it is the globalized world outside that holds most of the cards.

If the story of *Seven Years in Tibet* shows us anything, it is that the universe of virtual entertainment offers no certain escape hatch for Tibetans. No matter how much wisdom and power we invest them with and no matter how pure our intentions, in Hollywood Tibetans can never be more than glorified extras. The only way to begin to see Tibet clearly enough to imagine what if anything might be done to help its exiles and the various remnant peoples now inhabiting their partially dismembered homeland is to imagine Tibet in its own terms, not those of China, Hollywood, or any other of the Western aficionados who have ricocheted off its elusive, and illusive, peripheries.

One would think—or so we have been taught to imagine—that dreams are fragile things easily destroyed by reality. But increasingly, it seems, the opposite is true. As the tale of Tibet in the Western imagination illustrates so extravagantly, alongside reality there is often a parallel world, what we have come to describe as a virtual reality. But even in this there has been a change of remarkable proportions in recent years. For the urge to create virtual worlds—which once was by necessity relegated to individual consciousness, or at least to those dreams that an individual's own imagination could fabricate—has now been largely repossessed by a vast and ultimately impersonal entertainment machine that has taken over much of the job for us. This change has taken place at the very moment when so many vestiges of "mysterious" (or, in Chinese parlance, "feudal") Tibet have been expunged from the face of that occupied land.

The paradox is that even as it has become more physically accessible, Tibet has grown ever more virtual, while the many virtual environments of our modern world—the increasingly elaborate and bizarre holodecks on which we find ourselves—have gained a greater purchase on our time and our real lives.

When one looks back, in this context, at George Orwell's *1984* and Aldous Huxley's *Brave New World,* those two great dystopian visions of our century, it is striking that Orwell's book, with its "double-speak," "Big Brother," and "memory holes," has proved the lesser of the two, while Huxley's, with its cloning and its "feelies," its brightly colored, drug-ridden, shallow, shadowy, but feel-good world, seems, against all odds, more on target. It would be a mistake not to keep a wary eye cocked as we set about mass fabricating such worlds out of actual geographic places, because they all too easily become part of a larger distorting projection, however benign our intentions.

It is worth reminding ourselves, even in the case of *Seven Years in Tibet* and *Kundun,* where the reality of the situation is disheartening, that real life, real issues, real pasts, and real history still have power and can still play havoc with our even more enveloping virtual entertainment environments. However, so gripping and so convincing are the new virtual worlds enticing us that I would not bet on such corrective interaction to last long. For the truth is that we human beings have always wanted to believe in fanciful, even if largely imaginary, places to which we may mentally retreat. But if we could separate our dreams, individual and collective, from the lands we dream about and could instead create other imagined places out of whole cloth, that might be a good way to start reclaiming the boundary lines between the real and virtual parts of our lives.

There is, no doubt, something good and valuable in such dreams. In ways that even Tibetans themselves cannot quite discern, however, it may be an act more of respect than of neglect for us Westerners to pursue them in some other fashion. After all, it is always more difficult to solve a problem, such as the monumental standoff between China and Tibet, when it is not freighted with layers of sympathy and prejudice born of projection.

In a sense, Tibet should never have been—was truly never meant to be—"reached" by those of us in the West seeking solace from modern life, because it was never truly what was being aimed for (not to mention that it was never even really there). Perhaps it would be most accurate to say that there was always a part of us who yearned for Tibet that never really wanted to know what was being denied us, lest our longing be snuffed out by the act of arrival. That the real Lhasa had often disappointed those who finally managed to reach the elusive goal suggests that no borrowed land can satisfy yearnings that were never meant to be projected onto geography in the first place.

When I finally reached Lhasa in 1994, I experienced something of what Edmund Candler reported in 1904. "Having entered, the illusion is lost," he wrote of Lhasa attained. As we toured the largely defoliated city, I could not help thinking of something else Candler had written as he approached almost a century earlier: "Tomorrow when we enter Lhasa, we will have unveiled the last mystery of the East. There are no more forbidden cities which men have not mapped and photographed. Now that there are no real mysteries, no unknown land of dreams . . . children will be skeptical and matter-of-fact and disillusioned, and there will be no sale for fairy-stories any more." And then in a wistful cri de coeur he wrote: "But we ourselves are children! Why could we not have left at least one city out of bounds?"

I must admit that I felt an analogous set of emotions when I finally laid eyes upon the finished *Seven Years in Tibet* at its September 1997 premiere at the Toronto International Film Festival. For just a moment as I stood outside the theater amid Brad Pitt–crazed fans, a phalanx of Royal Canadian Mounted Police, a crush of TV cameras, and the usual parade of limos disgorging stars out onto a red carpet, I, too, felt a strange shimmer of hope. Especially when Pitt arrived, looking for all the world like a Catholic-calendar version of Jesus among the multitudes, it seemed possible that this roseate version of old Tibet might rouse the world from its neglect of Tibet's tragedy. But there was no deliverance to come.

In the darkness of Roy Thomson Hall, where every seat was taken and the audience was palpably eager to be transported, it did not take long to feel the flatness of Annaud's movie. Yes, there was the Jokhang and it was breathtaking (though I knew it was made of plywood and plaster); there were yaks, looking yaklike and authentic (though I was aware of all the complexities of getting yaks to Argentina); there was the ethereal roof of the Potala in Uspayatta (though I knew it had been spliced onto the real Potala through the wonders of computer graphics); and there were the magnificent tasseled hats (which I had watched Michael Jones make in the recreation room of the Hotel Valle Andino). The mountains soared (though I knew they were in Argentina and

Canada); the pageantry was elaborate (though I knew it had existed nowhere on earth for more than half a century); and the magic of Tibet was before me in all its refulgence (though I was aware that some of the monks were Bolivian Indians and Argentines of Japanese ancestry).

But just when I wanted most for all these carefully conjured-up images to overwhelm me and help us soar away to this fabled place, there would be Heinrich Harrer. His presence made me unbearably aware that the overexposed young face of Hollywood's Harrer peering out from the screen—as it had from so many magazine covers, posters, television screens, and other movies—was not "my" Heinrich Harrer. Each time I saw him, something in me would sag and my yearning to be borne away would lose traction.

It was hardly just the fault of Brad Pitt. After all, even the actual Heinrich Harrer had not proved to be my Heinrich Harrer, just as the Nazi Heinrich Harrer had not proved to be anybody's Heinrich Harrer (except the Heinrich Harrer of the Chinese) and just as Lhasa when I visited it had not quite proved to be my Lhasa. My Tibet, my Lhasa, my Heinrich Harrer, my Dalai Lama, even my yaks were to be found nowhere on earth other than inside my own imagination, my own childhood dreams, and several centuries of wistful imaginings in the West.

The critical assessments can be left to the reviewers, who mostly concurred with *Variety* in admiring the "magnificent widescreen lensing" while lamenting that the film "too rarely delivers at a simple emotional level." What can be said is that, when you sit watching the film in the darkness of a packed theater in the midst of a gala opening, you can feel something of the audience's collective response—and in that festival hall in Canada, as palpable as the initial yearning to be transported was, a sense of final epiphany was denied.

But here's the odd thing. I was not disappointed by either my Tibetan odyssey or the film. At the end of my long and circuitous journey from America to China, Tibet, Austria, Argentina, and now Canada, I found a strange if unexpected relief in the recognition that this film could not transport me to the Tibet of my childhood, that even the imposing heights of all its computer rearranged landscapes and elaborately and faithfully re-created sets were incapable of lifting me off the plateau of my own existence into that other dreamed-of realm. For me, at least, the film was a reminder that no Brad Pitt had ever been in my dream of Tibet.

Perhaps *Seven Years in Tibet* would have been a different matter if Annaud had cast a relative unknown as the Austrian mountain climber who, in the original book, could be viewed only in a few unprepossessing, milky black-and-white snapshots. Hollywood's craving for the well-known, the famous, the familiar, and the bankable star had simply run up against a land whose allure had depended for so long on its aloofness, self-absorption, and impenetrability. Perhaps all that care lavished on sets, costumes, props, and exotic locales only reflected a material culture at odds with our image of ineffable Tibetan spiritualism. Perhaps a small, noirish, or at least ironic film with little-known actors, a film about salvation in paradise without repentance, would have had some kind of strange appeal.

Then again, *Kundun,* which lacked stars or even familiar faces, fared far worse at the box office than *Seven Years in Tibet.* Admittedly released on many fewer screens, it dropped audiences into a completely alien world without a guide, much less a Western face. Without much in the way of explanation, it was a bold effort that left viewers more or less to make their way on their own through the young Dalai Lama's life. Visually sumptuous, musically exotic (with a score by Philip Glass), and religiously curious, it was an anthropological tour of otherness that ended up being as much a challenge as an escape.

Perhaps the poor box office returns had something to do with the fact that Americans found it unpalatable to have to mix their old escapist dreams of Tibet with the grisly reality of Chinese rule in that land. After all, such stern dominion over all that Tibet represented to the West felt very much akin to having one's own dreams occupied by interlopers. It's possible, too, that no film on Tibet—earthbound or spiritual, large or small, with or without megastars—could have attracted the tens of millions of viewers who now are the definition of success in Hollywood. At least, it's possible such success could not have been achieved in the face of the publicity generated by a suddenly Nazified Harrer, by China's demands, or, for that matter, by real Tibetans. In their real lives, it should be noted, some of them had refused to act the parts of cuddly, nonviolent naifs but had taken to the hills as guerrillas and to the streets in unruly protests and hunger strikes—sometimes even immolating themselves—to demand that attention be paid to them, their political cause, and their endangered culture.

Whatever the concatenation of negative forces may have been, one thing can be said with certainty: of all the "blank" places on the map that Hollywood had ever filled in, the blank space of Tibet (whether the fantasy Tibet of Western dreams or the culturally defoliated Tibet of the Chinese occupation) had proved less than fertile when it came to mapping the present-day dreams of global audiences. The stats on both pictures made this clear enough. *Kundun*—which Stephen Holden in the *New York Times* praised for its "dazzling, beautifully framed imagery," hastening to add, though, that "to call *Kundun* the most visually stunning religious storybook ever filmed is not to say it's a great movie"—performed dismally at the box office. Costing $35 million (including its publicity campaign), it took in less than $6 million during its four-month run, putting it well below Hollywood's blockbuster radar.

Seven Years in Tibet, which cost approximately $65 million, did not gross $38 million in its four-month run.

Not surprisingly, while books on Tibet and Buddhism continue to proliferate, Tibetan Buddhist centers continue to multiply, and the Dalai Lama continues to draw large and enthusiastic crowds wherever he goes, performing as himself on frequent visits to the United States and Europe, as the millennium arrived no Hollywood studio was rushing to situate its next big-budget virtual-reality production somewhere beyond the Himalayas. It seemed safer and more profitable to "map" the future, the past, the paranormal, and the outer spaces of our fantasy lives somewhere other than in places where our dreams of escape have begun to collide with reality.

As it turned out, while China had occupied Tibet, so, too, had Hollywood in its own inimitable way. And both of these kingdoms where gigantism reigns found it disappointingly indigestible. Unfortunately, only Hollywood showed signs of beating a retreat. Unlike China, after all, Hollywood does not need so much to physically occupy a place as to play on those virtual versions that have gained a life of their own in the imaginations of its potential audiences.

What's left of my Tibet remains today where it has long been, only a few feet from where I now sit and write these last lines about my own interior journey: that is, in a bookcase just behind my desk. There my Tibet books repose, many of them printed long ago on thick, yellowing paper and published in elegant fabric or leather bindings. Their presence provides a strangely reassuring connection to that time around the turn of the century when traditional Tibetan society not only still lived but our fantasies of it had not yet become hyperlinked to Hollywood. Some of these books—their covers detached and their spines broken as I myself trekked around the Tibetan Plateau—remind me that I, too, was enamored of the Holy Grail of Tibet and was part of the great tradition of trying to plumb its mysteries.

One day some months ago I discovered to my consternation that I had left my dog-eared original copy of *Seven Years in Tibet* on a plane. Somewhat mournfully, I asked my research assistant to pick up another copy for me when she next passed a bookstore. Several days later she handed me a new paperback, whose cover featured not the photo of the Dalai Lama, attended by monks and noblemen in exotic robes and hats, that had graced the cover of my 1953 original but a photo of Brad Pitt. He was striding through the portal of what I instantly recognized as Uspayatta's "West Gate," with towering computer-generated snow-capped mountains superimposed behind him. Above one of these majestic but misplaced peaks was a gold medallion inscribed: "Now a Major Motion Picture Starring Brad Pitt."

With mixed emotions I slipped this latest Hollywoodized version of *Seven Years in Tibet* onto my shelf next to the works of Father Ippolito

Desideri, Friar Orazio della Penna di Billi, George Bogle, Sven Hedin, Edmund Candler, Sir Francis Younghusband, Alexandra David-Neel, and Lowell Thomas. And so, where Jean-Jacques Annaud may have failed, Brad Pitt had nonetheless succeeded. He had won a place, however grudging, in what's left of my Tibet.

BIBLIOGRAPHY

During the five years it took to research this account, certain books proved particularly informative and useful. I have starred these works in the following bibliography. I would like, however, to make special mention of a few of them: Peter Bishop's *The Myth of Shangri-La: Tibet, Travel Writing, and the Western Creation of a Sacred Landscape;* Donald S. Lopez's *Prisoners of Shangri-La: Tibetan Buddhism and the West;* Karl E. Meyer and Shareen Blair Brysac's *Tournament of Shadows: The Great Game and the Race for Empire in Central Asia;* Sir Francis Younghusband's *India and Tibet;* William McGovern's *To Lhasa in Disguise;* Edwin Bernbaum's *Sacred Mountains of the World;* John MacGregor's *Tibet: A Chronicle of Exploration;* Victor Chan's *Tibet Handbook: A Pilgrimage Guide;* Filippo de Filippi's *An Account of Tibet: The Travels of Ippolito Desideri of Pistoia, S.J., 1712–1727;* Graham Sandberg's *The Exploration of Tibet: History and Particulars;* S. K. Sharma and Usha Sharma's *Encyclopedia of Tibet;* Edmund Candler's *The Unveiling of Lhasa;* Kenneth Wimmel's *The Alluring Target: In Search of the Secret of Central Asia;* and, of course, Heinrich Harrer's *Seven Years in Tibet* and *Return to Tibet.*

Other materials on which I regularly relied included the *China Journal,* the *China Quarterly,* the *Far Eastern Economic Review,* the *Hollywood Reporter,* International Campaign for Tibet's periodic reports, *Le Monde, Mandala,* the *New York Times, Premiere, Shambhala Sun,* FBIS translation service, *China News Digest, Tibet Press Watch, Tricycle,* the International Lawyers Committee for Tibet's *Tibet Brief,* the Tibetan government in exile's biquarterly *Tibetan Bulletin,* Human Rights Watch/ Asia's periodic reports, *Variety,* and *World Tibet News.*

Annaud, Jean-Jacques, Becky Johnston, et al. *The Seven Years in Tibet Screenplay and Story behind the Film.* New York: Newmarket Press, 1997.*

Avedon, John F. *Exile from the Land of the Snows.* New York: Alfred A. Knopf, 1979.*

Barber, Noel. *From the Land of the Lost Continent.* London: Collins, 1969.

Barnett, Robert, and Shirin Akiner, eds. *Resistance and Reform in Tibet.* London: Hurst & Co., 1994.

Bass, Catriona. *Inside the Treasure House: A Time in Tibet.* London: Victor Gollancz, 1990.

Batchelor, Stephen. *The Awakening of the West: The Encounter of Buddhism and Western Culture.* Berkeley: Parallax Press, 1994.

Bay, Jane. *Precious Jewels of Tibet: A Journey to the Roof of the World.* Santa Fe: Clear Light Publishers, 1998.

Bell, Charles. *The People of Tibet.* New Delhi: Motilal Banarsidass Publishers, 1992.*

————. *Portrait of the Dalai Lama.* London: Collins, 1946.

————. *The Religion of Tibet.* Oxford: Oxford University Press, 1931.*

————. *Tibet Past and Present.* London: Oxford Uninversity Press, 1927.*

Bernard, Theos. *Penthouse of the Gods: A Pilgrimage into the Heart of Tibet and the Sacred City of Lhasa.* New York: Charles Scribner, 1939.*

Bernbaum, Edwin. *Sacred Mountains of the World.* San Francisco: Sierra Club Books, 1990.*

————. *The Way to Shambhala.* Berkeley: Shambhala Books, 1986.*

Bernstein, Jeremy. *In the Himalayas: Journeys through Nepal, Tibet, and Bhutan.* New York: Lyons and Burford, 1996.

Berry, Scott. *A Stranger in Tibet: The Adventures of a Zen Monk.* London: Harper-Collins-Flamingo, 1990.

Bishop, Peter. *The Myth of Shangri-La: Tibet, Travel Writing, and the Western Creation of a Sacred Landscape.* Berkeley: University of California Press, 1989.*

Blavastky, Helena. *Isis Unveiled.* 2 vols. Pasadena: Theosophical University Press, 1960.

————. *The Secret Doctrine.* Los Angeles: Theosophy Company, 1947.

————. *Studies in Occultism*. Covina: Theosophical University Press, 1946.

Bonvalot, Gabriel. *Across Thibet*. 2 vols. London: Cassell & Co., 1891.

Breashears, David, and Audrey Salkeld. *Last Climb: The Legendary Everest Expeditions of George Mallory*. Washington, D.C.: National Geographic Society, 1999.*

Brignoli, Frank J., and Christine Johnston Brignoli. *Lhasa: Tibet's Forbidden City*. Ithaca: Snow Lion Publications, 1987.

Cambell, F. Bruce. *Ancient Wisdom Received*. Berkeley: University of California Press, 1980.

Candler, Edmund. *The Unveiling of Lhasa*. Berkeley: Snow Lion Graphics, 1987. (Originally published by E. Arnold, London, 1905.)*

Cao, Changqing, and James Seymour. *Tibet through Dissident Chinese Eyes: Essays in Self-Determination*. Armonk: M. E. Sharpe, 1998.

Capra, Frank. *The Name above the Title: An Autobiography*. New York: MacMillan, 1971.

Caraman, Philip, S.J., *Tibet: The Jesuit Century*. St. Louis: Institute of Jesuit Sources, 1997.

Carey, William. *Travel and Adventure in Tibet*. London: Hodder and Stoughton, 1902.

Case, Christopher. *The Ultimate Movie Thesaurus*. New York: Henry Holt & Co., 1996.

Chalon, Jean. *Le Lumineux Destin d'Alexandra David-Neel*. Paris: Perrin, 1985.

Chan, Victor. *Tibet Handbook: A Pilgrimage Guide*. Chico: Moon Publications, 1994.*

Chapman, F. Spencer. *Lhasa: The Holy City*. New York: Harper and Brothers, 1939.*

Clark, Leonard. *The Marching Wind*. London: Hutchinson, 1955.

Clarke, John. *Tibet Caught in Time*. Reading, Eng.: Garnet, 1997.

Coburn, Broughton, Tim Cahill, and David Breashears. *Everest: Mountain without Mercy*. Washington, D.C.: National Geographic Society, 1997.

Colman, Juliet Benita. *Ronald Colman: A Very Private Person*. New York: William Morrow & Co., 1975.

Cooney, Eleanor, and Daniel Altieri. *Shangri-La: The Return to the World of Lost Horizon*. New York: William Morrow and Co., 1996.

Craig, Mary. *Kundun: A Biography of the Family of the Dalai Lama*. Washington, D.C.: Counterpoint, 1997.

Cranston, Sylvia. *HPB: The Extraordinary Life and Influence of Helena Blavatsky, Founder of the Modern Theosophical Movement*. New York: Tarcher/Putnam, 1993.

Curzon, George. *Frontiers*. Oxford: Clarendon Press, 1908.

Dalai Lama. *Freedom in Exile: The Autobiography of the Dalai Lama*. New York: HarperCollins, 1990.

————. *My Tibet.* Photographs by Galen Rowell. Berkeley: University of California Press, 1990.

————. *The World of Tibetan Buddhism.* Boston: Wisdom Publications, 1995.

Dalai Lama and Jean-Claude Carrière. *Violence and Compassion.* New York: Doubleday, 1996.

Dalai Lama and Howard C. Cutler. *The Art of Happiness: A Handbook for Living.* New York: Riverhead, 1998.

Das, Lama Surya. *Awakening the Buddha Within.* New York: Broadway Books, 1997.

Das, Sarat Chandra. *Narrative of a Journey to Lhasa and Central Tibet.* Calcutta, 1885.

David-Neel, Alexandra. *Magic and Mystery in Tibet.* New York: Dover, 1971.

————. *My Journey to Lhasa.* Boston: Beacon Press, 1993. (Originally published in English by Harper and Brothers, New York, 1927.)*

————. *Immortality and Reincarnation.* Rochester, Vt.: Inner Traditions, 1978.

————. *Initiations and Initiates in Tibet.* London: Rider & Co., 1973.

David-Neel, Alexandra, and Lama Yongden. *The Secret Oral Teachings in Tibetan Buddhist Sects.* San Francisco: City Lights Books, 1990.

Dawson, Christopher. *Mission to Asia.* Toronto: University of Toronto Press, 1990.

Dutreuil, de Rhins, J. L., *Mission Scientifique dans la Haute Asia, 1890–95.* 3 vols. Paris, 1897–98.

Endres, Stacey, and Robert Cushman. *Chinese Hollywood at Your Feet: The Story of the World-Famous Chinese Theater.* Los Angeles: Pomegranate Press Ltd., 1992.

Epstein, Israel. *Tibet Transformed.* Beijing: Beijing Foreign Languages Press, 1983.

Evans-Wentz, W. Y. *The Tibetan Book of the Dead.* Oxford: Oxford University Press, 1960.

————. *The Tibetan Book of the Great Liberation.* London: Oxford University Press, 1968.

————. *Tibet's Great Yogi: Milarepa.* Oxford: Oxford University Press, 1951.

Fields, Rick. *How the Swans Came to the Lake: A Narrative History of Buddhism in America.* Boulder: Shambhala, 1981.

de Filippi, Filippo, ed. *An Account of Tibet: The Travels of Ippolito Desideri of Pistoia, S.J., 1712–1727.* London: George Routledge and Sons, 1931.*

Fleming, Peter. *Bayonets to Lhasa.* London: Oxford University Press, 1984. (Originally published by Rupert Hart Davis, London, 1961.)

Ford, Robert. *Captured in Tibet.* London: George G. Harrap & Co., 1957.

French, Patrick. *Younghusband: The Last Great Imperial Adventurer.* London: Flamingo, 1994.

Frutkin, Mark. *Invading Tibet.* New York: Soho, 1991.

Gelder, Stuart, and Roma Gilbert. *The Timely Rain: Travels in New Tibet.* London: Hutchinson, 1964.

Giorgi, Antonio Agostino. *Alphabetum Tibetanum: The Beginnings of Tibetology in the Western World.* Cologne: Editions Voce, 1995.

Goldstein, Melvyn C. *A History of Modern Tibet, 1913–1951: The Demise of the Lamaist State.* Berkeley: University of California Press, 1989.

———. *The Snow Lion and the Dragon: China, Tibet, and the Dalai Lama.* Berkeley: University of California Press, 1995.

Goldstein, Melvyn C., and Cynthia M. Beall. *Nomads of Western Tibet: The Survival of a Way of Life.* Berkeley: University of California Press, 1990.

Goldstein, Melvyn C., and Matthew T. Kapstein. *Buddhism in Contemporary Tibet.* Berkeley: University of California Press, 1998.

Goldstein, Melvyn C., William Siebenschuh, and Tashi Tsering. *The Struggle for Modern Tibet: An Autobiography of Tashi Tsering.* Armonk: M. E. Sharpe, 1997.

Govinda, Anagarika. *Foundations of Tibetan Mysticism.* York Beach: Samuel Weiser, 1969.

———. *The Inner Structures of the I Ching, the Book of Transformations.* New York: Wheelright Press, 1981.

———. *The Way of the White Clouds: A Buddhist Pilgrim in Tibet.* London: Hutchinson, 1966.

Grenard, Fernand. *Tibet: The Country and Its Inhabitants.* New Delhi: Cosmo Publications, 1974. (Originally published London, 1904.)

Guibaut, André. *Tibetan Venture: In the Country of the Ngolo-Setas.* London: John Murray, 1949.

Han, Suyin. *Lhasa, the Open City: A Journey to Tibet.* New York: G. P. Putnam, 1977.

Harrer, Heinrich. *Lost Lhasa: Heinrich Harrer's Tibet.* New York: Harry N. Abrams, 1992.

———. *Return to Tibet.* New York: Schocken, 1985.*

———. *Seven Years in Tibet.* London: Rupert Hart-Davis, 1953.*

Hedin, Sven. *A Conquest of Tibet.* New York: E. P. Dutton & Co., 1934.*

———. *My Life as an Explorer.* New York: Garden City Publishing, 1935. (Originally published by Boni and Liveright, New York, 1925.)*

———. *Through Asia.* 2 vols. London: Methuen & Co., 1998.*

———. *Trans-Himalaya: Discoveries and Adventures in Tibet.* 3 vols. London: Macmillan & Co., 1913.

Hilton, James. *Lost Horizon.* New York: Pocket Books, 1933.*

Holdich, Thomas. *Tibet, the Mysterious.* London: Alston Rivers, 1906.*

Hopkirk, Peter. *Foreign Devils on the Silk Road.* London: Abbot, Devon, 1981.

———. *The Great Game: The Struggle for Empire in Central Asia.* London: John Murray Ltd., 1994.

———. *Trespassers on the Roof of the World: The Race for Lhasa.* Oxford: Oxford University Press, 1982.*

Huc, Evariste-Régis, and Joseph Gabet. *Travels in Tartary, Thibet, and China: 1844–1846.* New York: Dover Publications, 1987. (Originally published in English by George Routledge and Sons, London, 1928.)*

Illion, Theodore. *In Secret Tibet: In Disguise Amongst Lamas, Robbers, and Wise Men—A Key to the Mysteries of Tibet.* London: Rider & Co., 1935.

International Commission of Jurists. *The Question of Tibet and the Rule of Law.* Geneva: International Commission of Jurists, 1959.

Iyer, Pico. *Video Night in Kathmandu and Other Reports from the Not-So-East.* New York: Alfred A. Knopf, 1988.

Jensen, Bernard. *In Search of Shangri-La: A Personal Journey to Tibet.* Garden City Park: Avery Publishing Group, 1993.

Kamenetz, Rodger. *The Jew in the Lotus.* San Francisco: Harper/San Francisco, 1994.

Katz, Ephraim. *The Film Encyclopedia.* New York: Harper Perennial, 1998.*

Kawaguchi, Ekai. *Three Years in Tibet.* Madras: Theosophical Publishing House, 1909.

Kelly, Mary Pat. *Martin Scorsese: A Journey.* New York: Thundermouth Press, 1991.

Kerr, Blake. *Sky Burial: An Eyewitness Account of China's Brutal Crackdown on Tibet.* Chicago: Noble Press, 1993.*

Knaus, John Kenneth. *Orphans of the Cold War: America and the Tibetan Struggle for Survival.* New York: Public Affairs Press, 1999.

Krakauer, Jon. *Into Thin Air.* New York: Villard Books, 1997.

Lach, Donald F., and Edwin J. Ven Kley. *Asia in the Making of Europe.* Vol. 3. Chicago: University of Chicago Press, 1993.

Lama Younden. *Mipam: A Tibetan Love Story.* Berkeley: Snow Lion Graphics, 1986.

Landon, Perceval. *Lhasa: An Account of the Country and People of Central Tibet and of the Progress of the Mission Sent There by the English Government in 1903–4.* 2 vols. London: Hurst & Blackett, 1905.

Landor, Henry Savage. *In the Forbidden Land.* London: William Heinemann, 1899.

Lehman, Steve. *The Tibetans: A Struggle to Survive.* New York: Eumbrage Editions, 1998.

le Sueur, Alec. *Running a Hotel on the Roof of the World: Five Years in Tibet.* West Sussex, Eng.: Summersdale, 1998.

Lopez, Donald S. *Prisoners of Shangri-La: Tibetan Buddhism and the West.* Chicago: University of Chicago Press, 1998.*

———. *Religions of Tibet in Practice.* Princeton: Princeton University Press, 1997.

MacDonald, David. *Twenty Years in Tibet.* London: Seeley, Service & Co., 1932.

McGovern, William Montgomery. *To Lhasa in Disguise.* New York: Grosset and Dunlap, 1924.*

MacGregor, John. *Tibet: A Chronicle of Exploration.* New York: Praeger, 1970.*

Maillart, Ella. *Forbidden Journey.* London: William Heinemann, 1937.

Maraini, Fosco. *Secret Tibet.* London: Hutchinson, 1954.

Marchetti, Gina. *Romance and the "Yellow Peril": Race, Sex, and Discursive Strategies in Hollywood Fiction.* Berkeley: University of California Press, 1993.

Markham, Clements R., ed. *Narratives of the Mission of George Bogle to Tibet and the Journey of Thomas Manning to Lhasa.* New Delhi: Manjusri Publishing House, 1971. (Originally published London, 1879.)*

Matthiessen, Peter. *The Snow Leopard.* London: Picador, 1980.

Mehra, Parshotam L. *The Younghusband Expedition: An Interpretation.* New Delhi: Journal of Indian History, 1955.

Meyer, Karl E., and Shareen Blair Brysac. *Tournament of Shadows: The Great Game and the Race for Empire in Central Asia.* Washington, D.C.: Counterpoint, 1999.*

Middleton, Ruth. *Alexandra David-Neel: Portrait of an Adventurer.* Boston: Shambhala, 1989.

Migot, André. *Tibetan Marches.* New York: E. P. Dutton, 1955.

Miller, Luree. *On Top of the World: Five Women Explorers in Tibet.* Seattle: The Mountaineers, 1984.*

Millington, Powell. *To Lhassa at Last.* London: Smith, Elder & Co., 1905.

Moorcroft, William, and George Trebeck. *Travels in the Himalayan Provinces of Hindustan and the Punjab; in Ladakh and Kashmir; in Peshawar, Kabul, Kunduz, and Bokhara.* Ed. Horace Wayman Wilson. London: William Murray, 1841.

Moore, Dinty W. *The Accidental Buddhist.* New York: Main Street Books, 1996.

Muir, John. *The Mountains of California.* New York: Doubleday/Anchor, 1961.

Normanton, Simon. *Tibet: The Lost Civilization.* New York: Viking-Penguin, 1989.

Olsen, Jack. *The Climb up to Hell.* New York: Harper and Row, 1961.

Paine, Jeffery. *Father India: How Encounters with Ancient Culture Transformed the Modern West.* New York: HarperCollins, 1998.*

Pallis, Marco. *Peaks and Lamas.* New York: Alfred A. Knopf, 1949.

Panchen Lama. *A Poisoned Arrow: The Secret Report of the 10th Panchen Lama.* London: Tibet Information Network, 1997.

Patt, David. *A Strange Liberation: Tibetan Lives in Chinese Hands.* Ithaca: Snow Lion Publications, 1992.

Peissel, Michel. *Cavaliers of Kham: The Secret War in Tibet.* London: Heinemann, 1972.

———. *The Last Barbarians: The Discovery of the Source of the Mekong in Tibet.* New York: Henry Holt & Co., 1997.

Pema, Jetsun. *Tibet, My Story: An Autobiography.* Rockport, Mass.: Element, 1997.

Powers, John. *Introduction to Tibetan Buddhism.* Ithaca: Snow Lion Publications, 1995.

Przhevalsky, Nikolai. *Mongolia, the Tangut Country, and the Solitudes of Northern Tibet.* London: Sampson Low, Marston, Searle and Rivington, 1876.

Rawson, Philip. *Sacred Tibet.* London: Thames and Hudson, 1991.

Revel, Jean-François, and Mathieu Ricard. *The Monk and the Philosopher.* New York: Schocken, 1998.

Rhie, Marilyn M., and Robert Thurman. *Wisdom and Compassion: The Sacred Art of Tibet.* New York: Harry N. Abrams, 1991.

Richards, Thomas. *The Imperial Archive: Knowledge and Fantasy of Empire.* London: Verso, 1993.

Richardson, Hugh E. *Tibet and Its History.* Berkeley: Shambhala, 1984.

de Riencourt, Amaury. *Lost World: Tibet, Key to Asia.* London: Victor Gollancz, 1951.

Rijnhart, Susie C. *With the Tibetans in Tent and Temple.* New York: Fleming Revell, 1901.

Rockhill, William Woodville. *The Land of the Lamas.* New Delhi: Asian Publication Service, 1975.

Rohmer, Sax. *The Hand of Fu Manchu.* New York: Robert McBride & Co., 1917.

Ross, Nancy Wilson. *Buddhism: A Way of Life and Thought.* New York: Alfred A. Knopf, 1980.

Said, Edward. *Orientalism.* New York: Vintage, 1979.

Salamon, Julie. *The Devil's Candy: The Bonfire of the Vanities Goes Hollywood.* Boston: Houghton Mifflin, 1991.

Salewicz, Chris. *Oliver Stone: The Making of His Movies.* New York: Thundermouth Press, 1997.

Sandberg, Graham. *The Exploration of Tibet: History and Particulars.* New Delhi: Cosmo Publications, 1973.*

Schary, Edwin G. *In Search of the Mahatmas of Tibet.* London: Seeley, Service & Co., 1937.

Schwartz, Ronald D. *Circle of Protest: Political Ritual in the Tibetan Uprising.* New York: Columbia University Press, 1994.

Shakabpa, Tsepon W. D. *Tibet: A Political History.* New Haven: Yale University Press, 1967.

Shakya, Tsering. *The Dragon in the Land of the Snows: A History of Modern Tibet since 1947.* New York: Columbia University Press, 1999.

Sharma, S. K., and Usha Sharma, eds. *Encyclopedia of Tibet.* 7 vols. New Delhi: Anmol Publications, 1996.*

Shen, Tsung-lien. *Tibet and the Tibetans.* Stanford: Stanford University Press, 1973.

Sinnett, Alfred Percy. *Esoteric Buddhism.* London: Chapman & Hall, 1885.

Sklar, Robert. *Movie-Made America: How the Movies Changed American Life.* New York: Random House, 1975.

Smith, Warren W. *Tibetan Nation: A History of Tibetan Nationalism and Sino-Tibetan Relations.* Boulder: Westview Press, 1996.

Snellgrove, David. *Himalayan Pilgrimage.* Boulder: Prajna Press, 1981.

Snellgrove, David, and Hugh Richardson. *A Cultural History of Tibet.* Boulder: Prajna Press, 1968.

Spence, Jonathan. *The Chan's Great Continent: China in Western Minds.* New York: W. W. Norton, 1998.

Sogyal Rimpoche. *The Tibetan Book of Living and Dying.* San Francisco: Harper/San Francisco, 1992.

Stein, R. A. *Tibetan Civilization.* Stanford: Stanford University Press, 1972.

Thomas, Lowell Jr. *Out of This World: Across the Himalayas to Forbidden Tibet.* New York: Greystone Press, 1950.*

Thomson, David. *A Biographical Dictionary of Film.* New York: Alfred A. Knopf, 1994.

Thurman, Robert. *Essential Tibetan Buddhism.* San Francisco: Harper/San Francisco, 1995.

Thurman, Robert, and Tad Wise. *Circling the Sacred Mountain: A Spiritual Adventure through the Himalayas.* New York: Bantam, 1999.*

Tibballs, Geoff. *Everest: The Struggle to Reach the Top of the World.* London: Carleton Books Ltd., 1998.

Tibet Information Network and Human Rights Watch/Asia. *Cutting Off the Serpent's Head: Tightening Control in Tibet, 1994–1995.* New York: Human Rights Watch, 1996.

Tibet: Myth vs. Reality. Beijing: Beijing Review Publications, 1988.

Tucci, Giuseppe. *The Religions of Tibet.* Berkeley: University of California Press, 1980.

———. *Tibet: Land of Snows.* New York: Stein and Day, 1967.

———. *To Lhasa and Beyond.* Ithaca: Snow Lion Publications, 1983.

Tung, Rosemary Jones. *A Portrait of Lost Tibet.* New York: Holt, Rinehart & Winston, 1980.

Waddell, L. Austine. *Among the Himalayas.* New Delhi: Pilgrim Books, 1998. (Originally published by John Murray, London, 1899.)*

———. *Lhasa and Its Mysteries: With a Record of the British Expedition of 1903–4.* New York, Dover Publications, 1972. (Originally published by John Murray, London, 1895.)*

———. *Tibetan Buddhism: With Its Mystic Cults, Symbolism, and Mythology.* New York: Dover Publications, 1972. (Originally published by W. H. Allen & Co., London, 1895.)*

Waller, Derek. *The Pundits: British Explorations of Tibet and Central Asia.* Lexington: University of Kentucky Press, 1990.*

Wang, Furen, and Wenqing Suo. *Highlights of Tibetan History.* Beijing: New World Press, 1984.

Washington, Peter. *Madame Blavatsky's Baboon: A History of the Mystics, Mediums, and Misfits Who Brought Spiritualism to America.* New York: Schocken, 1995.

Wilby, Sorrel. *Journey Across Tibet: A Young Woman's 1900-Mile Trek across the Roof of the World.* Chicago: Contemporary Books, 1988.

Wimmel, Kenneth. *The Alluring Target: In Search of the Secret of Central Asia.* Washington, D.C.: Trackless Sand Press, 1996.*

Woodman, Dorothy. *Himalayan Frontiers: A Political Review of British, Chinese, Indian, and Russian Rivalries.* New York: Praeger, 1969.

Younghusband, Francis. *Everest, the Challenge.* London: Thomas Nelson and Sons, 1949.

———. *The Heat of a Continent.* London: John Murray, 1937.

———. *India and Tibet.* Hong Kong: Oxford University Press, 1985. (Originally published by John Murray, London, 1910.)*

ACKNOWLEDGMENTS

Writing a book such as this is a mysterious task, because at the beginning one is never quite sure where one will end up. Indeed, a destination often does not reveal itself until near the end of the process. In this sense, the writer has to write his way out of an often compassless enigma.

The idea for this book began to germinate on a trip to Lhasa with two good friends, filmmaker and producer David Fanning and mountaineer and filmmaker David Breashears, as we were making a documentary for PBS's weekly program *Frontline* on Tibet's troubled historical relationship with China. The book took five more years, slowed in part by my job and family duties, which kept me from focusing exclusively on writing. Consequently, I was more dependent than usual on editorial help.

Thus I have dedicated this book to my longtime friend and editor, Tom Engelhardt, whose abilities and commitment to helping writers say what it is that they mean to say is legendary. But in Tom's case the appellation "legendary" does not come close to describing the magnitude of what he actually does or the painstaking care, thoroughness, and intelligence with which he approaches every stage of a manuscript. What marks him as an editor of the highest distinction is not only his ability to X-ray a piece of writing structurally and help reshape it into a coherent whole but the way in which he becomes intellectually attuned to the thematic import of what a writer is trying to convey.

Working with Tom, as I have for over thirty years, is a constant reminder that, while writing can be a very solitary undertaking, the best writing is also often an antiphonal process, especially toward the end of a project, when a manuscript is attempting to emerge from the dense underbrush of a first draft.

Thanks are also due Sara Bershtel and Riva Hocherman at Metropolitan Books and three of my students at the University of California, Berkeley's Graduate School of Journalism, Rob Selna, Iona Partengenaru, and Mathew Bell, who helped with bibliographic work, research, and fact-checking. I would also like to thank Jeffrey Hopkins and John Ackerley for graciously reading through the manuscript and pointing out errors.

Perhaps most of all I want to thank my wonderful wife, Liu Baifang, for her always good counsel and the enormous load she assumed in attending to our family—especially our three sons, Ole, Sebastian, and Sasha—during those seemingly endless years when I was closeted in my office at work.

Berkeley, California
2000

Index